Bob McGowan and Jeremy [...]
the former with the *Daily* [...]
Both set out on the now famous *Canberra* and moved to
the sister assault ships, HMS *Fearless* and HMS *Intrepid*
before going ashore on the Falklands. The Falklands
Crisis was Jeremy Hands' first war and Bob McGowan's
sixth.

Science is a 1st Rate

Piece of furniture

upper

for Mans own

Chamber

&

Only if he has

Common sense

on the ground

floor Oliver Wendall

Robert McGowan and
Jeremy Hands

Don't Cry For Me,
Sergeant-Major

Futura
Macdonald & Co
London & Sydney

A Futura Book

First published in Great Britain in 1983
by Futura Publications, a Division of
Macdonald & Co (Publishers) Ltd
London & Sydney

ISBN 0 7088 2390 4

Filmset, printed and bound in Great Britain by
Hazell Watson & Viney Ltd, Aylesbury, Bucks

Futura Publications
A Division of
Macdonald & Co (Publishers) Ltd
Maxwell House
74 Worship Street
London EC2A 2EN

Inspired by and Dedicated to
The men of 3 Commando Brigade

Acknowledgements

The authors gratefully acknowledge the help and friendship they received from the following, without whom this book would not have been possible:

The officers and men of

40 Commando, Royal Marines
The Third Battalion, The Parachute Regiment
The Second Battalion, The Parachute Regiment
42 Commando, Royal Marines
45 Commando, Royal Marines
The Special Air Service Regiment
The Special Boat Squadron, Royal Marines
Commando Logistics Regiment, Royal Marines
SS *Canberra*
Royal Fleet Auxiliary *Sir Lancelot*
HMS *Fearless*
Army Air Corps
Royal Navy helicopter aircrews.

Special thanks to:

Major Chris Keeble, 2 Para;
Surgeon Lieutenant-commander Rick Jolly, RN;
Sergeant Dave Munnelly, RM;
David Norris of the *Daily Mail*;
Ian Bruce of the *Glasgow Herald*.

Foreword

This book is not, as you might have guessed, the ultimate military history of what happened in the South Atlantic in the Spring and early Summer of 1982.

It is not likely to become the standard work of reference for historians who want to fathom the innermost depths of the minds of the generals and politicians who controlled the destiny of those Godforsaken monuments to desolation sometimes known as the Falkland Islands.

Indeed, it was what somebody else wanted to call them that was the reason for the British soldiers, sailors and airmen, and a posse of newsmen, going down there at all.

This is not a war diary or a chronological list of events. Many of the key events are mentioned only in passing. Some of the people who would consider themselves crucial to the whole effort are hardly mentioned at all.

But this is a true and accurate record of the experiences of some of the 10,000 men, and some women, who were involved in the liberation of the Falklands. This is the Falklands War without the false trimmings of pomposity and scholarly arrogance; the stories you won't find in any Very Senior Officer's memoirs, or the boring 'definitive' accounts culled from the reminiscences of people who were there, by others who were not.

Everything here comes from notes that were made at the time and on the spot by two men whose job it is to record what they see and hear. Indeed, we denied ourselves the option of adding to our notes later, lest we fall into the trap of embellishing or exaggerating.

No, this is a record of what we saw and heard at the time; nothing more, nothing less.

We would be the last to suggest that war is a joke. We have seen at first hand that it is not. We would be angry at any suggestion that the pain and anguish that inevitably accompany battle and death could, or should, be made light of.

That said, it is a fact that if you put any two men together for long enough, they will eventually make each other laugh. Put more than 10,000 together for three months and you have stories which will last forever.

There was humour that bound men together and kept them going when it was a simple choice of laughing or crying. And often, surviving or dying. There was laughing by one group at the misfortunes or incompetence of another, which human nature has decreed is the basis for so much humour.

There were the ludicrous situations that men found themselves in. And there was the simple, straightforward, sense of fun, not least in times of greatest danger, which, we venture to suggest, marked the greatest difference between the soldiers of the Queen, and those of the Argentinian Junta.

Of course, our men were better trained, better led and more professional than their counterparts, who were largely conscripted from the peasant communities of Argentina. Of course, Britain was right to reclaim that which had been illegally taken from us. The islanders did, and do, have the right to decide their own destiny. And, of course, mistakes were made in the reclaiming operation.

Let those facts be enlarged upon and dissected elsewhere. Here, we confine ourselves to what we were privileged to see and share with those caught up in it all, and to what kept them going in times of great adversity.

As professional reporters we, like the professional

soldiers under whose wing we were, had to justify the trust our employers had placed in us in sending us to war. Throughout the entire operation, code-named Corporate, we had our jobs to do. The soldiers had theirs.

At times, life was cold and wet. Mostly it was miserable and often it was frightening for us all. There were moments of great elation and others of bitter frustration. There was joy and sadness, feast and famine. Everyone made friends on their way to the South Atlantic. Everyone lost a friend, or saw one maimed.

In this book we have set out the feelings we and the soldiers we were with experienced, reflecting, we hope, the true spirit and the never-failing sense of humour of the fighting people of the Task Force.

The first two chapters, of necessity, feature the authors, during their separate journeys to Ascension Island. This is intentional. It is during these journeys that we introduce you, the reader, to the people who really matter – the soldiers, sailors and airmen of the South Atlantic Task Force.

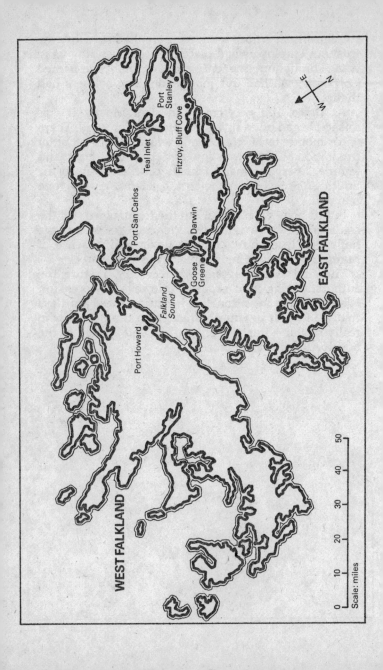

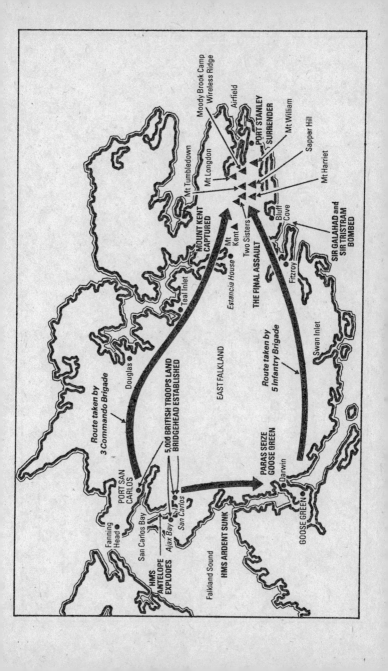

Chapter 1

Their faces showed all the emotion of a slab of granite as they moved slowly and purposefully towards the counter of the cafe, looking very hard.

On the serving side of the counter stood a woman whose face had always lived in the Coronation Street part of town, who probably spent nights exhausted before a rented colour television after a long day at work, and another cleaning house when she got home, wondering why everyone in the advertisements had a better kitchen than hers and if her husband would be home before closing time.

'Coffee's off. Not made yet, just tea. And if you want breakfast it's written on the wall what we've got, so don't ask.' She said it without looking up from the front page of the *Sun* while flicking the ash off her cigarette into an Embassy ashtray in front of her.

The granite cracked and the two Marines smiled, not that she noticed.

'Two wets, or I'll blow your tights off,' said one.

'Take more'n you, you fairy,' she said, the cigarette re-introduced into the vivid red circle that indicated the mouth in this former peach that had been too long left unpicked.

'Would you say,' said the other Marine, 'that she had a lived-in face?'

'Saying her face is lived-in,' replied his mate, 'is like saying they take paying guests in hell.'

'Nice,' said the woman. 'Bloody nice. Come in 'ere with your guns.' She stubbed out the cigarette, raised her voice a few ear-piercing decibels and screamed, 'Two teas!'

'With sugar.'

'On the table,' she said, flipping back to the front page. 'Says God Speed 'ere. All off to the Falklands and you buggers drinking tea.' Then with a wave of the arm she indicated the television set in the corner, and added, 'Old Hermers is off. There she goes. Bands playing. Navy, though, innit? Not bloody rude Bootnecks.'

Both Marines were looking at the television, across the floor beyond islands of plastic-topped tables on tubular frames with matching chairs sagging under the weight of more Commandos.

All the Bootnecks there were fresh-faced youths with an average age of just nineteen. All had faced the street corner threat of death in Northern Ireland but none knew what a full-scale soldier-against-soldier shooting war would be like. Bravado camouflaged their fear of uncertainty.

'There goes Jolly Jack,' said a voice among the islands. 'Bloody Navy getting all the glory while your fighting Bootneck sits around playing with himself. And no sod will even bang a triangle when we leave.'

He was right. No sod ever did. For these Commandos, like many others, left under the tightest security from ports along England's south coast.

A few days later, the P & O liner SS *Canberra* would leave Southampton in a blaze of patriotic emotion, recorded by television, radio and newspapers, carrying many more Marines and the Parachute Regiment's 3rd Battalion. But back in the cafe in Southampton, young Marines who would set sail before *Canberra* with some envy were watching on television the departure which they could have seen just by walking outside. The Falklands Task Force flagship *Hermes* and her support carrier *Invincible* were on their way, flight decks bristling with Harrier jump-jets, officers and ratings raising their hats to tearful relatives and well-wishers ashore, Sublieutenant H.R.H. Prince Andrew waving to his mother at home.

'Two teas,' said the lady behind the counter, with a voice deliberately loud enough to drown the noise of the ships' sirens on the television.

'Oh, ta,' said one of the Marines at the counter, handing over some money.

'Makes you wish you had the balls to go yourself, doesn't it?' she said, pushing back the change.

'If I had any tits, love, you'd be getting on them,' said the other Marine.

'Sorry,' said the lady. 'I was forgetting. You must have a tough job ahead, I mean, guarding all those pubs 'til the Navy gets back.'

'Key work, my love,' said one of the Marines.

'You coming back?' asked the lady.

'In 'ere?' asked one of the Marines.

'Yeah, in 'ere.'

'Not for a long while.'

Now she looked up from the *Sun*. 'Then, be careful. And come home safe.'

Both Marines smiled. One said, 'Keep your frock over it, love.'

The pair drank their tea, and left. Outside they encountered a Marine sergeant standing by a row of public telephones along their route.

'Hello, men,' the sergeant said. 'Pusser's holiday, is it?' he enquired, using another slang word for the Royal Navy.

'No, Sarge,' answered one Marine. 'Just going for a stroll.'

'No, mate,' said the sergeant. 'Forget it. Get to the ship. Would like to delay it for you but the colonel would have a hell of a time explaining it to Maggie. Any more in there?'

'Hundreds.'

'Shit,' said the sergeant. 'It wasn't like this in *The Longest Day*.'

Outside, a fine drizzle filled the air. Everywhere, columns of Marines and vehicles picked their way

17

through the dockyard towards two logistic landing ships, *Sir Lancelot* and *Sir Percivale*.

Scout helicopters droned in like bees and landed on the pocket-handkerchief flight decks on the stern of each ship. Men of the Royal Corps of Transport loaded trucks, Land Rovers, Volvo tracked vehicles, 105 mm field guns, fuel and ammunition, the ironmongery of war that was now choking the dockyard.

The two Marines climbed the brow to the port shade deck of *Sir Lancelot* and ran into another sergeant. He was not very happy, either.

'Am I a nasty bastard?' he asked of them.

'No, Sergeant,' they answered in unison.

'Do you want me to change?'

'No, Sergeant.'

' "No, Sergeant"!' jeered the sergeant, looking at the *Daily Express* team following the Marines up the brow, Robert McGowan and photographer Tom Smith. 'Doing conducted tours, are we? Who are these pricks?'

The Marines shook their heads and scampered inboard as the sergeant glowered at McGowan and Smith. 'Well?' he shouted. 'Not bloody deaf, are you? What's your game?'

Smiling courteously, McGowan replied, 'Bob McGowan, *Daily Express*, and my colleague, Tom Smith. We joined the ship last night with permission from the Ministry of Def . . .'

'Yeah, all right,' sighed the sergeant. 'Know about you. Come to tell a few lies about it all, have we?'

'Only write the truth,' ventured McGowan, lamely.

'Make a bloody change round here then, mate,' he snarled. 'Go on then, piss off out of the way.'

The two Press men made their way to Cabin G on the port side, which they were sharing with Alan Percival, an information officer from the Ministry of Defence. Percival is an extremely likeable young man who, for the duration of the campaign, was to try harder than his fellow Ministry 'Minders' in the other ships to get news stories back to London.

What he did not know then, what no-one embarked in the ships knew, was that this alone was to develop into a nightmare of delayed material, misinterpreted signals from London and hopeless communications, all combining in the coming weeks to give Argentina a vital edge in that other conflict, the Propaganda War.

'You didn't let me hear you when you filed your copy in the NAAFI,' said Percival to McGowan. 'I have to vet everything for security reasons.'

'I didn't think you'd let me get away with mentioning the tanks and the napalm,' lied McGowan.

Percival, wide-eyed with alarm and toying with the idea of being angry, snapped, 'But there are no tanks and napalm. You've made it up.'

'I'm joking,' said McGowan. 'I promise you, my story was so dull people in my office are even now falling asleep over it. I'm in the wrong place. We should be out there, with *Hermes* and *Invincible*, not on this bloody old tub. What's the good of being on here?'

'Luck of the draw,' said Percival. 'Take it or leave it, but you can't move to another ship. If you don't like it, you can go ashore now.'

'Great,' moaned McGowan. 'This the shape of things to come, is it? Tell me, how do I file my copy? How does Tom here get his pictures away?'

'There will be ways,' replied Percival. 'I'll go and check with the radio officer now.' He left the cabin.

'Fancy a sherbert?' said Smith to McGowan in his cheerful Cockney manner. 'I threw a roll of film to a bloke on the dock, so we've both got something past them already.'

Both men walked into the corridor outside the cabin which was crammed with men lugging their kit, looking for their accommodation. McGowan's tone slipped automatically into the peace-and-light mode

19

now, among men who might very easily give him a back-hander should he appear rude.

'Excuse me. Terrible weather, isn't it? How do you do? Where's the bar?'

'The bar?' bellowed Sergeant Dennis Brown, in his rich Liverpool brogue. 'This is a ship, not a bloody doss house. Are we referring to the mess, perhaps?'

'Don't start, Ace,' said Smith, using his usual epithet for McGowan. 'You don't want to peak too early.'

'Sorry, I mean mess,' snivelled McGowan.

Brown challenged, 'Which one? Who are you?'

'Press.'

'Oh, Christ,' said Brown. 'That'll be officers. Up the ladder through there and you'll see it.'

McGowan and Smith found the mess and the bar, and the man who was to strike more fear into McGowan than any battle-hardened Argentinian soldier could ever do.

Mr Chu stood four-square behind the bar, lank black hair framing a mustard face in which lurked two eyes of darkest brown that could pierce your soul, and a mouth fashioned into a permanent scowl. He wore crumpled black trousers that had not had the benefit of a visit to Sketchley's in many a long month and a sweat-streaked vest that, were it possible to get it off him and hold it up to the light, would have looked like a relief map of the Yangtze Delta.

The little man who must have obtained his clothes from a Mothercare dustbin now spoke, with a delivery no less disarming than an elephant breaking wind. 'What you want?'

Fearful that even a moment's delay in answering could bring about a spiteful karate chop a centimetre or so below his left, and nearest, ear lobe, McGowan said hastily, 'Two pints of lager, please.'

'Not ready yet,' snapped Mr Chu.

'Okay, we'll wait,' said McGowan. 'Doesn't look as though we're going anywhere.'

'I ready now,' announced Mr Chu, who in the bat of an eyelid had put on a once-white shirt that probably walked in by itself. 'Two pint lager?'

'Two pint lager,' replied McGowan, foolishly mimicking the man.

'You got mess number?' demanded Mr Chu.

'No mess number.'

'You pay,' ordered Mr Chu.

'I pay,' agreed McGowan. Percival walked in and McGowan added, 'You want pint lager? Don't upset my old China here, or he'll throw it at you.'

'Three pint lager?' asked Mr Chu, oozing venom.

'Three pint lager,' said McGowan.

Percival had not come in alone. With him were the ship's chief radio officer, Roger Sims, and the purser, Rab McKillop. Both men wore the uniforms of officers of the Royal Fleet Auxiliary, to which *Sir Lancelot* belonged.

McKillop sorted out the mess numbers with the irascible Mr Chu and Sims said: 'So far I see no problems about your filing stories, as long as they've been vetted in advance by Mr Percival. But there could be a problem over photographs.'

Smith groaned and as he did, Percival said, 'We'll get round it. There'll be other ships with us that may well have wire facilities for pictures.'

Two young men in flying suits came into the mess, both wearing the insignia of Royal Navy lieutenants. Vince Shaughnessy and Dick Nunn had just landed their Scout helicopters on board and now eyed the two journalists and the man from the Ministry with suspicion.

'Have to watch what we say, then,' said Nunn, a tall slim man with an expression that indicated that he would be a mean poker opponent.

They were followed by senior officers from the Commando Logistics Regiment, to which most of the Marines aboard belonged, the men whose job it would be to get vital supplies to the battlefields in the coming weeks.

One officer, holding a pint mug, said, 'The Press. How nice.' He said it with the diplomacy of a man who had just discovered a seagull dropping in his beer but did not want to let on.

Alan Percival then said, 'I have another problem.' He said he had received a signal from the Ministry of Defence, which he always called simply 'MOD', and added, 'I'm afraid that you can't name this ship in any stories. The Argies don't know about it so it stays anonymous.'

'Shit,' said McGowan, with the eloquence of a man who was not having a good day.

'I'm sorry, Bob,' said Percival to McGowan. 'But I'm sure it will be only temporary.'

'Well then,' said McGowan, 'can I make up a name? You know, explaining that it is fictitious but for security reasons the ship's real identity cannot be revealed?'

'Yes,' agreed Percival.

'Right, I'll call her Cinderella, on the basis that she knows she's going to the ball, but no-one else does.'

'Fine,' said Percival. Some officers in the bar laughed, some winced, and Mr Chu gave McGowan a look that seemed to bestow the Curse of the Boat People on him.

'What about the others?' asked McGowan. 'In *Hermes* and *Invincible*. Can they name their ships?'

'Yes they can,' said Percival, 'because they've been shown leaving on television and the Argies know they're coming.'

'Bloody marvellous,' blustered McGowan. 'How do you suppose I explain this little lot to my office? They'll go mad.'

Throughout this and other conversations, Percival always referred to *Hermes* and *Invincible* as 'Herms' and 'Invisible', a habit that was to annoy McGowan.

22

As *Sir Lancelot* made ready for sea, the three civilians argued on, wandering aimlessly through the ship, pausing only in either Cabin G or the bar in the officers' mess.

That night, 5 April, 1982, all three were to run into much more immediate problems than the trivia of informing a waiting world.

To reach the mess from their cabin, they had to traverse a minefield called The Sergeants' Mess, which no private, no officer and certainly no civilian could enter without invitation.

'Piss off,' shouted a very large sergeant who called himself Chris and everyone else 'Chalkie'.

'Sorry?' said Percival as he, McGowan and Smith made their way through the hallowed ground towards their cabin.

'Piss off, Chalkie,' repeated Chris. 'Sergeants' Mess, mate. Can't come in 'ere without permission.'

Smith tugged McGowan's sleeve and whispered, 'Let's go, Ace. Do a runner.'

The fearless hacks sped off to Cabin G, leaving the affable Minder in the lions' den.

'Fucking wonderful,' said Percival when he caught up, an hour later, to find the hacks slumbering peacefully in their bunks. 'I got a right savaging in there. You could have helped.'

'Takes a diplomat,' said Smith, soothingly. 'Me and Ace over there, well, we're more of your hooligan element. Would have done more harm than good.'

'Did that nice Mr Percival swear, Mr Smith?' said McGowan, buried under sheets and blankets in a lower berth.

'Yes, Ace,' said Smith. 'He doesn't swear, does he?'

'You'd swear if you'd been through what I've been through,' complained Percival. 'But I've smoothed it over. They want to see us in there tomorrow night.'

'It's a trap,' said McGowan.

23

'Yeah, they're planning something nasty,' said Smith.

Both journalists rolled over and went to sleep, no doubt leaving a disrobing Percival to ponder upon what he had let himself in for.

The following morning, 6 April, *Sir Lancelot* slipped her moorings and put to sea. No-one banged a triangle, no crowds wept and waved as they had for *Hermes* and *Invincible* the day before. A lone helicopter flew overhead and the pilot gave a thumbs up. On the shore, the headlights of one family car flashed a farewell. Sitting in it unhappily was Mrs Lynn Edwards, wife of the ship's second engineer Phil Edwards, who had driven down from Barrow-in-Furness just for this moment. It was a lonely, hollow departure for all on board.

Only four days earlier, an Argentinian invasion force had landed on the Falklands and overwhelmed the Royal Marines defending them. Now most of the Task Force was at sea and heading south, a monumental achievement in so short a time by a country renowned for being closed at weekends. It had all been done from Friday to Tuesday.

McGowan, chaperoned by Percival, left the ship's rail and went up to the radio room to call his office. He filed his 'Cinderella' story and asked his foreign editor to try to put pressure on the Ministry of Defence for clearance to use the true name of *Sir Lancelot*.

The ship's captain, Chris Purtcher-Wydenbruck, a friendly Austrian on his last voyage before retirement, and the commanding officer of the Commando Logistics Regiment, Lieutenant-Colonel Ivar Hellberg, a veteran Everest climber, both vowed to help both Smith and McGowan in every way possible; and whenever possible, they were true to their word.

The night came too quickly for Smith and McGowan. The Sergeants' Mess beckoned, and could not be avoided, since it lay between them in the officers' bar and their cabin.

'This is the Dodgey Optic,' announced Sergeant Sandy MacLeod, and pointing to a ginger bear hanging from a light, he added, 'and that's Teddy, the mess mascot. You are welcome to buy us all any amount you want.'

McGowan, Smith and Percival were then treated to a chorus of jeering along the lines of 'Gutter Press', then 'Bunch of poofs', and finally the soon-to-be commonplace 'Piss off, Chalkie'.

The evening developed into one of those that give you a head the morning after. 'It's good-oh, isn't it, Mac?' Sandy said to McGowan. 'Got all this together in a weekend. Bound to put the wind up the Argies. Always knew this country could hack it if it wanted to.'

For the three civilians the metamorphosis was beginning. Words like 'hack it', meaning you can do it, and 'yomping', and 'tabbing', meaning to hike across country, were to be firmly etched in their vocabularies for evermore. There would be many other strange phrases to follow.

A giant arm encircled McGowan's neck, with enough force to show its worth, but not yet causing pain. 'Little man over there says you'll break my back if I upset you, Chalkie. Is that right?'

Now, to describe Sergeant Chris as small would be much like saying the Matterhorn is a molehill. McGowan looked across at Smith, guffawing in the corner and muttered, 'Evil shit.'

Then to Chris, he blurted, 'Me? No, wouldn't hurt a fly. It's a joke. Have a drink. Or my watch. Anything.'

Chris laughed. 'All right, Chalkie. I'll buy you one. What happened with Spurs on Saturday?'

'Dunno,' choked McGowan. 'I'll find out. Promise.'

'Yeah, I need to know every Saturday. It's important to me. You going all the way?'

25

'To the Falklands? Yes,' said McGowan.

'Done it this time, haven't they?' said Chris. 'Gone too far. Don't care what the politicians say, we've got to go and sort them out. We've got to get a result. Give 'em a spanking, eh?'

'Yeah, well, absolutely,' agreed McGowan.

'You're all right, Chalkie,' said Chris. 'Just remember the Spurs results.'

There were too many more nights like that, but fortunately, few mornings like the following one.

Dawn broke with *Sir Lancelot* butting into a Force Eight gale and in the radio room Roger Sims said chirpily to a green McGowan, 'The old ship rolls on wet grass, you know. Flat bottom, you see.'

'Where's the toilet?' begged McGowan, an egg-and-bacon breakfast fighting to be free of him.

'Do you mean the heads, old chap?' asked Sims, mischievously.

'Look,' spluttered McGowan, in extremis, 'I don't have time for bloody semantics. Where's the bleeding bog?'

'Down there to your right,' chuckled Sims. 'Shade of an oak tree, that's what you want.'

If McGowan had the will then, had he had enough strength left after what was about to flow forth, he could have killed Sims right there. The moment passed in seconds, but in the wretched state of sea-sickness, the thought had gone through his mind.

The terrible time lingered all day as the ship headed through the Bay of Biscay. Out on deck, and fortuitously with the wind in the right direction. McGowan was soon at it again. A lusty Marine jogged by and said, 'Got your sea legs yet, mate?'

McGowan heaved over the side. 'No, see you haven't,' said the Marine. 'Still, you're doing it right. Keep chucking it up, but when you see a round brown bit, bite hard and swallow, 'cos that's your arsehole.'

'I'm in hell,' thought McGowan. 'It's a nightmare.'

The next day, the sun shone, the sea was like a mill pond and Marines were pounding the decks to keep fit.

A day or so later, *Sir Lancelot* was dead in the water, her engines giving trouble, awaiting a vital service before she reached the war zone. During the day, one at a time, chief engineer Andy Lauder and Phil Edwards would come out on deck, soaked in sweat, and look up at the funnel. Always, there was smoke billowing from it. Bad news in a war zone.

By the middle of the afternoon, the problem had not been solved. Phil came out and leaned against the rail. Four days after *Sir Lancelot* sailed he should have gone on leave, his first for thirteen months. Standing near him were Sandy MacLeod and McGowan.

'Fixed it?' asked MacLeod.

A puff of smoke drifted out of the funnel. 'Fuck,' said Phil, and disappeared.

'No, Mac. I don't think he's fixed it yet,' deduced MacLeod. 'They may have to start the war without us.'

The next morning, the supply ship *Stromness* came into sight. As McGowan watched it, knowing his friend, Dave Norris of the *Daily Mail* was on board her, Alan Percival appeared with radio officer Sims.

'Er, bad news, Bob,' said Percival.

'We're sinking?' asked McGowan.

'Gone to a ball of chalk,' said Sims.

'No, still not with you,' said McGowan.

'There's minimize on the radio,' Sims tried to explain.

'You mean it's shrunk?' asked McGowan, sarcastically.

'No,' said Percival. 'MOD has put us in radio silence. We can't send stories.'

'Shit,' barked McGowan. 'What's the point of having us here if we can't work? What about *Fearless*? Surely Brigadier Thompson can clear my copy?'

Brigadier Julian Thompson, commanding officer of

27

the Task Force Landing Forces, was based in the assault ship HMS *Fearless*, which had been in company with *Sir Lancelot* the day before, but now could not be seen.

' 'Fraid not, Bob. *Fearless* has gone ahead to meet up with "Herms" and "Invisible" at Ascension,' said Percival, unaware that his pet names for the two carriers were increasingly annoying to McGowan. 'Actually, it's not really on. We had agreed to see the brigadier today, but he's just gone. I could complain to MOD. After all, ministers eat brigadiers.'

'Right,' said McGowan. 'I want to send a snotty message to my office. Not a story, just an explanation to them for why we can no longer do our jobs. Can it be sent?'

'Not from here,' said Percival. 'I'll try to work something out with one of the other ships.'

Exasperated, McGowan stormed off, and later in the day he joined a physical training routine with some of the Marines.

'Old and bold,' said a drill sergeant as the hack panted by. 'Couple more laps will kill him off.'

But it didn't. Nearly, but not quite. McGowan staggered to his cabin and found Smith stretched out on his bunk.

'You're going to peak too soon, Ace. I'm warning you,' said Smith. 'What's the point? Why try to impress them? They won't let us work.'

In despair, Smith and McGowan went to the officers' mess that night and watched a war film in which Burt Lancaster got his come-uppance in Vietnam.

When Lancaster, playing a senior American officer, was interviewing new recruits, Smith nudged McGowan. 'Wouldn't have been any better out there, Ace. Look at that Burt. He's a wrong-un. He wouldn't let you file either.'

One deck below, the sergeants were conducting a bar-top court-martial. The padre stood accused.

28

Sandy MacLeod held a properly filled-out charge sheet, and read, 'You, Padre, stand accused of entering the mess and loitering, and with bringing no booze, which is vagrancy. Have you got a brief?'

'The officer here,' said the padre, cocking a thumb at a young sub-lieutenant beside him.

'Stop laughing, Padre,' warned Big Chris as the cleric struggled to suppress a giggle. 'It'll go badly for you.'

Sandy MacLeod asked of the young officer, 'Sir, can you explain his behaviour?'

The officer began the defence. 'He made a mistake. Never did he intend to break the rules of the mess. He is very sorry.'

'Guilty!' screamed the sergeants, making crosses with their forefingers and hissing at the padre as though he were a vampire in a Dracula film.

'We fine you a bottle of sherry,' pronounced MacLeod, 'and Sir here, too, because he did such a bloody awful job of defending you.'

The padre left, returning later with a bottle.

He didn't stand a chance. A sergeant examined the 'fine' and bellowed, 'Only half a bottle. You won't go to Heaven, Padre. Now piss off.'

The next morning, McGowan was told he could drop the Cinderella tag, and use *Sir Lancelot*'s real name. Permission came in a signal to the ship from the Ministry of Defence.

'Great,' said McGowan. 'I can't file a story, but I can use the right name. It's all going downhill.'

A helicopter piloted by Dick Nunn flew alongside, then inched over the flight deck and put down.

Out jumped Dave Norris, from *Stromness*. He was not best pleased with life.

'They won't let me use the name of my ship now,' he said. 'Been using it all the time. Now I can't.'

He shook his head and McGowan's hand and added in his endearing Manchester accent, 'Does anyone know what's going on? 'Cos I don't. It's daft. They've all gone mad. I don't think we're going to the Falklands after all. Bastards have kidnapped us.'

Sergeant Dennis Brown looked at Norris, who like McGowan, was the archetypal Fleet Street journalist in one sense at least, a study in misshapen physical disaster. Brown said, 'Bloody hell. There's another one of them. Look at the state of *him*!'

'Cheeky bugger,' said Norris, steadfastly showing no fear in the face of this rock-hard fighting man. 'Took me years and thousands of hard-earned pounds to look like this, and I'm proud of it. I suppose that clever sod McGowan has been jogging around like the crawler he is?'

'Polished him off yesterday,' said Brown. 'He's knackered, man. Gone a bit moody, he has. Can't send his stories. Like a bear with a sore arse, he is.'

'Good,' said Norris. 'Pleased to hear someone's still got some standards. Where'd he go?'

McGowan was now one deck up, at the officers' bar, trying to out-stare the inscrutable Mr Chu through the grill that proclaimed that the bar was not yet open.

'Savage little sod,' said McGowan as Norris walked in with Tom Smith. 'Little bugger knows it's opening time. He's got a whole new line in Chinese torture. Think about it. There are literally millions of Mr Chus around this planet who couldn't give a shit about opening time.'

The padre came in with Majors Tony Welch and Les Short, who should have been named Les Tall inasmuch as he was easily six feet four.

'Bar not open?' asked Major Short. 'I could use an orange squash.'

'Mr McGowan's about to break through the bamboo curtain,' said Norris.

'A visitor,' said Tony Welch. 'How nice.'

During the introductions, Norris said, 'Go on, you can tell me. This *is* the ferry to Ostend, isn't it?'

'You don't expect us to know what's going on, do you?' laughed Les Short. 'Only colonels and above know that.'

'Ministers eat colonels,' muttered a newly-arrived Alan Percival, slightly changing the quote. Then he added, 'These buggers are going to hang me if I can't get their copy out.'

'Clap 'em in irons,' suggested Les Short. 'Do 'em good.'

The grill clattered up and Mr Chu stood with his elbows on the counter as though he had been waiting for ages to serve his customers.

'Smug little shit,' whispered McGowan, but everyone heard. 'Sod it – sorry, Padre.'

'It's all right,' said the understanding cleric. 'If you can't swear, nor can I.'

'No swear,' hissed Mr Chu. 'Very rude person. No serve.'

The padre stepped in. 'Oh, he didn't mean it, Mr Chu. He's sorry.'

'Yeah, I'm sorry,' whimpered McGowan, convinced dehydration was setting in.

'What you want then?' demanded Mr Chu.

'Oh, yeah,' said McGowan. 'It's four pints of lager. Padre? OK, and a half. Tony? Les? Two orange squashes? Right.'

McGowan looked round to begin the order. Mr Chu had disappeared.

Exasperated, McGowan thundered, 'The little fart's pissed off. Would you believe it?'

'I here,' said a voice spitting from somewhere unseen. Then Mr Chu appeared from a crouching position behind the bar. 'I change barrel for you, rude person.'

The drinks were served and the three journalists stole off into a corner to bemoan their lot.

'The mad bastards on the *Stromness* are jogging round the deck chanting "Napalm sticks to Spicks," ' said Norris. 'They're a real hard lot, all in 45 Commando.'

Later, Norris returned to his ship. The next day, Sub-lieutenant Malcolm Hazell set about organizing a full-scale marathon aboard the *Sir Lancelot*, and two days after that, as the ship neared the Equator, it began.

Seven runners set out in torchlight before dawn on two measured courses on the port and starboard shade decks. Each runner had to cross a mark of masking tape at one end, turn round and run back to the other end, crossing a similar mark. The temperature was 79°F when they set off and 84°F when Marine Paul Brindley came home first after running 26 miles and 365 yards.

It took him four hours, four minutes and 15 seconds, in which time the ship had travelled 52 nautical miles.

It was the first-ever marathon, properly scrutinized, to be run on a ship heading towards a war. Morale aboard *Sir Lancelot* soared.

The next day, the ship crossed the Equator. Tom Smith, Alan Percival, and just about everyone aboard but an elusive chicken-hearted McGowan, were thrown into a specially rigged canvas pool to celebrate the event.

Twelve hours later *Sir Lancelot* anchored off Ascension Island, a day ahead of the SS *Canberra*.

'I'm sorry,' said Percival to McGowan and Smith. 'I had hoped you could go ashore and file your stories through Cable and Wireless. But the Americans who run the airbase here say you can't. It's out of my hands. Even MOD can't help.'

After the initial explosion, McGowan and Smith grabbed an empty bottle of Graves, scribbled a message which they sealed inside with a cork from the bar, and tossed it over the side.

It drifted out into the Atlantic. The message read, 'Mum, we want to come home.'

Chapter 2

Captain Christopher Peter Oldbury Burne, RN, strode into the Lounge Bar of the Post House Hotel, blinding the assembled hacks with the glare from the gold braid on his shoulders and the reflection of the sun from his hat, teeth and spectacles. Six foot plus, brimming with confidence and authority, this captain of the Queen's Navy was an awesome sight.

'He's a shit,' said one of the Minders from the MOD Press Office. 'We've been trying our damnedest to get your lot on to *Canberra*. Everyone from Downing Street to CinC Fleet has told him you've got to come. But you know what these passed-over captains are like. He's insisting it's all his show, and as *Canberra* is now his ship he's sticking out on this point just to be bloody-minded. We'll keep trying to get you on before she sails. But as that's tonight, you can take it from me you haven't got a hope in hell.'

Captain Burne put his hands on his hips, stood even taller, and spoke. 'OK; super,' he said. 'All right?'

Silence from the absorbed hacks.

'You're all coming with us. I insisted on it, and despite opposition from other quarters they let me have my way on this point at least. So I'm delighted to have you all with me. OK? Super.'

Nervous grins from the journalists. Purple blush from Alan George.

'OK, some of you will be in the Asian quarters, all right? But at least we'll get you there, OK?'

Nods of disbelief and relief from the hacks, and more grins towards the MOD, who had proved totally and prophetically, for the first time of many, that everything they said was going to be misleading if not completely inaccurate.

'OK; super,' said Captain Burne. 'We're sailing tonight at twenty hundred, OK? Want you on board by eighteen hundred. OK; fine. Jolly good. Right?' And with that, our leader left, sweeping out as he had swept in like the wake of the *Victory* under full sail.

Alan George saved face superbly. 'Told you we'd get you on,' he said, cringing. 'Leave everything to us, and it'll be plain sailing from here on.'

Nobody believed him, but nobody cared. We were going, and that's all that mattered.

With just four hours to get on board, Southampton's department stores, brimming with beachwear and summer fashions, didn't stand a chance. Crazed journalists rushed in demanding everything they hadn't got.

'Six thick arctic sweaters, three pairs of thermal underwear, four pairs of thick socks . . . oh, and some heavy walking boots,' was an average demand. Not a chance, but would sir like some swimming trunks instead?

But a compromise was reached, and the company American Express cards fairly melted with excess use. Ninety per cent of what was purchased in the spending spree was extremely pretty, but next to useless when put to the test.

Amongst many other bargains Hands picked up was an awfully fetching bright yellow waterproof jacket from C&A's. It looked fine in the fitting room and was sold immediately the salesman insisted on taking an inside-leg measurement to see if another size 'might prove a little less tight under the armpits'.

Even Sergeant-major Cameron March's first reaction was reassuring when he was treated to a viewing on *Canberra* later that evening.

'Very fetching bit of kit, that,' he said. 'Make a smashing target for an Argie pilot. Don't wear it anywhere near me when we land. Better still, chuck it over the side now.'

It stayed in the cabin for ever.

Were we going to war? Of course not, but why not enjoy the feeling of heroically riding off to the Crusades just the same? No *Canberra* cruise passengers had ever enjoyed a departure more. There we were, lapping up the envious glances of those who were being left behind, and trying to grit our teeth and kid ourselves that we were terribly brave and wasn't this what journalism was all about, and anyway it was better than being stuck in the office.

The last phone calls home: 'Don't worry, I'll be all right . . . we'll probably be back in a few days . . . for God's sake stop crying . . . of course I love you . . . no, there aren't any women on board.'

Then, with the Royal Marines, Paratroopers, Navy and everyone else already on board and beginning to look terribly professional, the fifteen media heroes shambled up the gangplank dead on eighteen hundred OK Super as Captain Burne had insisted.

'It's called a brow, so don't call it a gangplank,' said the diminutive fount of all things useless from the MOD. No, he didn't know what the difference was, but someone in a uniform had once said exactly the same to him, so that was good enough. It was a gangplank to us all from then on, just because the MOD insisted otherwise.

Captain Christopher Peter Oldbury Burne had been right. The accommodation was 'a little cramped' and we didn't need much prompting from the MOD to convince us that the real reason for our travelling in conditions that a self-respecting ship's rat would have deserted over was that Captain Burne, despite his plausible pleasantries, didn't really want us on board after all, and having had his hand forced was determined to ensure we had as uncomfortable a time of it as he could manage.

The ITN contingent, war veteran cameraman Bob Hammond, sunsoaked sound recordist John Martin and reporter Hands were led down a maze of corridors and staircases ('You've got to call them companionways and passageways,' said the MOD moron, who still had to realize that everything he said was going to be totally ignored). Three long and sweaty trips were required to get the mountain of camera equipment stacked outside the door of Cabin A281. The way through the door was blocked by the equally mountainous figure of the man who was to be our cabinmate; the enormously built man from the London *Standard*, Max Hastings.

Accommodation: four bunks, two up, two down, a wash basin, tiny wardrobe and shower closet in a space hardly large enough for the furniture, let alone four big men with all their equipment and personal baggage.

Hastings, ignoring our joint strainings under the weight of our equipment, was crouching on the cabin floor attempting to retrieve the contents of a large suitcase, which was strewn in all directions after an obviously impressive slapstick entrance which we had sadly missed. No clothes or survival kit met our gaze, but dozens of hardbacked books lay everywhere.

'Not to read, you understand,' said their owner. 'Just to make the place look a bit more like home.'

We could not gain entrance to our new home until the interior decorations were completed according to the fancy of our colleague. Protestations, groanings, even profanities were in vain. Eventually Hastings was satisfied that every volume was in a place where he could appreciate it, and we could get inside our cell.

Hastings and Hands had the top bunks, Hammond and Martin the lower ones. John Martin, whose neverfailing sense of humour did so much to keep us going throughout, immediately started referring to Hastings as 'Her Upstairs' when he was in a good mood, or 'Wendy' when he wasn't. Both fitted to a tee. The latter-day *Private Eye* epithet, 'Hitler Hastings', was, if anything, too kind.

Our neighbours were all young Marines from 42 Commando. Hands immediately upset them by referring to their beloved unit as 'Forty-two'.

'Forty-two is a position in the *Kama Sutra*,' said one. 'We are four-two, and we're still inventing positions you wouldn't believe.'

An early mistake was thus colourfully corrected, and we went upstairs to take a last lingering look at our green and pleasant land, in the shape of Southampton Docks, which are anything but green and pleasant.

Men in green and maroon berets craned over the rails and peered down on the mass of flags, banners and bands on the quayside.

The Royal Marines band played 'Hearts of Oak' and 'A Life on the Ocean Wave' as the band of the Parachute Regiment waited for their turn to let forth with 'The Ride of the Valkyries'.

Brave men wept, wives and sweethearts cried, and a Marine who had overdone the 'last chance' drink on shore was sick over the stern.

Banners urged us to 'Give the Argies some Bargie' and to 'Come back safe and soon'. Shouts from the quayside ranged from 'Oh, Bill, I love you', to 'Make the bastards die slowly'.

Everyone aboard felt braver than ever, and not a little choked by the emotion of it all. There were thousands of them wishing us well and tearfully waving their goodbyes. Nationalist fervour had soared to new heights, and a sailor said to his mate, 'If we don't come back without at least taking Buenos Aires, they'll murder us.'

To the strains of 'We are Sailing' the ropes were slipped and *Canberra* was off into the unknown. Down Southampton Water, past blocks of flats flashing their room lights, car horns wailing, distant cheering from jetties and small boats, even blue lights flashing from police cars. Nobody left the rails until we were well down into the Solent and the accompanying flotilla of small boats had turned back.

'God, I hope it's like this when we come back,' said a voice to Hands' left, 'and I hope some bastard's not screwing my wife in the meantime.'

'Could be a problem,' said whoever he was talking to. 'If she lets you anywhere near her, everyone's got a chance.'

And so the Paras went to their messes, and the Marines went to theirs. It was a pattern of self-inflicted separation that was to be followed throughout the operation. The reason quite simply is that the Marines believe the Paras are animals who eat their young, and the Paras look on the Marines as dimwitted clods who have their every whim pandered to by senior officers. This policy of keeping themselves to themselves was fostered lovingly by officers of both, who feared with some justification that fraternization would inevitably lead to attempted genocide.

Problems could arise too, it was felt, if too much drink was made available to the men. So each was rationed to two cans of beer a day. Now, either soldiers have an astonishing ability to get totally paralytic on two cans a day, or someone wasn't very good at counting, as groups of men propping each other up as they tried a joint rendition of 'Eskimo Nell' were not an uncommon sight from the first night onwards. Yet drunkenness was never a problem. The soldiers had an ability to fall over only when nobody with pips or crowns on their shoulders was watching. Only one man was ever caught, charged and fined (£200).

But if the Marines and Paras tolerated rather than enjoyed each other's company, they were bonded together in a common loathing of the Royal Navy.

Captain Burne had about twenty men under his

command. But *Canberra* being a ship, the Navy being the senior service, and Captain Burne being Captain Burne meant there was never a moment's question that the twenty were in complete control of the 2,500. Well, that was the theory.

In fact, the Crow's Nest Bar, where the officers of all units and the gentlemen of the press used to drink, was a hotbed of indignation at the Navy's impertinence. The Crow's Nest was surely an officers' mess, as that's where the officers messed. So how dare the Navy try to insist that it was to be called a wardroom? They certainly tried.

Signs went up: 'Wardroom' and 'Wardroom Notice Board'; even 'Wardroom, Officers Only'. They came down quickly, only to be replaced by others declaring, 'Officers' Mess', and 'Officers' Mess Notice Board'; and so on. It was open warfare before we had even got to the Equator.

In the end the matter was permanently resolved in a non-diplomatic way, when the Navy were informed they would be 'filled in' if they continued with their misguided behaviour.

'It's in your own best interests not to interfere with officers of the Royal Marines and the Parachute Regiment,' they were told. It was the Officers' Mess from that moment on without further question.

But the Navy, still brimming with the spirit of Trafalgar, had one last attempt at keeping alive the traditions they hold so dear. At seven p.m. the Tannoy system ('It's called a "pipe",' said the MOD cretin) burst into life with the announcement, 'Sunset. All those on the upper deck face aft and salute.'

It was a nice thought, and well-meaning enough, but they don't do that sort of thing in the Paras. The exercise was cancelled after the second evening, when the Naval party realized that they could never stop the moving little ceremony being interrupted each time by 2,500 voices shouting in unison 'Bollocks!'

Those early days of the cruise, for it was no worse, were full of bravado and high expectation. General Galtieri was the butt of a hundred jokes, and what our shipmates were going to do to his poor, cold, useless army was nobody's business.

Canberra plodded rather than charged towards the South Atlantic, and her passengers set about improving their already well-proven skills in killing people.

Fitness plays a major part in being a soldier, and as *Canberra* bears little or no resemblance to Dartmoor, or Crystal Palace Stadium, improvization was needed. It was found on the Promenade Deck, which some PTI paced out and discovered was exactly a quarter of a mile once round. So round and round we all went day after day after day, as it got hotter and hotter and hotter, and everyone grew a little fitter and a lot more fed up with each circuit.

Out came the tee-shirts with their scores of different motifs, all leading the casual observer to the inescapable conclusion that the wearers were not in any way connected with Gay Lib or the Women's Institute. Some tee-shirts simply proclaimed the wearer's unit, others what the wearer had allegedly done to Linda Lovelace's throat, and some more optimistically what they were going to do to the Argentine Army.

One set of shirts, a leftover from a section's duty in Northern Ireland, sickeningly alluded to the effectiveness of the plastic bullet with the words 'X Troop, Plastic Killers'.

'Falk off, Galtieri', was a hurriedly produced specimen, as was 'Start Crying for Us, Argentina, we're Coming to Bomb the Shit out of you'.

Beneath the vests lay the full gruesome range of what the tattooists of Plymouth and Aldershot can do. Every Marine had his blood-group tattooed on his left shoulder with garish embellishments. Other tattoos swore everlasting devotion to 'Mum and Dad', or a wife or girlfriend. There were the tough-guy types, too, promising 'Death before Dishonour' with decorations of daggers and snakes. Comedians had 'Cut here' around their necks, and there was at least one 'Go and Fuck Yourself', tattooed on the outside of the little finger of the right hand which only showed when saluting.

The work rate increased both on the physical side and in the *Canberra*'s public rooms, which were used for briefings on everything from what the Argentines had waiting for us on the Falklands to first aid and signalling. There was a real fear that the men would 'peak' too soon, and get off the ship at the other end exhausted and useless. But anything that kept the Marines' and Paras' minds off attacking each other was considered a worthwhile exercise whatever the consequence.

New bulletins were avidly listened to, the to-ings and fro-ings of Al Haig monitored and argued over in every mess, until someone, who understandably had lost complete track of where the worthy Secretary of State was, suggested it was Haig who put the 'lag' in jet lag and that it was bound to be left to the soldiers to sort it out in the end.

Others disagreed. How could that Dago dunderhead in Buenos Aires possibly keep holding out now we were on our way? He was bound to give in soon, wasn't he? Diplomacy was bound to provide the answer in the end, wasn't it? The Yanks would step in and stop it, and even if they didn't, they'd never let Maggie re-invade . . . would they?

But why, oh why was *Canberra* bumbling along so incredibly slowly? Surely if we were on our way to liberate those poor oppressed sheep-shaggers we ought to be hurtling along at warp factor nine, not practising how to replenish at sea and go through anti-submarine manoeuvres at a miserable 12 to 15 knots.

The *Canberra* Owners' Handbook said the ship could do over 23 knots, so who the hell was playing at what?

It was all very frustrating, and the one thing the fighting men aboard *Canberra* didn't lack was self-confidence or the desire to start making Argentina cry. If they'd known it was going to take the best part of two months to get to the Falklands, Captain Burne, who had earned himself the temporary nickname of Captain Bligh, would have had a real mutiny on his hands.

In the early days, the inevitable question, 'How long to you think we'll be away?' was met with a stock answer: '43 days. That's three weeks to get there, one day to kick the Argies off, and three weeks to get home.' Now the jokers and pessimists began to wonder.

Rumours, naturally, had started on Day One. They're called 'buzzes' in the Services, and so it was that the *Canberra*'s daily news-sheet, the *Canberra Buzz*, came into being. The prime function of the paper was to entertain and misinform as much as possible. Anything which bore a faint resemblance to the truth was relegated to the lower paragraphs; anything which was libellous, scandalous or hilarious given the splash headline. Rumours like 'Prince Andrew is being flown home because the Queen insists', or 'Russia is supplying the Argentines with something nasty' were played up prominently.

If any of the 14 P&O girls on board were seen as much as looking at, or being looked at, by anything in army uniform, the *Canberra Buzz* would report fully in grossly exaggerated detail, to the delight of everyone except the innocent parties. Nothing on board ship can be held sacred or kept secret.

One of the chaplains found that out the hard way, when he was caught in his cabin one afternoon with a girlie magazine in one hand and his wife's best friend in the other. In the Marines such a practice is known as 'giving it the nifty fifty', but a padre who forgot to close the curtains was too good an opportunity for the *Canberra Buzz* to miss, and the following morning in the small ads section he was reminded of his indiscretion with a curt line, 'Who's a randy boy, then, Harry, RN?'

In the end the *Canberra Buzz* was murdered by a few Very Senior Officers, who laughed like drains until the jokes started being aimed at them. Then it was all thought to be in 'terribly bad taste' and under the pretext of the *Buzz* becoming a security risk by being a little too close to the truth on issues that mattered it was summarily executed.

In fact the editors, Lt-Cdr Nick Brown and Lt Tony Maclinski, were offered the opportunity to continue publication on the condition they submitted each edition for 'editorial screening', as the Very Senior Officers called it, or 'Moscow-style censorship' as everyone else did. They refused, and the *Buzz* was no more. It was one of the sadder tragedies of the whole campaign.

But true to the finer traditions of the press, the erstwhile editors refused to be silenced, and what they couldn't pass on in print they tried to pass on by word of mouth. They might have lost their credibility, they might even have lost their commissions. In the end they lost their nerve and simply carried on doing what they were being paid for, namely to be the education officers trying to instil matters of moment into the brains of 42 Commando.

Maclinski, a Polish Scot ('Actually, I'm from the better part of Dundee') devoted his free-time activities to keeping relationships between the military and the press on an even keel. He succeeded by using a subtle technique involving passing on information in one direction and cadging drinks in the other, which led to him earning the nickname 'The Greasy Pole'.

In fact, thanks largely to the goodwill and good

43

humour of Lt Maclinski, there were never any of the problems regarding the press which cropped up in *Hermes* and *Invincible*.

But problems within the ranks of the press did arise, not least in cabin A281, where 'Her Upstairs' was becoming increasingly disliked by the ITN trio. It was mutual.

Mr Hastings kept remarking loudly about the awful stench, which he alone was able to detect, and made unmistakable allusions as to where he thought it was coming from, namely his cabin mates. Exception was taken and revenge planned.

With Hastings absent, John Martin and Bob Hammond stood awaiting his return, each armed with a vile-smelling eau de toilette they'd picked up from somewhere. As Hastings walked in, both sprays were raised as though to neutralize the offending armpits, but deliberately aimed right into our companion's startled face. He smelt sweetly for days, but never complained again. However, a move had to be arranged.

And so with the help of one of the most amiable men on board, Sergeant-major Bob 'Buster' Brown, the parting of the ways for the incumbents of A281 was brought about.

The worthy sergeant-major, at considerable risk to his career prospects, sorted out two new cabins, each of them much larger than A281, and for two passengers apiece only. Hammond and Martin seized one, leaving Hands still incarcerated with the man from *The Standard*. Was there no justice? Wasn't going to war bad enough without this?

But there was the one single compensation, which made it a lighter cross to bear. It was a simple and extremely moving daily ceremony which was to become known as The Hastings Dawn Chorus. It became a legend. Men were prepared to part with money to witness it, but few were ever privileged enough to get a sighting.

Hands and Hammond used to rise shortly after six each morning for half an hour's horrifyingly strenuous PT with 42 Commando. On his return to his new abode, cabin A22, Hands was greeted by the sight of the half-naked Hastings torso, still dormant. It was not pleasant viewing, particularly after the PT.

Once the man-mountain was alive, his brain went into auto-pilot as the rest of his body grew accustomed to the fact that it was alive. A loud 'herrumph!' would ensue, between four and six seconds after the initial explosion, and the white frame would raise itself to the sitting position, eyes still shut, arms flailing in search of spectacles. An inane tune would start to be hummed as the body was steered, still under remote control, across the floor to shower closet. All this in under ten seconds.

It was hilarious. It was wonderful, and there could be no better way to get Hands' day off to a start with a smile. It was a latter-day wonder of the world, and Hands made sure he never missed a single performance. An offer was made from the 3 Para sergeants to be present on one occasion to place a cork between the White Mountains before the earthquake, so that the force with which it would be fired against the cabin wall ('They're called bulkheads,' said the brainless one) could be measured. Hands declined. How could perfection be improved upon? Why ruin a masterpiece with over-embellishment? The sergeants conceded, grudgingly.

As *Canberra* kept up her southward track, so the Marines and Paras came to tolerate each other a little more willingly. Friendships grew, trusts were forged, hostilities declined. Inter-mess socializing was still banned between the units, but the spirit of co-operation which was to prove so invaluable later on was born.

There was the time, much enjoyed and admired by the Paras, when the Marines nearly sank our floating companion, *Elk*, by sheer accident, and bad management.

Elk, a North Sea ferry, was a cavalier little ship which bounded around *Canberra* as a puppy plays with its mother. Whenever you looked for *Elk*, she was somewhere else.

Her master, Captain John Moreton, and senior naval officer Commander Andy Ritchie, had aboard enough ammunition to take out half South America. But how they loved to show off the manoeuvrability of their happy charge. *Elk* would dart about as though trying to prove she was as versatile as any frigate, as indeed under her enthusiastic drivers she was.

But one fine morning the eternal leaping around the ocean nearly proved to be *Elk*'s undoing. Some Marines were firing at gash-bags off *Canberra*'s stern, to test and zero their rifles. Suddenly, there was *Elk*, right where she shouldn't be as usual, and in the sights of the Marines, who were far too busy blasting away at the rubbish bags to notice.

'Check, check, check!' yelled Captain Burne into the Tannoy. 'Cease firing, cease firing, cease firing!'

Reluctantly the Marines stopped, but not before *Elk* had been hit on the bow by at least one high-velocity round. By a miracle, but as proof that there is natural justice in this world, it turned out to be the only hit *Elk* received during the entire campaign.

No damage was done, and the Very Senior Officers tried to hush the incident up, which was the best possible way to ensure that everyone knew about it within minutes. It became joke-fodder on the mess decks for days afterwards.

But three days later *Canberra* recorded her first 'kill', which did not provide so many laughs.

Hands, in an article for the late lamented *Canberra Buzz*, had coined the nickname the White Whale for *Canberra*. It had stuck. But the first real whale we came across was black and far from well.

It was first sighted three cables off the starboard bow.

'Look, there it is, half a mile off the front to the right!' squealed the man from the Ministry, completely forgetting himself in the excitement.

Everyone rushed forward to see, and to take its picture. The whale was a friend, a good omen, a sight that was bound to cheer seafarers. But it really was very poorly.

The unfortunate animal kept coming straight for us. 'It thinks we're another whale, the randy sod,' said Lt Tony Hornby, still clinging to his pint glass. 'But I've a feeling it's bitten off a bit more than it can fellate.'

And so it proved. *Canberra*, on business far too urgent to worry about what conservation groups might think, kept steaming straight ahead at a steady 15 knots, and suddenly it was apparent that someone was going to come off second best. It was no contest. 45,000 tons of metal powered by the finest turbo-electric engines that were available in 1960 wasn't going to divert by an inch. 'This ocean just ain't big enough for the two of us, sweetie,' would have been the last thing the whale would have heard, if it had been listening, which it obviously wasn't. *Canberra*'s sharp bow struck the whale amidships. It was sliced neatly in two. Moments later our wake turned red, and well-prepared and sliced whaleburgers slewed out from the propellers.

The whale, which had been diagnosed by *Canberra*'s medical squadron as being 'bloody daft', was no more. We had found our Ancient Mariner's albatross; the omen was bad, and all aboard mourned.

But the gloom was lifted with the news that Sierra

Leone was just over the horizon, where we would call in for refuelling and taking on stores.

It first appeared as a grey dot on the horizon. Spirits and expectations rose. Surely there would be at least a few hours' shore leave. The first sighting of a civilian woman for a week; a bit of fun with the natives.

Canberra and *Elk* slipped into Freetown past the wrecks of other ships, which were a sorry testament to the skills of the local harbour pilots, who must have muttered, 'Damn, got it wrong again', on at least a dozen occasions. *Elk* tied up near the town centre; *Canberra* on the outskirts by the oil jetty.

'Forty thousands gallons of four star, and hurry up,' shouted a Marine to a native in a white coat who was picking nits out of his friend's hair.

Some men had gathered near the gangplank, anxious to be the first to sample the local delights.

'Do you hear there? Do you hear there?' rasped the Tannoy. 'Nobody, I say again, nobody, will go ashore due to the unsuitability of the local conditions. That is all.'

Stunned silence, followed by boos and catcalls.

Apparently Sierra Leone, once called the Fever Coast, was rife with disease, hostile natives and muggers. At least that's what the Very Senior Officers gave as their basis for it being unsuitable, although any local mugger who tried his luck with 3 Para would have quickly learned that crime does not pay.

And so our brave shipmates, who felt once again that naval officers should be gassed at birth, could only line the rail and leer at the one pretty English girl who came down with her family to see the ship and wave a couple of union flags.

The family had come in a spirit of goodwill and patriotism, with words of cheer and comfort for the troops. They soon wished they hadn't bothered. Mother was fat, and told so many times by the men at the rail. Father was offered everything from light tanks to cases of small arms for the loan of his buxom daughter. Ten-year-old son was ignored, except when he shouted out 'Rule Britannia', in an attempt to boost morale. The troops replied loudly with such replies as 'Piss off, you little queer', or 'Here's a fiver, go and fetch your other sisters'.

A tender moment of Royal Marine courtship followed, as a member of 40 Commando leaned over the rail and politely invited the young lady to 'Get your kit off and show us your tits'.

The invitation was captured on television, and shown in edited form on ITN and BBC two days later, which resulted in the poor Marine being deluged by letters from his irate wife and relations back in Plymouth.

Eventually the disillusioned family decided that the oil jetty was not after all going to provide the social event of the year, and they sadly moved away.

'Don't go, little boy,' yelled out a joker from 42 Commando. 'Come up here. We've got some sweeties for you.'

So there's at least one kindly family in Sierra Leone whose once proud and loyal feelings towards the British Army will never be quite the same.

Trading with the native pedlars was also banned. The risk of bringing disease on board was the reason sent down from the bridge, but bumboats don't come under Naval Orders, and dozens of them swarmed round *Canberra*'s port side. Fresh fruit, coconuts, native spears and even monkeys were offered. *Canberra*'s fire party was ordered to turn the hoses on them, which didn't work at all. In fact the hawkers seemed to enjoy a mid-afternoon shower in the steamy heat.

3 Para, sensing a problem and anxious to sort it out in their own more positive way, discovered that a well-aimed half brick thrown down on the thin dugouts from *Canberra*'s flight deck a hundred feet above could have a devastating effect.

The natives, realizing that they had incurred the wrath of the British Tommies, struck out for the shore at speed, even ditching their cargoes in their haste. One received a direct hit amidships, and went down like a stone. It was the first sinking of the campaign and was accordingly received with jubilation. Delighted Paras cheered and whistled as the stricken bumboat captain started swimming home with the chant 'One nil! One nil!' ringing in his ears.

Closer inspection of Freetown through the binoculars convinced all in *Canberra* that they had been spared in the long run, and the place wasn't worth visiting anyway. 'A septic spot on the arse of Africa,' was one description, not too far from the truth.

Any further proof that the Sierra Leonese needed that the British were completely mad, and just as hostile as they were in colonial days, was provided by the strains of martial music blaring from *Canberra*'s flight deck as she basked in the noonday sun. The Royal Marines band had decided it was a good time to give an impromptu concert.

Then at midnight, *Canberra* slipped out, or as Lt Hornby so eloquently put it, 'buggered off on the second leg of our magical mystery tour'.

Nobody saw us go, and it wasn't until months later that we realized that the Big White Ship going to the Falklands had provided the talking point of the year in Freetown.

Apparently the Sierra Leone government would never have given us permission to dock in the first place, if Whitehall hadn't somehow convinced them that we were nothing more than an ordinary merchant ship in urgent need of a little sustenance. It appears that the Freetown Government spent many a sleepless night wondering what Argentina would do in reprisal after we had gone.

Somehow Sierra Leone marked the end of the holiday, the point where the serious intentions began.

The pervading feeling of 'tee-hee, bet we never get there' suddenly changed to one of 'Jesus, we really are going all the way'.

Suddenly we weren't so sorry that we'd wasted all that time going through anti-submarine practice, life-boat drills, and darkening-ship routines at night. Even *Elk* stopped darting around, and fell quietly into line a mile or so astern. Brazil was a bit too close for comfort, and it was suggested that we should paint 'Good luck in the World Cup' on *Canberra*'s flight deck in Spanish, just in case the Brazilian Air Force should decide to play in Argentina's forward line. And in view of the obvious lack of humour from everyone in Buenos Aires it was further suggested that *Canberra* should camouflage herself by painting jokes all over her sides and superstructure 'as the Dagoes would never see them'.

Crossing the Line came and went without ceremony, as the Very Senior Officers didn't want to upset the ship's routine, and suddenly *Canberra* was in the wrong half of the world, alone and vulnerable. We all looked forward to seeing the rest of the Task Force for a bit of company and protection.

Then, at last, there was Ascension Island: a little pimple in the South Atlantic, where Britannia's might was waiting for us, we had been told. We arrived soon after dawn, everyone with a camera up early to take pictures of the great fleet welcoming the White Whale.

We'd expected to see the great carriers, the destroyers, frigates and merchantmen in their dozens. All we saw was a pile of volcanic ash and dust, a couple of landing ships, and a frigate or two.

Big deal, we thought, and went down to breakfast.

Chapter 3

Now most of the Falklands Assault Group was assembled in some disarray around this scorpion-infested scab in the ocean waiting to pack up and go home, or get on with it.

In the next two weeks, in which no-one was to go anywhere except round in circles to avoid a phantom underwater threat from tenacious long-distance Argentinian frogmen or in pursuit of whales classified as hostile by myopic naval lookouts, other ships joined or rejoined the group.

The assault ship HMS *Fearless* and her escort the Type 21 frigate *Ardent* must have glanced casually astern one morning, and realizing that their vulnerable charges had not bothered to follow them, immediately put back to Ascension in some haste.

They were joined by the sister ship of *Fearless*, HMS *Intrepid*, saved at the eleventh hour from the knacker's yard, and two other frigates, the Exocet-carrying Leander class *Argonaut* and another Type 21, *Arrow*. Others would follow.

During this frustrating fortnight, equipment put on the wrong ship in haste in Britain was being moved to the wrong ship again, and then to the right one, in a bizarre game of checkers, while combat troops were put ashore by landing craft to play war games in the blistering heat in some sort of act of strategic brilliance which would hopefully equip them for fighting in the snow.

Also shuffled around were the hacks. The MOD 'Minders', having unsuccessfully attempted the divide and rule theory, now thought it prudent to put all their eggs in one basket.

That basket was *Canberra*, and McGowan, with photographer Smith, accompanied by the bewildered Alan Percival, were summoned by Gemini inflatable from *Sir Lancelot* in a ploy calculated to soak them through and wash away any semblance of dignity, while Dave Norris was dragged screaming from *Stromness* where his beloved 45 Commando were developing new warlike techniques which, had they been discovered at the time, would have led to a rapid rewriting of the Geneva Convention. The pride of the Press Corps was now in one ship.

At first, not everyone in *Canberra* was pleased to see the newcomers. This feeling was hammered home that first night in the Meridian room, once a dance hall, now the sergeants' mess, when Smith foolishly decided to give the gentlemen of 3 Para the benefit of his Cockney wit.

'I hear you fairies are going ashore in Para frocks,' jibed Smith, sucking sustenance from a can of Tennents. With him, and sensing the rumble of distant thunder, were McGowan and *Daily Mirror* reporter Alastair McQueen who six times suggested that the words 'Para smock' would take some of the feeling of impending doom out of the evening.

The words 'fairy' and 'frock' are the last the Paras would themselves choose to describe their demeanour or their attire, and Smith's fate was sealed.

He said it one more time and in an instant Sergeant John Ross was on his feet and Smith was on his back, the left-hand side of his face bearing the unmistakable evidence that it had been in collision with a Para's right fist.

For days afterwards Smith looked as though he had been in a war already, and his mood was not heightened by McQueen's habit of referring to him as The Panda because of his bruise-blackened face.

But there were those on board who looked less

53

macho and, indeed, prided themselves on appearing rather beautiful.

Not all the *Canberra*'s crew, it must be said, were entirely heterosexual. More than once a steward had to be reminded that lipstick and mascara were not the kind of warpaint likely to endear them to the fighting men of the Royal Marines and the Parachute Regiment.

One such member of the crew, wearing such make-up and using a strangely high-pitched voice, was invited by the men he was hoping to impress to leave the room. When he hesitated he was propelled through the door by two Marines who had not bothered to open it first. His dismissal from the ship and an ignominious journey home was delayed only by a brief visit to the ship's surgery.

The door needed surgery too, and a carpenter was called to put it back on its hinges.

Sadly, this lesson was not taken to heart by all the ship's crew. A likeable steward in the Crow's Nest bar called Geoffrey, who looked like Humpty Dumpty in a cummerbund, was quietly minding his own business, polishing glasses during a lecture in the bar to Marines on survival. Suddenly the lighting failed. The room was in darkness and silent, a silence broken only by the soon-to-be immortal words of Geoffrey: 'Ooo, fancy me in the dark with all these soldiers!'

Later, one Para decided it would be a laugh to have an assignation with another member of the ship's crew of questionable sexual persuasion. Halfway through the evening, the Para changed his mind and beat the hapless poof to a pulp.

Events such as this are difficult to keep quiet aboard a troopship, and within hours the Marines' bingo session in the Peacock Room was punctuated by the call, 'The Para and the crewman, Sixty-nine.'

At the back of people's minds then was the thought that there might soon be a war on; and sure enough, the following morning, the reality was brought home.

Instead of the sophisticated monitoring aids of a technological world it was the keen eyes of an off-watch radio officer having a quiet cigarette on *Canberra's* bridge wing which first noticed an Argentinian freighter stooging around on the horizon.

Instant panic.

The crew of the 9,500-ton bulk freighter *Rio de la Plata* could hardly have been surprised at the reaction. Indeed, they must have been amazed that they got so close without being seen off earlier. Now, however, the game was up. The frigate *Ardent* shot off with a roar from her twin Olympus engines (as used in Concorde) at more than 30 knots, straight for the interloper, then shadowed her for about six hours.

The freighter was unarmed. But was she harmless? Had the dirty deed been done? Were there even now swarms of enemy frogmen thrashing their little flippered feet towards the hulls of the assault group ships? Were there shoals of miniature submarines circling ominously, waiting shark-like to close in for the kill?

The truth is, no-one had a clue. So, from a page from the text book of modern naval strategy, the fleet did the sensible thing. It ran away.

The Navy's phrase for it was, 'Tactical evasion in the face of a potential underwater threat.'

The troops said it was 'the nautical version of "Here We Go Round the Mulberry Bush"'.

The Press did not call it anything because the Ministry 'Minders' put a block on the story.

Troops armed to the teeth were rushed ashore, by landing craft and Sea King helicopters, to ferret out any saboteurs that the freighter might have landed when nobody was looking. Very Senior Officers despatched Scout and Gazelle rocket-carrying helicopters to aid the search.

Was disaster imminent? Certainly, Navy and Marine divers were sent over the side, to look for limpet mines, and reassured by their manual that sharks 'very seldom attack Royal Navy divers'.

Then, there it was: the enemy, a few miles out to sea.

'Unidentified submarine,' screamed an alert marine, manning his general-purpose machine gun on *Canberra*'s bridge wing. Instantly, the frigate *Antelope* surged off to engage the intruder. This, surely, was it. Argentina was making a pre-emptive strike against the Task Force.

The intruder dived and sped out to sea, with *Antelope* closing fast. The chase was on. As *Antelope* drew closer, she was able to identify her quarry . . . Nothing more sinister than a whale, which was allowed to go in peace and pass on confirmation to its friends that hanging around the British Task Force did indeed constitute a serious health risk.

Later, some wit put a signal around the fleet to the effect, 'The whales have surrendered.'

Also caught up in this farce of mistaken identity were the crew of the *Elk*, who were ordered to stand for several hours with rifles trained over the side and shoot anything they saw beneath the surface.

The two captains of this container ferry were still trying to turn their charge into a man-of-war, but were at this time somewhat dejected by Whitehall's refusal to allow them to rig a ski-ramp on the bow, and thereby become HMS *Elk Royal*, the Harrier-carrier. But to their delight certain lesser modifications were permitted. Some of her sides were cut away to allow helicopters to land on and two World War Two Bofors guns were specially flown in, along with a team of engineers to fit them to her bow.

Should the guns ever have to be fired in anger, Moreton and Ritchie had devised a sporting way of deciding who would be first to pull the trigger.

Commander Ritchie explained, 'When that time comes, we'll have a Le Mans start from the bridge. First there gets the honours. We don't think we'd stand a chance in hell of hitting anything but if we scare a few pilots we'll be happy.'

Ritchie had earlier beaten the bumboat embargo at Freetown and acquired a rather shaggy parrot, about which he said, 'I'm not sure if it's Nelson or Lady Hamilton, if you know what I mean.' At the time he was gazing sadly at the bird's broken wing. 'But don't worry. We'll soon have it flying again,' he added optimistically.

Captain Moreton, who did not like the bird anyway, had other ideas. He said, 'The only way that thing will fly again is if we stick it in the barrel of the Bofors and blast it off at mach five.'

Meanwhile, back in *Canberra*, other colourful characters were emerging through the smokescreen of panic over phantom enemies.

Captain Christopher Peter Oldbury Burne, RN, had been relieved of his nickname Captain Bligh, only to have it replaced with the now far more appropriate Captain Fawlty.

He had a long-suffering yeoman signaller, whose job it was to send by morse lamp the many signals that his lord and master always wanted flashed to other ships. Captain Burne was of the opinion that this particular signaller was 'not quite all there upstairs' and consequently wanted him examined by *Canberra*'s naval psychiatrist, Surgeon Commander Morgan O'Connell.

But the worthy Morgan, who was later to be pleasantly surprised how few mental problems resulted from the war, tactfully declined.

'I didn't want to examine the man until I was at least satisfied there was a reasonable chance there was something wrong with him,' he said. 'My preliminary enquiries ended with me being quite certain there was nothing I could do, so I didn't see him.'

Captain Burne was not convinced, and the signaller was flown back to England at the first opportunity.

Morgan continued to be amazed how the pressures

that were bound to arise never led to any serious psychiatric problems in *Canberra*.

'All those fighting men in one ship for so long,' he said. 'I am sure that morale was kept high by the presence of the civilian ship's company and the Royal Marines Band.'

And certainly, despite attempts by some sections of the embarked force to inflict grievous bodily brain damage on others from time to time, everyone stayed remarkably sane.

As the relentless sun beat down on the befuddled brains of all gathered at Ascension, the Senior Minder, Martin Helm, felt it was time to stamp the authority of his position on the now unified hacks.

Each morning he called the fifteen stalwart media men for a conference in the Pacific Restaurant. The idea was to tell the reporters what they could, or more often could not, say in their stories. Top of the list of un-reportable facts was that we or anybody else was at Ascension. Even more emphatically denied was any possibility of any one of us getting ashore.

Reasons for this denial of facility ranged from 'Direct orders from Number Ten', to 'We'd love you to go ashore, of course, but the Americans are awfully twitchy about their airfield and the satellite communications gear.'

We were not allowed now or ever to cast even an inquiring glance in the direction of Wideawake Airfield, which lay tantalizingly just out of sight behind a hill.

So there was total panic from the Minders when on one of *Canberra*'s 'keep moving so the subs won't get us' trips, we sailed within a few hundred yards of the airfield, with a perfect view of the vast array of aircraft lined up on and near the runway.

Godfrey Hilliard, the chaplain to 40 Commando, obliged by giving us all an exact run-down of what each aircraft type was. There were rows of Victor tankers, Vulcan bombers, Nimrod reconnaissance planes, Harriers, American Starlifters, VC10s, and the inevitable Hercules transports.

Suddenly up rushed Alan George, squealing in horror. 'You mustn't look! It's secret! Stop looking!'

The press didn't even take their eyes from their binoculars, and totally ignored the little man, knowing full well that he and his cohorts would ban all reference to what they'd seen in all subsequent stories.

Max Hastings, detecting a possible heart attack from the Mini Minder, tried to ease the situation. Soothingly he said, 'Umm, I don't think you can complain, Alan. After all, umm, we cannot be held responsible for where the ship takes us.'

Hastings' favourite word was 'umm'. He used it all the time. In fact on one historic occasion he was recorded by Hands as 'umm-ing' at the rate of 23 times during each five minutes of conversation in which three speakers were taking part.

Perhaps the finest example of the art of 'umm-ing' was Hastings trying to explain how grave he thought the South Atlantic situation was.

'This, umm, has all the makings of being the greatest umm in the history of umm.'

Nobody could argue, and few could put it better.

It was a prophetic remark, as that very night the news was piped through the ship that the Royal Marines had retaken South Georgia. In fact they hadn't, the SAS had, but that didn't stop the celebration or the Minders stopping the story being released from the ship, despite the fact it was already being broadcast on the BBC World Service.

Further proof, if proof were needed, that a brain addled by bureaucracy is a prerequisite for every civil servant in the Ministry of Defence, was acquired by a Royal Marines major who had just joined *Canberra*.

Major Mike Norman had led what was called Naval Party 8901, the group of Royal Marines who had by coincidence arrived on the Falklands to relieve those who were finishing a tour of duty there when the invasion came, some three weeks earlier.

Major Norman and the other Marines had fought valiantly against the invaders before being ordered by Governor Rex Hunt to surrender, as further resistance against so many would have been futile.

Now Major Mike was back with most of his men, ready to go south to 'finish the job' as he put it.

So far, things had not been going too well for him. He had been landed with the on-board job of military censor which meant being the meat in the sandwich between the Ministry Minders and the by now bitterly frustrated newsmen.

It could not get worse, he thought, but it did.

Major Mike had taken with him a Service Land Rover on his trip to the Falklands before the invasion. Now, through no fault of his own, that vehicle was being operated by another Ministry of Defence.

In Whitehall, they were clearly blind to this new turn of events, and sent Mike a note telling him so.

His face a mask of disbelief, Mike sat in the Crow's Nest bar, staring at a piece of paper that had arrived with his mail.

'Would you believe it?' said Mike. 'Because I can't. I've been through a bloody invasion and I get this!'

He held up the offending document which read:
'Urgent:

Return of receipted voucher. We have not received from you a receipted No. 3 Blue copy of our issue voucher which is returned for audit. Please be kind enough to receipt and return either the original or the attached photocopy as soon as possible. Signed D. R. King, Stores Office Supervisor, Ministry of Defence.'

'I know what it's about,' fumed Mike. 'Apparently I didn't sign a receipt for five sodding tyres. Not ordinary tyres, mind you; these are Michelin radial steel-braced tyres for the Land Rover the bloody Argies are now driving around. They should have sent it to them.'

Mike walked off to ponder this dilemma alone as a group of young Marines trooped in behind a sergeant for a briefing on survival.

With the young fighting men around him, Sergeant Roy Pennington launched into his favourite subject: how to kill things.

'Right, lads,' he began. 'listen in. What I'm about to tell you just might save your lives when we get there. First priority, shelter. Well, there ain't no bleedin' trees, so living like Tarzan's out for a start. Holes in the ground, I hear you suggest. Nice idea, but go down more than a couple of feet and you'll hit water, and we don't want to drown in our little beddie-byes, do we?'

Heads were shaken. 'No, Sarge,' they mumbled.

'Right. So find yourself a bit of ground that's dry, and looks like it's firm beneath. Then dig away with your little shovels and home sweet home is made. Failing that, of course, you can always live in a hollowed-out elephant seal, which you will of course have killed first.

'But you've got to watch these, 'cos they're bad bastards, and might not entirely go along with your ideas. Always approach these big buggers from the front. They are not known for their nimbleness. But should you be cunt enough to try to surprise it from behind you should remember it is well able to roll backwards quickly and be on you. If that happens you are well fucked.'

Throughout his talk, Sergeant Pennington kept tapping his palm with a bayonet, which few of his audience doubted would come scything towards them if they answered one of his curt questions incorrectly.

'Sometimes you will see,' he went on, 'little holes in the ground. Do not go sticking your finger in them because there are little penguins what live inside with razor-sharp beaks who will have it off with one nod of their little heads.'

A few questions and answers later, Sergeant Pennington turned his attention to the main survival aid on the Falklands.

'Sheep,' he said, 'can be an endless source of amusement. First you catch one of the pretty ones, and ask it to come home for dinner, being careful not to arouse its suspicions. Then you take your bayonet in your right hand, pull out the loose skin from underneath its throat, and stick your bayonet through, twist and withdraw, pulling upwards.'

The sergeant's face glowered at his listeners.

'But make quite sure you don't stick your bayonet in too far, or you'll put it right through your left hand. And we don't want that, do we?'

'No, Sarge.'

'Right. Any other uses for a sheep before you kill it, except the obvious one, for which you can still get five years?'

Alan George, who was looking paler and sicker than usual, decided he could curry favour with the sergeant, not realizing that he does not suffer fools lightly.

'Why not use the sheep as a pack animal? It could carry your kit,' he asked.

Sergeant Pennington's eyes narrowed. His head tilted backwards. His grip on his bayonet tightened. He paused before replying.

'Cunt,' he hissed, barely audibly.

A few sensible suggestions, like skinning it for its thick fleece, or curling up next to it to keep warm if stuck in the open up a mountain at night were put forward, and Sergeant Pennington concluded his lecture.

He left his audience with a word of advice.

'If you haven't got any thermal underwear, nip down to the ship's shop and get a pair of tights. They really do keep your little leggies warm.'

Alan George realized that this was his chance to redeem himself. 'Should we cut a little hole in the front so that we can have a pee?' he ventured.

'Oh Jesus,' said Pennington, casting up his eyes, and left the room.

At that moment, Minder-in-Chief Martin Helm pranced into the bar, beaming from ear to ear. He was carrying a piece of paper, and scoffed at the journalists present, saying he had just been with Captain Burne and explained to him that the newsmen were a wingeing bunch of ungrateful morons.

On the piece of paper were the words, ' "Everything is very simple in war, but the simplest thing is very difficult. These difficulties accumulate and produce a friction which no man can imagine exactly who has not seen war." ' It was a famous quote Captain Burne had given Helm to subdue the hacks, and was attributed to C. von Clauswitz [sic]: *On War*.

The Marines and hacks who were there had never heard of von Clausewitz, but deduced that he was German and since they had lost both major wars this century, 'What did he know?' they asked Helm.

The Marines, whose predecessors had been on the winning side, had spent some time at Ascension writing a song to commemorate what was inevitably going to be another glorious chapter in the history of the Corps.

It was simply called 'The Malvinas Song' and was loosely attributed to 42 Commando. It was sung to the tune of the old Cliff Richard hit 'Summer Holiday'. The chorus went like this:

'We're all going to the Malvinas,
We're all going to kill a Spic or two,
We're all going on a pusser's holiday,
For a month or two . . .
Or three or four.'

And one verse:

'We're going to kill the wops with phosphorous
We'll get them with our GPMG's.
They'd better not try to take cover,
'Cos they're ain't no fucking trees.'

The song was given a rousing debut in the 42 mess that night, as news came in that RAF Vulcans and Task Force Harriers had bombed Port Stanley airport.

Again it was first heard via the BBC World Service, and again the Minders refused to let the reporters on *Canberra* mention it in stories.

The following night the troops heard of another successful British initiative outside the 200-mile Total Exclusion Zone which had been imposed around the Falklands two weeks earlier. The British nuclear Fleet Submarine *Conquerer* had fired a pattern of World War Two torpedoes into the Argentine cruiser *General Belgrano* and sent it to the bottom with the loss of more than 300 lives.

The Paras and Marines did not rejoice at the news. Instead the mood was almost sullen, a realization at last that they were on their way to join in a war in which people were already dying.

In the Meridian Room, used as the sergeants' mess, Tony Dunn of 3 Para sipped his beer and said sombrely, 'Well, that's it. The politicians can't stop it now. We'll be getting on with it soon.'

But soon the humour returned. Preparing for the worst, the Marines compiled their own list of 'Essential Spanish Phrases to be Used in the Event of Capture'.

Amid howls of laughter in the messes, the choice of words to be uttered to an Argentinian soldier while your hands were raised in surrender would be: 'You are trespassing' or 'Can we talk this over?' or 'Is this Guernsey?' or 'Do you want to buy some dysentery tablets?' or 'Some of my best friends are Dagoes'.

In the officers' mess, spirits had also returned to banal normality.

The film *Straw Dogs* was getting an airing on the video, and when it came to the scene where Dustin Hoffman was avenging the rape of his screen-wife Susan George by almost decapitating an attacker with a steel bear-trap, Lieutenant Martin Eales of 40 Commando leapt to his feet.

Enthusiastically he shouted, 'Yes, yes, yes!' as the screen villain went to his maker, and turning to a senior officer he pleaded, 'Please, can we have them issued as kit?'

But the seriousness of the escalation in activity further south was not lost on the men. Last will and testament forms were issued, and little groups of Marines and Paras gathered around the ship debating what to do with their worldly possessions should they not come home.

Heated discussions between friends who were to witness each other's wills broke out.

'All right, then, I'll leave you my stereo system, on condition you leave me your motorbike, OK?'

'Done.'

Even the civilians were advised strongly to fill out the forms, and most of them did. The sombre scribbling went on for a couple of days, and did not do much to boost morale.

Attendance at that Sunday's church service in *Canberra*'s cinema was better attended than on previous occasions. 3 Para's padre, Derek Heaver (known, of course, as 'Derek the Cleric'), was giving the sermon.

It was based on a story of a film crew going by sea to a distant location when a storm broke. The crew, who had previously ignored the ship's captain, suddenly pleaded with him to save them. But he didn't, as he had other things to do. Derek's moral was that now was the time to turn to God, so that he would in turn look after you when the going got rough.

Godfrey Hilliard, 40 Commando's padre, was

furious, and the next Sunday preached a sermon along the lines of 'It's never too late to turn to God'.

Each service opened with the dramatic entrance of *Canberra*'s captain, Dennis Scott-Masson, preceded into the cinema by a young cadet carrying the massive ship's Bible. Each Sunday Captain Scott-Masson read the lesson from the Bible, placed by the cadet on a music stand which doubled as lectern.

But someone decided that the captain's attitude was altogether a little too pompous, and arranged for a staggeringly successful collapse of the music stand the moment the Bible was placed on it.

Derek Heaver was having his own fight with the forces of evil, which he saw in the form of the British Forces' Post Office. As mail started arriving on *Canberra*, Derek noticed that our address was BFPO 666. He was furious and mumbled darkly about someone playing a practical joke.

'Can't they see the effect this will have on morale?' he asked angrily. 'Can't they understand the damage they're doing?'

It was a puzzling riddle, to which only Derek could provide the answer.

'It's the mark of the devil. The anti-Christ. The Beast,' he said.

'What is?' came the response.

'666!' he said. 'It's in the Book of Revelations.'

In fact 666 was the mark of the Beast, and had been used as such in the book and film *The Omen*. The double meaning of our BFPO number spread round the ship, and became the source of much amusement.

'At least it's better than 999,' suggested a Para, and from then on sections of *Canberra* were caught up in what became known as 'The Doom Syndrome'. Troops and pressmen greeted each other in the corridors and on the decks by throwing their hands in the air and wailing, 'We're doomed. We're doomed.'

McGowan had a home-made Task Force calendar

pinned above his bunk, on the bottom of which was written in letters two inches high those very words: 'We're Doomed!'

Godfrey Hilliard, trying vainly to stop the pessimism, added in ballpoint underneath, 'Oh ye of little faith.'

Some of the phoney fatalism even reached the bar in the officers' mess. New cocktails were invented by barmen Joe and Alan to fit the mood of their customers. The ingredients of the Harvey Wallbanger were mixed, shaken and poured under the new name The Argie Doombanger. Yet another, of dubious contents but high potency, was called The Exocet Cocktail, about which Joe warned, 'Just one, and you're fucked.'

A few hours later Commander Tim Yarker made the nightly broadcast over the ship's Tannoy, which was by now known as the 'Dead and Alive Show'. During his talk he said there was a row in Britain over the sinking of the *Belgrano* outside the TEZ, and that more British aircraft had been bombing Stanley Airport.

He did not say anything else about the day's actions. But McGowan had taped from his own radio the World Service news that evening. He took the recording to the Meridian Room and played it to the hushed assembly of sergeants. It had been reported that a British Harrier had been brought down and the pilot lost, and even more gravely that the destroyer HMS *Sheffield* had been severely damaged and was in danger of sinking.

Sergeant-major Sammy Dougherty of 3 Para summed up the mood of everyone in the room. He said, 'There's no turning back now. We are in a war. We'll be getting our orders to sail on south any time now.'

It was 5 May 1982.

Chapter 4

Everybody on board sensed it. *Canberra*'s endless meanderings around the mulberry bush of Ascension Island were over. The Very Senior Officers refused to confirm it, but with every ship in the Assault Group on ten minutes' notice to sail, there was really nothing more to say, except, perhaps, goodbye to this forlorn and festering staging post. Until now, Ascension had looked like hell. Now, too late, it began to look quite good.

Thursday, 6 May, dawned like many earlier days, with Paras and Marines pounding the decks, but this time instead of training shoes and tee-shirts, they wore full fighting kit.

'Faster, you bastards,' bellowed a drill sergeant at the head of one group. 'Keep tight. No lagging behind.'

A panting voice from somewhere amid the jogging throng moaned, 'Shit, are we sailing down there, or do we have to run all the bloody way?'

The morning sky was alive with helicopters criss-crossing between the ships in a last vain attempt to get everyone and every thing in the right place before the armada sailed to war.

'Are we really ready?' asked a young soldier of an officer standing by *Canberra*'s midships flight deck.

'No, but we're going anyway,' replied the officer.

'I only asked,' said the soldier, 'because I'm supposed to be on *Intrepid*.'

The officer turned, gave the soldier a superior glance, smiled, and said, 'You're fucked, then.'

He was not the only one. Lieutenant the Lord Robin Innes-Ker of the Blues and Royals should have been elsewhere polishing his Scimitar tank. Instead, there he was in the Crow's Nest bar of *Canberra*, looking sheepish.

'I'm shopping,' he said. 'Looking for some things for my chaps. Some want cigarettes. I don't use the ghastly things myself. Tell me, what sort of cigarettes do soldiers smoke?'

He did not get much help with this one, so he wafted away in his green wellington boots towards the ship's shop.

As the civilian stewards were serving coffee in the bar the word came. The Assault Group was on its way. Barmen Joe and Alan were preparing their stock for opening time when the news was made official.

'Bloody hell,' said Joe in his Irish brogue. 'We're supposed to be getting off here. They told us we'd go as far as here and no further.'

Alan, not an easy man to ruffle, said calmly, 'We've been conned.'

And Geoffrey the steward said simply, 'I suppose sailing with you boys is some consolation for me missing my holiday in Jersey.'

The unmistakable sound of anchor chains being winched up ended the conversation. *Canberra* edged to starboard, picked up speed, and headed south, escorted by the frigate *Ardent*. Ships soon to follow sounded a God speed on their sirens and hundreds of troops stayed on deck until Ascension disappeared over the horizon.

Now events had entered a new phase. Until now, only combat troops had been involved in rehearsing for war. But everyone in *Canberra* was on their way to the battle zone, so life-boat drill meant no-one wanted to be, or was allowed to be, left out.

At the most unexpected times of day or night, the klaxons sounded. 'For exercise, for exercise. All ship's company and embarked forces proceed immediately to your muster stations,' the chilling voice of P and O deputy captain Mike Bradford echoed through the ship.

Pandemonium.

Bodies collided on corridors and staircases throughout the ship. Public rooms filled with servicemen pretending to be frightened.

'It wasn't like this on the *Titanic*,' joked one Marine as strains of 'Abide with Me' wafted across the Meridian room, sung by men of 42 Commando who were not taking matters as seriously as the captain would have liked.

It took anything up to twenty minutes for people to gather in the right place. It was common knowledge that had *Canberra* been hit in the vitals by a torpedo, it would have gone down in about three minutes.

'That means,' said 3 Para Sergeant Chris Phelan, sprawling in an armchair, sweating under his warm clothing and lifejacket, 'we all drowned seventeen minutes ago. So what are we doing here?'

Sometimes Captain Bradford tried to make the exercise more interesting and realistic. 'Assume Meridian and Peacock rooms on fire. All personnel normally using these rooms as their muster station, proceed to the cinema on "A" Deck,' he announced during one drill, clearly forgetting that there were already some 400 would-be survivors crammed inside.

The arrival of another 600 battle-trained bodies determined to get in too, put the fear of God into the sitting tenants.

But they had been told to get in, and get in they did.

Bodies were piled four deep in places, and still they kept pouring in. 'This isn't working, is it?' was one helpful observation.

'Not quite,' groaned a voice from beneath a heap of paratroopers. 'Doesn't bother me though. I always had this fear of dying alone.'

From his eyrie on the bridge and oblivious to the chaos below, Captain Bradford further announced,

'Ship's company and embarked forces are to proceed in an orderly fashion to their lifeboat stations.'

Marine Lieutenant Tony Hornby, his head protruding from a pile of bodies, asked, 'Have I got time for a wank first?'

The scrum slowly broke up as men streamed into the corridors, which were soon blocked by a seething mass of people going nowhere.

'What would it be like if the ship really was sinking, we were listing 45 degrees to starboard and the corridors were full of thick smoke?' asked a voice in the queue.

'This is nature's little way of telling you you are going to die,' replied a Marine corporal.

Eventually, everyone reached their lifeboat station on the promenade deck to be congratulated by the voice of Captain Bradford, which said, 'Well done. You did it all in fifteen minutes.'

Comforting but not true. In fact it had taken at least 45. Again, there was the odd muttering of 'We're doomed'.

And a Marine captain said to his commanding officer, Lieutenant-colonel Malcolm Hunt, 'This is one hell of a way to disband the brigade.'

Then came the voice of Surgeon Lt-Commander Rick Jolly, which said, 'The time will come when you will put your lifejacket on in your sleep. Those of you who do not have your lifejackets and warm clothing with you now are dead.'

More cries of 'We're doomed'.

They were followed by a statement from a realist among the troops, 'All this farting about would turn to ratshit if it was the real thing. We'd all jump straight over the side.'

As *Canberra* sailed on towards colder weather, she was joined by *Fearless* and *Intrepid*, *Norland* the North Sea ferry carrying men of the 2nd Battalion the Parachute Regiment, the frigate *Argonaut*, *Atlantic Conveyor*

71

with her helicopter cargo, *Elk*, the fleet tanker *Tidepool*, the supply ship *Stromness* carrying 45 Commando and the repair ship *Europic Ferry*.

All the while *Canberra*'s medical squadron were practising putting up and taking down their 'emergency medical facility' in what had once been a large games room on 'A' deck.

Surgeons, medical assistants and orderlies became lightning fast at getting their makeshift hospital ready, to the annoyance of officers staggering in or out of their bar, which lay on the other side.

It was all under the control of Surgeon Captain John Wilkes, aided and abetted by ship's surgeon Peter Mayner, Surgeon Commander John Williams, Mayner's deputy, Dr Sue West, and Rick Jolly and the other medics.

It was one of the few contingencies on board which worked smoothly and almost exactly as planned, but was only put to the test briefly under war conditions before being transferred ashore on the Falklands.

The Royal Marines band, under Captain John Ware, was seconded to the medical squadron to act as stretcher bearers. They willingly set to in their new role, even offering tubas as makeshift bedpans.

The call went out around the ship for blood donors, leading to the medical squadron becoming known as the vampire unit.

'You'll never know when you might need it back,' said Rick Jolly to a Marine who was unable to decide whether or not to bare his arm.

'That's settled, then,' said the Marine, rolling down his sleeve before the needle got too close. 'I'll leave it inside in the first place.'

Sunday Telegraph reporter Charles Laurence, a wiry individual, tried in vain to give blood. Try as the medics could, and no matter where they punctured his arm, they could only get half a pint out of him. From then on he was known as Half-Pint Charlie.

First aid lectures too became more frequent. Everyone became thoroughly conversant with the details of sucking chest wounds, how to cope with white phosphorous burns and more importantly what was meant by your 'one per cent'.

In military jargon burns are classified by the Rule of Nines. The head is nine per cent of the body, each arm is nine per cent, each leg 18 per cent, the chest and back 18 per cent each, and a soldier's manhood, no matter what its proportions, the remaining one per cent.

The expression 'one per cent rise' took on a whole new meaning.

Leading Medical Assistant Terry Bradford was detailed to give a series of lectures. Terry's instructions were based on common sense. 'Give first aid whenever you can,' he would say. 'But don't hesitate to leave the poor sod where he is if someone starts shooting at you.'

Other little pearls of wisdom included never using your own phial of morphine on an injured colleague.

'Find his and use it,' Tony said. 'You might need yours later. And if he's really badly hurt, and you don't think there's a lot you can do for him, start telling him lies. Always tell the patient he's going to be all right, even if it's patently obvious that he isn't. And mentioning that you're a qualified doctor usually goes down quite well too.

'If he's out cold, you've got to clear his airway so that he can breathe. Stick your finger in his mouth and whip out his false teeth in case he chokes. It's more than likely he'll have some, because Marines are violent buggers who are always punching hell out of each other.'

LMA Bradford even knew what to do if the patient died. 'Stick his rifle in the ground to mark the spot, then nick his water bottle and anything else you haven't got and leg it.'

73

In a question and answer session, LMA Bradford asked what should be done if it appeared a patient had stopped breathing.

'Kiss of life,' ventured an avid listener.

'Only if you love him,' said young Terry. 'In fact you're quite right, but only after other methods have failed first, and in civvie street you can get prosecuted for not doing mouth-to-mouth properly. Down there if it doesn't work I shouldn't worry, though. Just put it down to experience.'

Another essential piece of advice on the subject of stopping profuse bleeding was never to tie a tourna-quet round a patient's neck 'no matter how bad his nose-bleed'.

On personal hygiene in the field, the golden rule was to keep yourself clean.

'Dysentery spreads like wildfire,' said Terry. 'And a battalion which is forever running off to have a shit isn't going to be a lot of use. And another thing: don't have a crap too close to somebody else's trench, or you're likely to get a 7·62 round up your arse before you get your trousers back on.'

The Marines raced off from the lecture looking for one of the 14 P and O women on board to practise the kiss of life on.

Other lectures included the handling and interro-gation of prisoners. 'Under the Geneva Convention you are not, I repeat not, allowed to stick a bayonet in a newly captured prisoner,' explained the instructor, a sergeant in 42 Commando. 'So what do you do if you capture an enemy trench with a couple of wounded Argies still inside?'

'Shoot their heads off,' came the reply.

'Quite right. But remember if there's a TV crew nearby you've got to go through all the first-aid rubbish just as if they were your best mates.'

As he spoke a four-man squad of Paras stormed past the room looking evil.

It was something they practised long and hard at, looking evil, and they were consequently very good at it.

What they were brushing up on in this instant was a skill they had acquired for duties in Northern Ireland, and were now adapting for use on the Falklands. Basically it was the four man 'brick' which moved through an area of suspected terrorist activity looking hard at every potential hazard, whilst covering themselves at the same time.

It looked ridiculous in the cocktail lounges of a cruise liner: groups of four creeping forward, rushing round corners, aiming their rifles down corridors in the 'hard targeting'.

On the streets of Belfast, of course, they would encounter hostile welcomes from the local population. On *Canberra* they only encountered other soldiers and the ship's crew. The former totally ignored the Paras, the latter thoroughly enjoyed it, neither of which added much to the realism. But if it came to street fighting around Port Stanley, it would be the Paras who would lead the way, as the best unit in the British Army at such things.

The body searching, with a suspect spreadeagled against a wall, was a particular favourite with some of the ship's crew. Suddenly a group of four Paras would hurtle round a corner, grab the extremely willing 'suspect' and start giving him a thorough and quite rough search. A few of the not-totally-hetero stewards could be found on occasions wandering hopefully along corridors waiting to be grabbed and searched.

To add variety, whilst maintaining the same theme, the Paras also went through house-clearing routines. But with no houses available, they trained instead on cabins. One hapless civilian was dozing peacefully on his bunk one afternoon when the door of his home was opened in a way that can only be described as impolite. How it stayed in one piece remains a mystery.

The incumbent shot bolt upright at the intrusion, saw four fully-camouflaged soldiers brandishing rifles in his direction and could have been excused for enquiring what was going on.

Something round and small was tossed into the cabin, the soldiers stepped out, slammed the door shut and yelled 'Grenade!'

The poor civilian, who had been asleep three seconds earlier, understandably thought the end of the world had come.

The 'grenade' turned out to be an apple.

The waning rays of the tropical sun were used three days out of Ascension for what was to be the last day of relaxation for over two months. In England, the London Marathon was being run, so as consolation for those aboard who were unable to take part, The *Canberra* Olympics were staged.

Each unit on board, and the ship's crew, were invited to put up teams for the tug-of-war, 10,000 metres, and deck quoits. Comedians who suggested hang-gliding and ski-ing as extra events were told the venue was hardly suitable.

The tug-of-war on the midships flight deck was expected to be a pushover for the Marines. The Paras admitted they stood little chance due to the fact that, as an observant Para corporal put it, 'Bootnecks have got the brains of gorillas and figures to match.'

The ship's crew did better than expected, with the heavyweights from the engine room having at least a two-stone advantage per man over everyone else. But they lacked style and cohesion, and ended their challenge in an undignified heap.

40 and 42 Commandos nearly came to blows after their tie, which would decide the championship. 40 believed they had pulled their opponents just far enough over the line to win. A quick-thinking member of 42, sensing imminent defeat, yelled out, 'OK, that's it.' 40 released their grip, thinking they'd won. But

instead 42 gave two mighty heaves, pulling the startled 40 team to an ignominious and hotly disputed defeat. 'Foul play,' yelled 40's second in command, Major Andy Gowan. 'We've been cheated.' They had, but the result stood.

In the deck quoits, as expected, the ship's crew won easily. It's not the sort of sport that Marines and Paras practise a lot.

The 10,000 metres was a foregone conclusion, with the Paras fielding a couple of long-distance running champions, which they tried to keep quiet about so that they could clean up with the unofficial bookies.

But it nearly all went wrong for them. The Marines knew they didn't have too much of a chance, but the ship's crew had a secret weapon . . . laundryman Frank Taylor.

To everyone's total amazement, Frank shot off into the lead from the start, leaving startled Paras trailing in his wake.

'No probs,' said the Para's commanding officer Hew Pike. 'He'll burn himself out in a couple of laps.'

But he didn't, and if anything increased his lead as the race developed.

Frank was cheered all the way.

'Come on, darling! Oh, Frank, I love you! Keep going, my darling!'

Despite a few incredulous glances from other spectators at where the encouragement was coming from, all was well. It was Frank's wife Anne, leaping up and down in her pride and excitement.

But Hew Pike was right, and at the end of the gruelling race, Frank could only manage a creditable third place, behind the Paras who sensed severe reprisals from their messmates if they had been beaten.

But Frank was the only runner to end the race in the arms of a beautiful woman, being smothered in kisses.

'There's no fucking justice,' said the winner, as he trooped off to collect his certificate.

The day of the *Canberra* Olympics also marked the end of the sunbathing. Men who had left England a pasty white were now golden brown, a state they had reached after most of them had suffered agonies at the lobster-red stage. But now the weather was cooling again, and time off would be spent below decks.

But there was still one more chance for the privileged few to remind themselves what the shape of a woman looked like in a scanty bathing costume.

The girls on board were allowed to use the Monkey Island above the bridge for their sunbathing, supposedly out of the gaze of all the embarked forces apart from the Very Senior Officers who were allowed the same facility.

More than once visiting helicopters had hovered low over the Monkey Island as the crews looked lovingly down on the pretext of making absolutely sure that the flight deck was clear, and they were absolutely clear for their landing.

Officers who were not in the slightest bit interested in getting sun tans turned brown as berries on the Monkey Island. The fact they had forgotten to pack their beachwear did not put them off, and one commanding officer used to turn up regularly wearing a pair of ancient rugby shorts that no self-respecting boy scout at the turn of the century would have been seen dead in, as they went half way to his ankles.

One innocent but attractive young lady used to go through a strenuous PT routine on the fo'c'sle, believing she was away from the lecherous glances of the soldiers. She wasn't.

Officers peered down from the Crow's Nest bar through binoculars as she went through her routine in shorts and a flimsy tee-shirt. One deck below, the other ranks ogled too. But the display ended abruptly when some over-enthusiastic Marines invited her to carry on with even less clothing.

'Come and bounce 'em over here, love,' was the first

shout. 'You can practise your press-ups on me,' was the second.

Red faced, the girl picked up her bag and ran off. From then on the girls who wanted exercise had to use a lonely little deck at the after end of the ship, and then only after dark.

For many on board Olympics Day was to be the last time they were ever to see the frigate *Ardent*.

She came close alongside that day and showed her fire-power by pounding away with her 4.5 inch gun. As she pulled away at speed, most of her crew came out to line her decks and wave farewell before *Ardent* steamed off south. Both ships saluted each other with their sirens.

Later the fortunes of war decreed that the small and well-armed *Ardent* was to die in the waters of Falkland Sound, whilst the massive and unprotected *Canberra* escaped without a scratch.

A few miles to port, *Norland* with 2 Para on board had edged ahead, to the disgust of 3 Para in *Canberra* who were going frantic at the possibility of their comrades getting anywhere ahead of them.

But it was a Sunday, and a well-loved padre in *Norland*, with no sports day to interfere, wanted to keep his shipmates occupied. He walked into the main mess deck dressed in clerical garb. At the end of the room he turned and faced the men of 2 Para, who were idling away the morning with cards and coffee.

'Gentlemen!' called the chaplain. 'The next entertainment this morning is a church service. All those not interested, fuck off.'

As the convoy grew in size, ships of all shapes and sizes could be seen from horizon to horizon, zig-zagging. No two ships appeared to be going in the same direction.

Elk, our faithful companion, suddenly shot off to the west.

'Oh, look,' called Captain Rod Boswell, of the Royal

Marines Mountain and Arctic Warfare Cadre. 'For Christ's sake stop her. She's off to take Buenos Aires singlehanded.' The laughter stopped for a moment when everyone realized that with Captains Moreton and Ritchie in control, that was indeed quite possible. But *Elk* fell back with a zig when the particular zag had been completed.

The ill-fated *Atlantic Conveyor* passed close to *Canberra*'s port side heading in exactly the opposite direction.

'Very sensible, that,' said a voice. 'She's had enough already and is going back home.'

Sadly for *Atlantic Conveyor*, she was only zig-zagging her way towards destruction at the hands of an Argentine Exocet missile two weeks later.

On this day, Harriers from the Royal Navy Carrier Group ahead of us brought down three Argentine Skyhawk fighter-bombers, and the pride of the Cunard fleet, Queen Elizabeth 2 sailed from Southampton with the Guardsmen and Gurkhas of Five Infantry Brigade.

A Russian 'Bear' spy-plane flew low over *Canberra* and the rest of the assault group. It flew off peacefully after a couple of low passes, unworried by shouts from *Canberra*'s deck of 'Shoot the bastard. Bring it down!'

Shortly afterwards another speck appeared in the sky heading for the group.

'It's OK, it's only the Crabs,' said a man with a pair of high-powered binoculars – Crabs being the military nickname for the Royal Air Force. It was the welcome sight of a Hercules transport plane, which dropped three large canisters under orange parachutes.

The mail had arrived, or as the Marines called it, the flying postman.

Military jargon was used all the time, and could be confusing to the uninitiated. The Paras, for instance, called every serviceman not graced with a red beret a crap-hat. To 'hack it' simply meant it could be done. Marines referred to everything naval as 'pussers', being a derivative of pursers. *Canberra* had become a 'pusser's ship' for the duration.

'Blagging' was a Paras' term for acquiring something, usually in a less than hundred per cent honest way. The Marines called the same exercise 'proffing'. 'Rassing' was a Marines term born out of the initials of Replenishment At Sea, and used when an item was obtained without any shady methods being employed.

Paras referred to a forced march at speed in fighting order as 'tabbing'. The Marines instead went 'yomping', which was by necessity a slower operation as they carried their 'bergans' or back-packs which could weigh anything up to 100lbs. When the Marines moved at a slower pace they were 'bimbling', and sneaking up on an unsuspecting enemy was 'snurgling'.

Any drink was a 'wet' and food was 'scran' or 'scoff'. Paras when they disposed of an enemy position said it had been 'banjoed'. The Special Air Service described a similar scene of destruction as having been 'malletted'.

The Army helicopters were always known as 'Teeny Weeny Airways', due to the fact that they were the little Scout and Gazelle aircraft, believed by the troops to have only one purpose, namely to provide a VIP taxi service for Very Senior Officers. In fairness they played their role in many ways, including 'cas-evaccing' or casualty evacuation.

A best mate was always an 'oppo' and officers always 'pigs'. Marines called lance-corporals 'stripeys', but always knew sergeant-majors as 'sir'.

The base camp of a unit moving forward was known as its 'echelon'. Hence those who never went to the front line, but stayed with the echelon were known as 'Remfs' or Rear Echelon Mother Fuckers.

Any meeting at which orders were given was an 'O group' at which usually officers only were filled in on the future intentions of their commanders.

81

Artillery rounds were referred to as 'shit', particularly when incoming, and a target which had been wiped out with casualties had been 'greased'.

Marines called anything good 'wazzer' or just 'wazz', a term which caught on with some Paras by the time they landed.

So a Bootneck whose oppo had proffed some scran, was a Marine whose best friend had got some food. In the weeks to come it would be considered very wazzer to banjo a spic.

A phrase not so popular but never out of mind, was 'Air Raid Warning Red', which because of its almost constant usage was abbreviated simply to 'Air Red.' It was at first followed by the order 'take cover' but the appendage was soon dropped as being superfluous.

A lesser air threat, meaning enemy aircraft were not too close but somewhere in the area, was 'Air Yellow', and 'Air White' meant the threat had passed. The Argentinians had a knack of turning up during more than one 'Air White' in the ensuing weeks.

On 18 May the first real 'Air Red' was flashed to every ship in the assault group, and men raced, as they had practised, to their emergency stations. Argentinian fighter bombers were in the air somewhere to our west, and an attack was considered likely.

It had by this time been agreed that all newsmen in *Canberra* could go aloft to the Monkey Island during an attack, so they could see what was happening.

Captain Burne changed his mind, and refused permission for the journalists to go up. Then a Very Senior Officer pointed out to him that the Monkey Island was probably the most dangerous and exposed part of the ship, and the reporters had an excellent chance of getting killed.

Captain Burne immediately suggested that all newsmen go up.

But the attack never materialized.

The next day, 19 May, the assault group arrived in the war zone.

The Very Senior Officers realized that had the previous day's air threat been a real one after all, the entire landing force was in just three ships, *Canberra*, *Norland* and *Stromness*, and if they had been sunk everybody else might just as well have packed up and gone home.

With undignified urgency two of the three units in *Canberra* were hustled off to other ships. 42 Commando stayed back in reserve.

40 Commando were cross-decked by landing craft to HMS *Fearless*, with Hands and the ITN crew in their midst.

3 Para went to HMS *Intrepid*, with McGowan and photographer Smith. Just like the troops, the journalists were now committed, way beyond the point of no return, to going all the way.

Chapter 5

Whatever else the assault ships *Fearless* and *Intrepid* were designed for, it was not for assaulting. Both these ageing, rusting and overcrowded scrapyard escapees were to be the spearhead for the British landings.

The combat troops, who had for six weeks been living in the comparative luxury of the third largest cruise liner in the world, were in for a rude awakening. Creature comforts were not high on the list of the Navy's priorities.

The fun of sailing 'Grey Funnel Line' style began the moment the landing craft buffetted their way through the South Atlantic swell into the stern docks of the sister ships, chicks returning to a mother hen.

In these caverns of steel, piping, heavy equipment and men shouting like banshees to make themselves heard, the newcomers were given a passing notion of what Hitler's gas chambers must have been like.

Thick, choking diesel fumes hung like a fog.

If ships are always ladies then 600 men were almost suffocating up *Intrepid*'s backside. It was the same in *Fearless*.

For half an hour the pride of 3 Para and 40 Commando were left stranded in their landing craft while some poor naval officer tried valiantly to work out where he was going to put them all.

Sergeant Chris Phelan of 3 Para said, 'Ten more minutes and we'll all be dead. Then the Navy's problems will be solved.'

The Navy solved the problem in its usual simplistic way. 'There are no bunks, so you sleep on the floor. Officers get carpets; the rest of you get the decks.'

It was a foretaste of the rigours to come.

First hurdle was the assault course to the 'quarters'. Maybe that is why they were called assault ships. With full kit the men had to scramble up ladders, along slippery companionways half as wide as they were, round impossibly narrow corners, then through more hatches and up more ladders. It made the Commando 'Tarzan' course at Lympstone look like a gentle stroll. And as one Marine pointed out, 'At least they don't gas you as well at Lympstone.'

In fact, most of the men never walked on the deck at all. So cramped were the ships with everything from men to equipment, floors were literally carpeted by cardboard boxes of 'rat-packs', the 24-hour ration packs the fighting men would live on once ashore.

Another Marine, not happy with his lot, groaned, 'It's like a mass audition for the Quasimodo part in *The Hunchback of Notre Dame*. The floor's so high and the ceiling's so low, you can't bloody stand up straight.'

In *Intrepid*, a group of Paras tripped over a pile of books, one ominously entitled *The Cruel Sea*, as they staggered along to find what they called their 'grots'.

'Who the hell left these here?' growled a private.

'We did,' replied a voice from inside the bookcase beside the offending pile. 'And we ain't fucking moving.'

There they were, two enterprising soldiers, or 'Toms' as they called each other, settled for the night. One was on the top shelf, the other below him, curled up, using a few copies of *Yachting World* for a pillow. They had even taken the trouble to close the glass doors of the bookcase to avoid disturbance.

Life was not any better in *Fearless*. The Marines, who are supposed to be used to such discomforts at the hands of their parent service, the Royal Navy, were complaining too, or 'dripping', to use one of their quaint, and not totally inappropriate, expressions.

'This is going to give the Black Hole of Calcutta a

good name,' said a sergeant from 40's headquarters company. 'For God's sake don't everyone roll over in the night together or we'll capsize.'

If the erstwhile inhabitants of *Canberra* had been a little apprehensive at what might lie ahead, it did not take the newly-arrived Marines in *Fearless* long to realize that their hosts were positively evacuating their bowels at the prospect.

It had been easier in *Canberra*, as during the Red and Yellow alerts they had at least been able to see what was going on outside. And that is a distinct psychological advantage. In *Fearless* imaginations and fear of the unknown had run riot.

For hours at a time during the alerts, the men had been forced to sit in their cabins unable to see anything but the dim red lighting which filled the ship. They had to wear the anti-flash hoods and gloves too, which meant they couldn't even recognize each other as only their eyes were visible through the white masks.

It had done terrible things to their state of mind. The newly arrived Marines, who had not stopped joking for six weeks, suddenly found that the 'we're doomed' mentality had taken over for real in their new ship.

In *Fearless* everyone was quiet. Nobody spoke unless spoken to first. There was no laughter as we steered nearer to the Falklands. Tension rose and brave hearts pounded.

The Marines and the Paras were never given anti-flash clothing. It just was not available.

One Para in *Intrepid* had sneaked out on deck with a member of the press, McGowan, for a moment's escape from the claustrophobic atmosphere below. 'Fucking arseholes,' he said a trifle despondently. 'Have you ever seen so many flaming ships?' He had a point. Warships, tankers, supply ships, cross-Channel ferries with the British Rail sign on their funnels defying any concession towards camouflage and the seemingly mountainous white presence of *Canberra*, which had yet to master the art of darkening ship and was still lit up like a Christmas tree, were steaming in close convoy for the Falklands.

At last, the great armada was together in one pack. The Para, clearly impressed by the awesome sight, said, 'They are so close. Christ, we could all crash into each other in the dark.'

In *Fearless*, the obvious question was asked, 'How could enemy aircraft fail to find such a fleet, so many ships so close to each other? They would have to be blind to miss us.'

Captain Jeremy Larken provided the answer. 'It's just what the doctor ordered,' he said over the Tannoy. 'The worse the weather, the better our chances of getting in undetected. And we've got a real peasouper out there.'

Incredibly, perhaps, with all the modern technological hardware available, finding a fleet in foul weather is not a lot easier than locating a needle in a haystack.

But the Argentinians tried. In *Intrepid*, the klaxon wailed, 'Air Raid Warning Red.'

'Bloody hell,' bellowed one of the two Paras in the bookcase. 'For Christ's sake let us out.' As they flung open the glass doors to race for the emergency station in time to take cover in the threatened air attack, a crush of bodies with the same objective bashed them closed again. They were trapped behind glass, fearing it was for eternity.

Again, prowling Skyhawks had passed to the south. The fleet was not attacked. It was not even detected, despite by now being well within the 200-mile Total Exclusion Zone around the Falklands, and with far from peaceful intentions.

An old lady in a rowing boat could have thrown a well-placed hand grenade at any time during that day and General Galtieri would still be enjoying being carried shoulder high through the streets of Buenos Aires.

'Don't worry, if their air force doesn't get us their submarines will,' said Lieutenant Mike Hawkes of 40 Commando, a man who did not like optimism to get out of control. 'And if the subs don't, they are bound to have laid mines all across Falklands Sound,' he added, with sarcastic reassurance.

In *Intrepid*, a Para officer went to the bar in the wardroom and asked if he had been given a mess number, vital if he was to get a drink. 'Yes, sir,' said the naval steward. 'It's 007.'

'Oh,' said the officer, turning to his peers, 'I'm licensed to kill.'

'Or licensed to be corpsed, cunt,' whispered the steward, fortunately out of earshot.

It was at this time that the first photographic evidence of the RAF Vulcan raids on Stanley airfield was released. It did not do a lot to improve morale.

'I don't believe it,' said Captain Alan Berry of 40 Commando, through clenched teeth. 'How can they only have got one bomb on the runway after dropping 42?'

Captain Berry looked close to tears, realizing that all the triumphant shouting from the MOD in London was farcical. He grumbled, 'Another magnificent chapter in the history of the Crabs.'

A Marine later received a letter from home proudly announcing that the highlight of the Air Day at RAF Halton had been two Vulcans re-enacting the bombing of Stanley airfield. The reply was hastily despatched, inquiring, 'How many of the spectators were killed?'

As the welcome cloak of darkness enveloped the Assault Group, Captain Larken came back on the Tannoy in *Fearless*. He announced, 'We're almost home and dry. It's been the trickiest day so far.'

He added that the Argentinian air force was incapable of flying at night, which, although said in good faith, turned out to be another of the great misconceptions under which British Intelligence was labouring.

But at the time it did a lot to make the men breathe more easily on what was to be their last night at sea.

In *Intrepid*, final beach assault plans had been laid. Colonel Hew Pike, the commanding officer of 3 Para, was sure his men would fight like lions once they were ashore. It was getting them ashore in the first place that caused him concern.

Gravely, he told his company commanders, 'The Navy has promised to get us ashore with dry feet.' He paused, then added, 'But you know what cunts they are.'

Each of the Para companies in *Intrepid*, A, B, C and D, had been given their jobs for what was called, rather unimaginatively, D-Day. A sergeant in D Company, careful not to be explicit, said, 'We've got our job, mate. Ultra vandalism.'

The Marines in *Fearless* had also been given their orders.

Much of the landing plan, which was given the specific code-name of Sutton because, it was said, that is where Task Force commander Admiral Sandy Woodward lived, was devised by Marine Major Ewen Southby-Tailyour, principally because he had spent some time sailing around the islands.

The men of 40 Commando were to land at the settlement of San Carlos on a beach code-named Blue Beach 2, a colour arrived at because of the lanyard this unit wore on their left shoulders.

Other beaches were designated in the same manner. 45 Commando would land at Red Beach 1, at Ajax Bay, across the water from San Carlos; 2 Para at Blue Beach 1, further up San Carlos Water from 40 Commando; and 3 Para were to go ashore at Green Beach 1 around the headland a mile from the settlement of Port San Carlos.

Men of the Special Air Service Regiment and Special Boat Squadron of the Royal Marines were already ashore, and had secured the beaches.

They'd also been usefully employed keeping the Argentinians busy before the main landing force arrived. The most successful pre-landing action had been the SAS raid on Pebble Island, which they later admitted had been their most enjoyable and unexpected operation of the whole war.

Under the cover of a diversionary bombardment, a party from the SAS were put ashore near the Argentine's makeshift airbase at Pebble Island. Their orders were to do what the SAS like doing most: 'go in and cause a bit of trouble, then get out fast.'

De-briefings afterwards, extensively reported at 0 Groups for other units, related that the SAS 'thought Christmas had come early'.

They couldn't believe their luck. There were at least eleven Argentine aircraft virtually unguarded, and instead of the quick hit-and-run, the lads from Hereford could not resist 'hanging around a bit, and really ruining their day'.

As their commanding officer, Lt Colonel Mike Rose said later, 'Three times they were told to stop having a good time and get the hell out of it, and three times there was some strangely suspicious reason why they never got the order.'

When at last a small squad of Argentinian soldiers arrived to see what was happening, a few shots from the SAS had them running away again. They returned being waved on by an officer, who was promptly shot dead, and his men ran away again.

'There's a valuable lesson in that,' said Lt Colonel Malcolm Hunt to his men of 40 Commando as they were preparing to go ashore themselves. 'If you see an officer or anybody else urging men on, shoot them first.'

A voice from the back of the room asked, 'Can we have a practice now, sir?'

'Fuck off,' said Colonel Hunt with a grin.

Stories were told of the SAS on Pebble Island having

the time of their lives blowing up everything in sight, raising their eyes to Heaven and saying, 'Thank you, thank you, thank you,' for providing such an opportunity.

At last, with total destruction all around them, fires that could be seen miles away, and some frightened Argentine soldiers making good their escape, the SAS reluctantly called it a day and returned to their ship.

Sadly, the story was reported with such glee and gusto that an impression was instilled in some minds that the enemy were a bunch of comical cowards, and the Falklands would be recaptured with as little trouble and just as much fun.

The truth began to dawn a few hours later when the landings started.

In *Fearless*, Brigadier Julian Thompson, commander of 3 Commando Brigade, which included the three Royal Marines Commandoes and the two Parachute Regiment battalions, was smiling. He was confident, and satisfied with the landing plans, and even allowed himself time to walk around the ship chatting to the men and sharing a few jokes. It did a lot to quell last-minute nerves.

'Everything looking OK?' inquired Hands.

'Everything's looking OK,' assured the brigadier.

In *Intrepid*, though, the SAS were not quite as happy as their recent exploits would have led one to expect. This was understandable. Sadly, off the stern of the assault ship a Sea King helicopter had crashed, while bringing 22 troopers back from a mission. All aboard were lost.

These hardy men, also with nothing but decks to sleep on, treated the newly arrived Paras and pressmen with suspicion.

Captain Bob Darby, air adjutant of 3 Para, said to one newsman, 'For Christ's sake don't ask any silly questions. You're not supposed to be here, and the gentlemen across the room with slightly long hair wouldn't be all that bothered if you all fell over the side.'

One SAS man, obviously in a mischievous mood, frequently stalked around the wardroom muttering, '25th of May, glug, glug, glug.'

Asked to explain this strange sentence, he replied, 'Name of their carrier, isn't it. If it comes out to play on the 25th, it will get sunk. Glug, glug, glug.'

The 25th of May was five days off. The *Veintecinco de Mayo* wisely had run for its home port after the sinking of the *Belgrano*, never to stick its nose out to sea again until after the war.

Company commanders were now giving final briefings to their men for the pre-dawn landings, scheduled to take place in just a few hours.

Colonel Pike told his men, 'We are going in. The Navy has got us here. Stay flexible. Good luck.'

Captain Berry was telling his men of headquarters company, 40 Commando, that the signal for all being clear on the beach would be the morse letter 'Alpha' flashed from a red torch by the SBS.

'That will mean everything's fine, the landing is clear,' he said. 'Morse letter "Bravo" means there could be a bit of trouble, and "Charlie" means there will be a lot of trouble.'

'What happens if there's no signal?' inquired one of his men.

'Probably means the Argies have captured the SBS and are waiting for us in their hordes.'

'What do we do then?'

'We go in anyway,' said the captain.

'Shit.'

Colonel Pike, meanwhile, had told his men in *Intrepid* that the SAS would have secured Green Beach 1 and in the darkness they could be identified by white bands round their helmets.

'A point of warning, though,' he said. 'The Argies

92

appear to be in the habit of wrapping their field dressings around their helmets.'

'Bloody confusing,' said one Para. 'Who the hell do I shoot?'

The reply: 'Any silly sod who shoots at me.'

The wardroom of *Intrepid* now looked anything but the quiet and dignified refuge for officers off watch. SAS men were now walking around carrying their Armalite rifles, and wearing grenades on their camouflaged windproofs.

Anyone who was not carrying a weapon ashore had each collected two canisters of 7·62 rifle rounds to be taken ashore and then dumped on the beach. This included the Press.

McGowan and Smith were to go ashore with 3 Para's spearhead, 'A' Company, commanded by Major David Collett. Collett said, 'There is a possibility that there are Argie troops in Port San Carlos. We've got guns, you haven't. So there are two things to bear in mind. Keep out of the bloody way, and duck when the mood grabs you.'

In *Fearless*, Hands, with Bob Hammond and John Martin were to go ashore with Alan Berry's headquarters company and the Commanding Officer of 40 Commando.

'Party frocks and make-up on, girls,' said a sergeant-major. 'It's time to go.'

And it was. Full camouflage clothing, black cream smeared over 'all exposed parts, so your little faces don't shine out like the Eddystone Light', and the heavy bergans pulled on.

All this at one in the morning.

Everybody looked the same. Even the machine gunners had heeded Captain Berry's warning and stowed their ammunition properly, not, as he had feared, 'walking round with bandoliers slung across their chests like a bunch of Mexican bum-bandits'.

He enforced one last point as his men started the

long, tortuous descent to the landing craft. 'Dead quiet. Not a sound,' he said.

'No trouble,' said a voice on the ladder. 'Quick run ashore, into the nearest pub, then back here for lunch.'

'Shut up,' called Captain Berry.

Then into the dim red glow of the dock, with the landing craft waiting. Queues of men from other parts of the ship were slowly balancing their way along narrow walls to get to them too.

In *Intrepid* the same pattern was being followed. The Tannoy crackled into life: ' "A" Company proceed to their landing craft.'

As in *Fearless*, combat troops filed towards the dock in silence, a silence broken only by a forlorn voice with a Yorkshire accent: 'I've lost me coat,' wailed Derek Hudson, who would be going ashore with 3 Para's headquarters company.

'Oh, for Christ's sake,' boomed 3 Para's second in command, Major Roger Patton. 'Where the hell is it?'

Hudson, chief reporter of the *Yorkshire Post*, replied, 'I don't know, I just put it down, and now it's gone. It looks just like yours.'

'Well it would, wouldn't it?' said Patton. 'They're all exactly the same! It's only a major landing you're delaying here. I hope you realize that.'

Hudson's windproof was found under a wardroom table.

'Put it on, do it up, and never, never take your bloody eyes off it again. If you lose it ashore, you've had it,' said Patton.

Suddenly it felt cold after the warmth of the cabins, and there, at the end of the dock, was the black, moonless sky. Sounds of heavy naval gunfire rumbled into the dock, and eyes grew accustomed to the dark. As they did, a shape took its form over the stern of the ship: a long, black mass, gently breaking the horizon – the hills of East Falkland.

Chapter 6

Preconceived ideas drawn from the films of John Wayne and Audie Murphy perished in the chill of the morning air. Hollywood had got it wrong. On 21 May, 1982, the British returned to the Falklands in a way that the cinema just would not have believed.

The men of 40 Commando were loaded into their landing craft, hearts pounding bravely in their chests, full of evil intentions. For six weeks they had been psyched up for this moment.

'It's just not working,' said their colonel, Malcolm Hunt. 'They can't possibly expect us all to get in that,' he added, pointing disbelievingly at an already jam-packed boat.

The loadmaster had tried to cram a quart into a pint pot. There were just too many men trying to get into too small a vessel.

'Don't worry, this won't be for very long,' said Colonel Hunt. 'We will do a bit of cross-decking once we get away.'

His men nearly did not get that far.

'Air Raid Warning Red. Air Raid Warning Red,' screamed the Tannoy.

'Oh fuck,' said Lieutenant Mike Hawkes. 'They might have the decency to at least let us get away from the ship before bombing us.'

'Don't worry,' said a voice to his right. 'They've got it wrong. We all know the Argies can't fly at night.'

It was indeed pitch black. But faith in Intelligence reports that the Argentinian air force could not operate in the dark was beginning to dwindle.

Every man in the landing craft just wanted to get away from *Fearless* and start acting like a real soldier.

95

'Good luck and God speed, 40 Commando. It's been a pleasure to have you on board,' said the Tannoy as the stern gate lowered and the open sea at the mouth of San Carlos Water flooded in.

'No it fucking hasn't,' said a voice in the landing craft. 'I hope you bastards sink.'

The four landing craft pulled away from *Fearless* and into the gentle swell. This was it, the landing was under way.

But in Foxtrot 1, the code name given to the boat carrying 40 Commando's headquarters company, all was not happy. There were 30 too many bodies on board to make breathing possible. Everyone knew the trip to the beach would take over an hour, and everyone knew survival in such conditions was unlikely.

It was hardly the way John Wayne would have planned it. After circling for what seemed like hours, Foxtrot 1 was joined by one of the smaller landing craft, called an LCVP, from *Fearless*.

'Where the hell have you been?' inquired Malcolm Hunt.

'Sorry, sir,' came the reply. 'There seems to have been a bit of a fuck-up on *Norland* and the Paras aren't ready.'

The men of 2 Para had been held up because in the crush to get to his boat station one soldier had fallen in the darkness on a staircase inside the ferry and had broken his hip. The war was over before it began for him, and would take a little longer to get to for others. The man had to be hauled out of the way so other Paras could get to the boats.

This simple, but painful, slip, put the entire landing behind schedule.

The extra bodies in Foxtrot 1 made their way through the scrum to the port side. They then had to scramble up and over into the LCVP. 'A' Company was now, at last, all together and in the right place to spearhead the Marines' assault.

The phalanx of 40 Commando chugged expectantly up

San Carlos Water through the blackness before the dawn. Around them a continual crashing and crumping of Naval gunfire, as the warships relentlessly pounded the Argentinian positions on Fanning Head. Above them, the beautiful but incongruous sight of a magnificent display of shooting stars, around the Southern Cross.

'It was never like this on Dartmoor,' said a voice.

The black hills on both sides echoed to the sounds of the Naval gunfire. For all the men knew, and indeed feared, those hills were swarming with Argentinian troops just waiting for the right moment to blast them to oblivion as the landing craft groped through the darkness.

'I don't suppose,' said the same voice, 'this is the right moment to volunteer for parachute training?' From the rumble of expletives from others in the landing craft, he gathered it was not.

All eyes then were turned towards land. Where were the reassuring red flashes from the SBS which would signal that all was well to come in?

'Can you see anything from up front?' inquired Colonel Hunt, hopefully.

'No,' came the frank, if unhelpful, response.

Captain Berry had been right. His men were going in anyway, and the landing craft veered towards Blue Beach 1.

'Don't forget,' Lieutenant Hawkes had instructed his charges. 'The moment you get on shore, head for the large white rock and regroup there.'

It was not his fault that there was not a single white rock anywhere on the beach the landing craft was making for. So he could not be blamed for the confusion that was to follow.

Twenty yards from the beach, the man at the front of the landing craft called out, 'Brace yourselves, we're 'ere.'

And with a sickening thud, they were.

The ramp went down and the two light tanks in the

bows of the craft spluttered into life. After a delay that seemed to last a lifetime, one of them lurched off into the water.

'I have not heard its engine die, so it must be all right,' said a Marine near the stern. 'The driver must have found the beach.'

The tank was indeed on the beach, but the Marines stood fast on the boat. It was agonizing. Nobody moved.

Perhaps they were waiting for someone to be given the privilege of being first to put his boot on the beach. Maybe they had all changed their minds about the whole thing anyway. The fact was that no brave Marine seemed over-anxious to take that first giant step for Maggie Thatcher.

'Get on with it, this is supposed to be a fucking invasion!' said a voice with enough polish and authority to make it sound like it belonged to an officer.

Thus inspired, 40 Commando got on with the invasion. They waded through the ice cold water and up onto the beach . . . the wrong beach.

Where was the large white rock Lieutenant Hawkes had been looking for, and had promised would be there? No-one knew.

'We are quite sure this is the Falklands, are we?' asked a voice in the darkness, not terribly impressed by the way things were going.

In fact, and quite understandably, the landing craft had in the gloom and confusion missed its mark by 100 yards. In fairness, after 8000 miles, missing by 100 yards was not at all bad. But it was enough to throw the best-laid plans into some disarray.

For nearly an hour Marines stumbled about looking for the right place to be. God knows what it would have been like if the Argentinians had after all been waiting in force to push them back into the sea.

One machine gun or mortar would have decimated the Marines before they had even got ashore. And there had actually been enemy troops near Blue Beach 1 as

98

they approached but they had heard the landing craft a good half mile away, and decided they could best serve the Junta by beating a hasty retreat into the hills.

If Prime Minister Margaret Thatcher had known then exactly what was going on, she might well have been chewing her fingernails in No. 10 Downing Street.

The stalwarts of 40 Commando had made a landing, with the grace of God, without opposition. *Norland* had finally disgorged 2 Para and they, too, were now swarming ashore.

Out in San Carlos Water, 3 Para's 'A' Company had left *Intrepid* but were apparently more interested in sailing round the old ship to check its paintwork. Where they were not going, was ashore. This trip around the bay was anything but fun. Like just about every other landing craft that morning, this LCU would have encouraged the inmates of a sardine can to put out a 'vacancies' sign.

'I want a piss,' said a young Para, wedged in a forest of bodies in the centre of the boat.

'Do it over me and we'll fall out,' said his mate. 'If I could reach my bayonet, I'd stab you. Should have listened to your mum and gone before you left.'

One soldier had managed to kneel down and check his belt order. 'Get up, you idle shit,' shouted an officer on the craft's tiny bridge. 'Sod about like that, and you'll sleep for ever.'

No-one could move. So cramped were the men, breathing was no walkover, either.

'Look, cunt, either marry me or get your shovel out of my crutch,' snarled a sergeant.

'Can't move,' said the soldier with the shovel on his back. 'You'll have to live with it.'

If the discomfort was bad, so was the mood of potential doom. Because of 2 Para's mishap in *Norland*, 3 Para had been delayed in leaving *Intrepid*.

The Landing Forces commander, Brigadier Julian Thompson, had refused to change the order of landing after the accident on *Norland*. 3 Para were to go to Green Beach 1 after 2 Para had gone to Blue Beach 1, and that was it.

The worrying factor was that *all* the landings were to have been in darkness. Because of this delay, 3 Para were now chugging about, trying to group for the beach assault, in broad daylight.

Sergeant Chris Phelan, in the bow, chanted from time to time what everyone aboard knew. 'Paras don't like boats, Paras don't like boats.'

Any one of them would have preferred to drop out of a Hercules at 10,000 feet rather than go to war like this.

Their mood did not improve with the words from the man driving the little boat.

'Air Raid Red. Air Raid Red,' he boomed. A Para on the bridge roof cocked his machine gun. The soldiers moved the only parts of their bodies they could, their heads, and anxiously scanned the sky.

'Fucking 2 Para,' shouted a voice. 'Done it on purpose to screw us up.'

'What does it look like?' Colonel Pike asked the landing-craft crewman with a radio.

'Pucaras, sir,' said the crewmen. 'Heading our way.'

Pucaras are Argentinian-built piston-engined anti-insurgency aircraft, slow but with devastating capabilities to deliver bombs, rockets and cannon fire. It was not good news.

Two more landing craft joined 'A' Company's and the three headed for a distant headland two miles from the assault ships.

Under the lee of Fanning Head, red and green tracer arched towards an Argentinian position. The SBS were ashore to give an enemy company a 'malletting'.

Word spread throughout the 'A' Company landing craft that enemy troops were near Green Beach 1. There was every chance that the Paras would have the only opposed landing.

'Oh, good,' said a private. 'Now if I could reach my

weapon, I'd be able to do something about that. As it is, all I can do is shout rude things at them.'

'Quiet in the boat,' ordered somebody with the right to.

' 'Ere,' said one of the Para medics. 'Thought's just occurred to me.'

'What's that, Steve?' said his oppo.

'Bloody Navy took our lifejackets off us when we got into this thing. What if it sinks?'

'Then you're dipped, mate,' came the reply. 'It won't do me a lot of good, either.'

'Beach secure,' shouted the man driving the LCU. 'We still have an Air Red.'

Then he muttered to Colonel Pike, who shouted, 'Prepare to beach. Brace yourselves.'

Then it all went a little wrong.

The man in the bow, acting as a sort of combat doorman, would have liked at this time to lower the bow ramp and watch these young lions whizz out and start savaging the odd invader.

It was not to be.

'Too bloody deep, sir,' he reported.

'What?' screamed Colonel Pike.

'Can't land here, sir,' said the doorman. 'More than six feet of water.'

'This is the bloody beach, isn't it?' demanded the colonel.

'Right beach, wrong slope, sir,' said the man in the bow. 'Hang about, I've got an idea.'

He had, too. From no-one knows where, this enterprising character found a long white pole.

'Fuck, he's blind,' said Sergeant Phelan. 'That's all we need.'

The reality was that on the doorstep of what could be a battleground, the man with the white stick was probing the depth of the water, while the driver edged the landing craft out and made several attempts to nudge it in to more shallow water.

'Oh, for Christ's sake,' groaned Colonel Pike. 'Could we please get on with it?'

But it was no good. To land from the LCU would be to introduce the Paras to that which is most abhorrent to them: swimming under water.

In near panic, with the dreaded Pucaras buzzing around somewhere if not yet in sight, the colonel ordered the smaller LCVPs to land their men and then come alongside.

This done, the Paras began to cross-deck to the smaller craft and thereby reach water shallow enough to wade ashore.

Some, desperate to get off boats after six weeks at sea, leapt over the side into what was then chest deep water, and waddled up the shingle to set foot on the peat turf of East Falkland.

McGowan, ever keen to impress, did the same, missed his footing, and disappeared beneath the water.

On emerging, drenched and devoid of any respectability, the man with the white stick shouted at him, 'Who's a stupid cunt, then?'

Adjutant Captain Kevin McGimpsey then helpfully threw McGowan a camera he had been entrusted to take ashore for Independent Television News. His aim was reasonably good, but McGowan was not at that moment in a fit state to catch anything other than pneumonia. The camera disappeared into the water and was ruined.

The Paras fanned out and the lead company ran forward towards Port San Carlos settlement a mile away, while ammunition boxes and mortar rounds were heaped on the beach for following units to collect.

Now the distant noise of aircraft could be heard. Whatever the aircraft were, they could not be seen.

Someone shouted the words that were to be commonplace every day for three weeks. 'Take cover!'

Simultaneously, the phrase was being repeated at each beach-head. Somehow, and not exactly as the

102

brigadier had planned it, the invasion troops were back on the Falklands and largely intact.

The Argentinians had not, after all, been aware of their approach until it was too late.

Now they were determined to make up for being wrong-footed. Wrongly, they had assumed that the British would land closer to Port Stanley, not on the far end of East Falkland. Their air force was to begin that morning a demonstration of heroic flying that would soon gain them grudging respect from the British.

But before they arrived, 40 Commando had been doing its best to win friends and influence people. The door of a local sheep-station labourer was tentatively knocked upon. All around Marines took up firing positions, not yet sure whether or not enemy troops were there to meet them.

The sound of sleepy footsteps came from within. The door creaked open to reveal an ancient dressing gown containing the portly figure of one of the 1,800 Falklanders they had come to liberate. It was a female of the species.

She stared blearily into her garden, now infested with anxious-looking Marines. She had been waiting 49 days for this moment, yet she reacted as though it was the milkman calling for his money.

'Oh, you're back then,' was all she could muster on this historic occasion. The Marines smiled, lost for words.

Next morning, another islander, similarly unimpressed, wanted only one question answered. With aching sincerity he asked, 'Have Leeds United been relegated?'

There had been a race among the units to see which would be the first to raise the Union Flag once more over the Falklands. Arguments still rage to this day as to who actually made it.

40 Commando swear blind it was them, and on this day, there were no witnesses from rival units to dispute

their claim. However, even this simple act did not go without a hitch. They found a flag-pole near the settlement manager's house and they had brought the flag with them. Then came the problem. They could not get it up.

It had been so long since the flag-pole had been used that the pulley for the halyards was jammed with rust.

A couple of local farmworkers, who had come to see the momentous, symbolic return of British rule, had to shin up the pole so that the flag could at last be raised.

The flag's valiant flutterings were short-lived. The following day Brigade Headquarters was established in its shadow. It was decided that a large Union Flag in the middle of a well-concealed brigade headquarters would prove to be an irresistible aiming point for Argentinian pilots. Without ceremony, the flag was pulled down again.

Meanwhile, 45 Commando had landed across San Carlos Water and 2 Para were tabbing up Sussex Mountains, the high ground overlooking San Carlos settlement.

Now the elusive Pucaras had arrived, and unlucky 2 Para was to have the dubious honour of their first fire-power demonstration.

As men weighed down with Blowpipe shoulder-held anti-aircraft missiles struggled up the slopes, the dreadful droning of these aircraft grew louder. 2 Para were strafed, and fired back, and those edging uphill slowly were now moving with renewed energy.

Those units left behind at the beach-heads were already digging in for all they were worth, fully expecting the full weight of the Argentinian air force to be upon them at any minute.

The Junta's planes were indeed on their way in force. Mirage and Skyhawk jets were even now screaming at low level towards the British. The real battle for the liberation of the Falklands was on.

Understandably, the impending arrival of hostile aircraft instilled fear into everyone in the Task Force, but most were sure that the British Harriers would soon sort them out. After all, Rear-admiral Woodward had promised almost total air superiority on D-Day to enable the troops to get established ashore.

Wrong.

The first of many cries to echo above the noise of bandits in the sky reverberated through the bridgehead: 'Where's the fucking CAP?'

This reference to Woodward's air cover, the Combat Air Patrol, rarely received a satisfactory answer. Those who knew weren't there. Those who did not, were taking cover.

Instead of the friendly Harriers, the skies were seemingly full of Mirage and Skyhawk jets.

'It's OK,' said a disbelieving Marine, pointing at the incoming jets. 'As we've been promised it can't be the enemy, you're looking at proof that Harriers are just as good at camouflaging themselves as we are.'

There was, of course, one flaw in this. Normally it is frowned upon for Harriers to drop bombs on their own men and ships, so if these were Harriers, 'someone's in for a bollocking', pointed out the Marine's mate.

Wave after wave of enemy jets screeched in spitting cannon shells and dropping 500lb and 1000lb bombs among the ships in San Carlos Water. Not for nothing was it soon to be nicknamed 'Bomb Alley'.

Frightening fields of fire were put up in front of the warplanes as men in the ships blasted away with everything they had. Green and red tracer laced webs of fire in their paths, but on they flew, often at wave-top height.

Ashore, the men could only watch, horrified. 'I thought the Argies were supposed to be a bunch of wankers,' suggested a Marine in 40 Commando. 'Forgive me if I'm wrong, but these bastards seem to be quite good.'

Captain Berry, also observing not only the total lack of Harrier protection, but the daring brilliance of the Argentine pilots, tried to provide the answer.

'It's all to do with temperament,' he said. 'Just think of Fittipaldi and Fangio and you've got the Latins off to a tee. They may not like slogging around on foot, but give them something fast to play with and you can see what flash bastards they are.'

Then Berry added, 'Instead of watching the fireworks, I strongly recommend you get on with digging in, before they turn on us.'

As he spoke evil hissing sounds and the odd explosion caused anxious glances from the men ashore. It was the beginning of a trend that would soon have to be discouraged. Troops and seamen, in their enthusiasm to bring down the enemy aircraft, had not stopped to consider for a moment where the thousands of rounds they were firing every minute, would end up if they missed their targets.

Bullets zipped into the turf on both sides of the anchorage, narrowly missing the troops now digging feverishly, like moles, to get out of the line of fire.

Over on Port Carlos, lead platoons of 3 Para had engaged 47 Argentinian troops who had been sent there for rest and relaxation, on the misguided premise that this, of all places, was likely to be far away from any British landing.

Wrong again.

The Paras, psyched up and keen to get on with a 'bit of banjoing', could hardly believe their luck. The chill morning came alive with rifle and Sterling sub-machine gun fire as the hapless enemy ran like hell out of the settlement.

'For Christ's sake,' bellowed Colonel Pike, 'pick your targets. Don't just fire off in all directions.'

While this show of brutal manliness was being played out, the 52 civilians in the settlement, including 14 children, stood and watched.

'Been a bit dull round here for weeks,' said Stan Heathman, at 75 still a farmworker. 'Used to go to the store and have a drink and play bingo at night, but since the Argies came, we haven't been allowed.'

'I didn't know you were coming,' he said to a Para sergeant. 'Don't look as if those buggers did, either, does it?'

Those buggers, the enemy troops, were now going like greyhounds up a slope overlooking the inlet beyond the settlement. Paras' mortar rounds were thumping into the peat turf around them.

Then came tragedy. Two British Gazelle helicopters came beating in low and flew over the fleeing enemy troops.

'No. For Christ's sake, *no!*' shouted Colonel Pike, but in vain. The Argies opened up with everything they had, including a heavy machine gun. One chopper crashed in flames on the hillside. The other ditched into the inlet.

The two crew of the latter struck out for the shore as the Paras poured fire at the enemy. One airman virtually disappeared as machine-gun bullets danced around him in the water. He was hit in the stomach.

Local schoolteacher Susanne McCormick, just 18, dragged the wounded man out of the sea and she and other villagers took him to the nearby bunkhouse. They were too late to save him. His fellow crewman lived.

'Bastards,' said Susanne, in tears. 'I only hope I've got my own back on them. The water here has liver fluke in it. They asked me if I could drink it and I told them it was perfectly all right. Have they got a surprise coming.'

Even while all this was happening, the other villagers looked upon the morning more like a carnival than a war.

Stan Heathman's wife, Violet, said, 'It's been the worst winter here for ages. We used to have whist drives and everything. We haven't been able to hold the dance on Saturday nights because the Argies put a curfew on us. Then these Argies came and lived in the dancehall. Really it's the community hall.'

107

Stan added, 'Shit all over it, they did. Came and stole our food, too.'

He went on, 'We expected you all to be here a bit earlier. Still, better late than never. Never thought I'd be so pleased to hear artillery.'

As he spoke, the Argies fired back. All the Paras around him and his wife dived for cover. The old couple stayed at the garden gate, smiling with pride.

'Stupid old cunts,' said a soldier, lying covered in mud in a trackside drainage ditch.

One house away, taking cover was low on the list of chores that morning for Mrs Jeanette Bernston. As her husband, Olaf, boiled a kettle indoors, she touched a burly sergeant-major on the arm as he stalked by with intent to cause grievous bodily harm to anyone fool enough to mutter the odd 'olé' and asked him, 'Good morning, dear. Would you like a cup of tea?'

The sergeant-major couldn't believe it. Colonel Pike turned away in carefully controlled disgust, and a line of beaming Paras queued for a nice cup of tea.

'Take sugar?' asked Mrs Bernston.

'Jesus Christ,' muttered the colonel as he walked off. 'Keep apart. Keep your distance. One burst would get the bloody lot of you.'

The natives weren't being quite so friendly round the headland, where 40 Commando were by now nearly all 'heads below ground', as the Argentine air attacks kept pouring in above them on their way to the ships.

No tea was offered to the Marines; few people came up for a chat. It was two ten-year-olds who eventually came forward from the houses.

'Want a hand?' they said to a sweating Marine half-way through digging his trench.

He looked up at the volunteer labourers. Resisting the temptation to point out the obvious fact that he was extremely busy, and that two kids would inevitably slow down his digging, he smiled up at them instead and rested on his shovel for a moment.

'Yeah, why not?' he said in a kindly voice.

'Oh great,' said the young boy to his sister, and they set to work with pick and shovel while the Marine, a fatalist to the core, stood aside, and lit a cigarette.

Colonel Hunt, on the other side of the small valley, looked on with a grin.

'Typical Royal,' he said. 'Always ready to take advantage of facilities when they're available.'

Lt Hawkes was having less luck with his trench. His first attempt came to an abrupt halt when his shovel struck a boulder a few inches below the surface. The second attempt ended in a soggy mess as water came gushing through.

'That's it,' he said, throwing his shovel to one side in mock disgust. 'I'm booking into the hotel instead.'

His third try ended slightly more successfully, and although less than two feet deep, it was piled high with earthworks and neatly covered in turf, which inspired the massively built lieutenant to give it a proper name, culled from the backstreets of Belfast.

'Turf Lodge,' he called it. 'And not at all inappropriate, is it?'

Other members in the unit were still finding it hard to believe why on this first day of the landing, the Argentinian planes were flying right over their heads and still pounding the shipping.

'What's wrong? Have we got BO, or something?' asked one.

'Shush. Keep your big mouth shut,' said his mate. 'No-one's told them we're here. They must still think we're in the ships, so don't you go spoiling everything by telling them our little secret. Anyway they seem to be enjoying themselves enough even without playing with us, so leave the bastards alone.'

A few hundred yards away in San Carlos Water the bombing raids were, if anything, intensifying. Great white plumes of water shot into the air as the bombs missed their targets by a matter of feet. Planes screamed in and out of 'Bomb Alley' surprisingly aiming more for the smaller warships which could defend themselves, instead of the larger merchantmen like *Canberra* and *Norland* which could not.

'Serves the buggers right,' said a man to Colonel Hunt's right, as *Canberra* again disappeared behind a sheet of water. 'She should have stayed a liner.'

Canberra did not receive a scratch that day, but having by now become more than used to doing things the Royal Navy way, that night she kept up the old tradition of running away.

Captain Burne on the bridge of *Canberra* was, by all accounts, magnificent on that day, but he knew it would have been suicide to keep the ship in the anchorage any longer.

The P&O women members of the crew also lived through a day that bore little resemblance to the careers they had gone in for. They hurriedly did their work between air raids, then dived for the nearest solid object and crossed their fingers when the jets and the noise of explosions came back.

Even the 'not terribly hetero' stewards came through the day in a far better state than anyone could have expected. As one explained later, 'Well, we're all boys together, and at least we were among friends.'

A Marine with 40 Commando thought of the stewards as he watched the ship coming under attack.

'I'll bet they're having the time of their lives,' he commented. 'All cuddled up together, arseholes twitching in unison.'

As another three Argentinian jets screeched over, a Marine shouted up at the pilot. '*Fearless* is the one with the two black balls on the mast,' he called. 'There's a fiver in it for you if you get the cooks on board.'

Occasionally a Skyhawk would fly over the Marines with smoke pouring from its tail, obviously destined never to make it back to the mainland. Marines cheered, waved two fingers at them, and whistled triumphantly.

One Skyhawk, riddled with machine-gun bullets, and out of control, disappeared over the Sussex Mountains and inevitably crashed, with a shout of, 'Serves you right. Now fuck off', from a Marine's trench.

Young girls barely in their teens walked around Port San Carlos handing out tomato and vegetable soup to Paras now digging in on the slopes on the edge of the settlement, and on the high ground of Settlement Rocks overlooking the entire area.

Mirages and Skyhawks swooped in low but pressed on for the ships instead of hitting positions ashore. None-the-less, all troops took cover just in case. 'Do make your arse twitch, dunnit?' said a private to his mate in the shallow hole that was now rapidly getting deeper.

'One more foot, and I'll have you buggers for desertion,' said a passing sergeant, using an old World War Two grumble.

By now, the battalion's medical team had moved into the bunkhouse. Their doctor, Captain John Burgess, told the occupants, 'Put blankets up over all the windows for a blackout when it gets dark. If you don't, you're likely to get a 7·62 round up your arse.'

The civilians could still not quite understand that the British being with them was not only a welcome state of affairs, but also highly dangerous.

Captain Giles Orpen-Smellie, 3 Para's Intelligence officer, told a group of them around the manager's house, 'Look, the Argies are going to get a trifle annoyed about us being here sooner or later, and come and hit us. You must dig trenches and keep under cover.'

Colour-sergeant Brian Faulkner told a knot of kids playing around the bunkhouse, to make sure they got the point, 'You have to dig holes. They are the safest thing. If the Argie planes fire cannon at these houses, the rounds will go through them like shit through a goose.'

It made no difference. Not one civilian that day picked up a shovel to get on with some steady digging. They made tea, cooked mutton, and walked around meeting their new friends.

Just before dusk, men of 42 Commando came on to 3 Para's flank at the settlement. They had been put ashore from *Canberra* before she sailed for safer waters.

Major Mike Norman, having now shrugged off his chore as Press censor aboard the liner, was now in command of Juliet Company. Somewhat peeved, he said, 'Bloody Paras have let those Argies go. Now we have to fuck off up into the hills after them without sleeping bags and ponchos. It's going to be bloody cold up there.'

Outside the community hall, where the Argie troops had lived, Para Sergeant Tony Dunn pulled out a pickle jar. 'It's ears I'm after,' he said. 'Not just any ears. I want Argie ears. They'll keep nicely in here.' He picked up a long ceremonial sword and added, 'Christ, I could have a few off with this. Pity I can't keep it. Too bulky. Have to use the old bayonet.'

Soldiers began to cook their meals, the start of a long love-hate affair with the item always on the top of the menu, a dehydrated goo laughingly referred to as Chicken Supreme. It had to be done before dark on their hexi-stoves, small tin frames heated by a kind of fire-lighter, because to show any kind of light after darkness might well give away the position.

'Our big fear tonight,' said Orpen-Smellie, 'is infiltration and counter-attack. If we were them, we'd hit us very hard about now.' He added, 'So far, the war goes well for us.'

Perhaps he was right. Nine enemy aircraft had been shot down.

But the frigate *Ardent*, whose crew gave the fighting men in *Canberra* such a rousing farewell at sea on the way down, had been lost outside 'Bomb Alley' in Falkland Sound. 24 of her crew died and 30 were injured.

Chapter 7

Day Two of the British landings dawned to find the bridgeheads established. 40 Commando were now four feet under the soggy peat of San Carlos Settlement; 45 Commando were similarly installed across the water at Ajax Bay.

3 Para and the bulk of 42 Commando were round the headland at Port San Carlos, and 2 Para, who had seen enough of Bomb Alley, were 'tabbing' their way over the Sussex Mountains, hoping they'd get to Port Stanley before the brigadier noticed they were missing. Unknown to them at that time, there was an appointment with the Argentines at Goose Green before they got there.

Brigadier Thompson and his staff, meanwhile, were thinking about moving away from their floating headquarters aboard *Fearless*, and establishing themselves not far from 40 Commando at San Carlos.

The priorities for the troops were taking shape. After holes had been dug to provide as much shelter as could be found under the circumstances, the next most important factor in life had to be attended to with some haste. Unfortunately, at Port San Carlos, 3 Para found that most if not all the available women in the area were either too young to consider, or too ugly.

There was a dilemma.

One young lady in particular caught the Paras' eyes. She was lovely but unattainable. Kia Miller, the daughter of Alan, the manager of Port San Carlos settlement, was, without being unduly unfair to the other women there, like a canary in a cage of crows.

As she walked among the trenches handing out soup and soothing words, she was unaware that had the men not been forewarned with one nugget of information she would have been propositioned every ten feet. She was only 13. In fairness to the Toms, she looked easily 17, and most of them weren't a lot older than that.

Kia's mother, Mrs Carol Miller, was not there. She had for some time lived apart from her husband in Congleton in Cheshire, and it was her information on East Falkland that had played a major role deciding where the landings should take place. It was good information, as apart from the Argentinian air force there was no major enemy military presence anywhere near the D-Day beaches.

There was no pretty face to serve the Marines with their daily sustenance at San Carlos. Nor indeed were there the dubious luxuries of dehydrated chicken supreme. No, the Marines were living on what quarter-masters refer to as 'GS' rations. The Marines called them something else.

The primary difference between the dehydrated 'Arctic' rations and GS was that the latter came in tins and did not have to be reconstituted.

The Arctic rations were so named, and indeed so prepared, to be mixed with ample proportions of snow, as found in the Arctic. Sadly, nobody had informed the quartermaster general that the landings would occur when there was no snow on the ground. Water was in short supply or contaminated. Each man could only be sure of about a pint and a half of water a day to live on. The Arctic rations required at least that, if not more, to reconstitute. So shaving, washing, and even drinking were technically out of the question. The majority of rations would prove to be Arctic. GS would come to be regarded as a luxury; the two were often interchangeable.

The beauty of the GS rations was that no water needed to be added, and they could, if absolutely

114

necessary, be eaten without pre-heating. It was vile either way.

But the GS 'rats' had another virtue. They provided the calories in such a way that a visit to the 'lats' to evacuate the bowels was only required once every three days. It all sounded good in theory as that meant operational requirements need never be interrupted by men asking to go off for a few minutes to dig a hole and dispose of the aftermath of the GS rats.

But it was short-sighted, as so many Army contingencies have a habit of being. The 'third day' was not taken into consideration.

It was common-sense that if a battalion had not had to have a 'tom tit' as Cockney rhyming slang would have it, for three days, the 'third day' was likely to be a bit special. And so it was. Any military genius in Argentina would have known that to launch a full-scale attack on a 'third day' would have been literally to catch the enemy with their trousers down.

A way of turning this obvious flaw to a British advantage was suggested to Colonel Hunt, who was pondering the problem. 'It's easy, sir,' said the adviser. 'All we have to do is wait until the next "third day", then march the entire unit up to the top of the Sussex Mountains, drop their trousers, and aim their backsides at Port Stanley.' It was immediately conceded that an Argentine surrender in the face of such a bombardment would be instantaneous, but might be difficult to explain in the press, or indeed to the authors of the Geneva Convention, not that Argentina had signed it.

It had also been forgotten, or ignored, that both Arctic and GS rations, apart from being almost inedible, do not provide quite the requisite amount of calories for a fighting soldier in the field.

It was a problem beyond the responsibility of 40 Commando's quartermaster, Captain Geoff Whitely. So long as he could keep the food coming, he knew he would have a regular supply of customers. Variety was not the spice of life, and Geoff had other things to worry about, like keeping the ammunition and hardware flowing.

But eventually, either through economy or complaining Marines, a change in the daily fare was brought about.

A field kitchen was built, for communal messing. In the pitch blackness of pre-dawn or after dusk, men could be seen queueing for their hot meals. As it was in the dark, all did not go smoothly.

The evening meal was advertised as 'Babies' heads and train smash', which should have meant a steak and kidney pudding followed by jam sponge. In the rush for food, one did not always follow the other. More than once a steaming plate of main course could only be admired in the gloom for an instant before a ladle full of sponge and custard was heaped upon it, leaving the most unutterable, if wholesome, mess writhing in the unfortunate recipient's mess tin.

'You cunt,' said a voice in the gloom, peering horrified.

'Take it or leave it,' came the reply. 'I've got far less troublesome clients waiting to be served, so fuck off and eat your supper.'

Major Andy Gowan, standing by with two mess tins, each filled in the correct way, believed the whole communal messing was a great success from the start.

'Do you realize,' he said to a neighbour standing in the freezing darkness, 'this is the first time ever that a field kitchen has been set up and operated entirely in the dark?'

'Let's hope it's the last, then,' said a listener, his tin overflowing with a mixture of steak and kidney, custard and coffee.

Moving about after dark was a pastime beset by pitfalls. After supper the Marines would move back to their trenches for the night. Anybody moving around after that had to know the password. For the first week the correct procedure when challenged was to give the second half of a two-word phrase, the first of which would be offered by the sentry.

In Port San Carlos, well out of the way of the anchorage, there was absolutely no light at all after dark. A man five feet away could not be seen.

One young Para making his way from the echelon stores area (in a sheep shed) to the command post beside the manager's house could hear nothing but dull thuds and muffled cries of 'shit', as his mates crawled out of their trenches to do just that, and fell into drainage ditches or other people's trenches.

Nothing, that is, until he heard the sound of rifles being cocked. A voice shouted out, 'Dark!'

The young 'Tom' replied, 'I fucking know that. Can't see where the hell I'm going.'

The voice, unamused, came back, 'Password.'

The Tom said, 'Oh, shit. I've forgotten it.'

'Dark, you cunt.'

Suddenly it was flooding back. The soldier knew that he had to give the second word, but he couldn't remember it. So, using his initiative, he guessed.

'Night?' he ventured.

'No,' came the reply.

He tried again.

'Crusader?'

The reply: 'No. Try again.'

'Side?'

'What the fuck's the point? Where are you from?'

The hapless soldier, expecting to be cut down by the sentry at any moment, shouted, 'HQ Company.'

The sentry said, 'This *is* HQ Company. Come forward.'

The soldier did, and as he passed the sentry he asked what the second word of the pass phrase was.

'Tyrant.'

'Gave you the right fucking job, then,' said the soldier as he passed through.

In the manager's house officers were sipping Scotch and eating mutton while their men were forbidden to touch alcohol and lived off their 'rat packs'. The officers were there for an O-Group with the colonel.

All the men had been told not to scrounge food off the locals or take showers, which were available in the bunk-house, because this would be bad for the morale of men several miles outside the settlement who were unable to enjoy such luxuries. What those men would have felt had they known how convivial the O-Groups were is open to conjecture.

In fact many of them, instead of taking food from the villagers when it was offered to them, in many cases gave up their own. For weeks the people of Port San Carlos had not been able to get hold of sugar and were running short of tea. In every house after a while small piles of these commodities were stacked on kitchen tables from the soldiers' own rations.

At San Carlos, an ancient privy had been discovered at the settlement hall. The hall was being used as a regimental aid post, but the privy with its adjacent wash basin was a closely guarded secret.

Officers, and indeed some men, who had discovered it and were tired of sneaking off with a shovel on the 'third day', had decided to make use of this God-sent facility.

The word spread. Shovels were laid aside as more and more men headed for the porcelain haven. Hardly surprisingly, the ancient loo gave up under the strain.

The last Marine successfully to bolt himself inside had little idea that the toilet was about to give up in such a dramatic manner. He was heard entering by impartial observers, who with great glee related the event in every detail soon afterwards. He was heard sliding the bolt across. Some witnesses, not known for their realiability, even said they heard the muted, sound of his trousers hitting the concrete floor. What happened a few minutes later was beyond contradiction.

There was a muffled explosion, taken by those outside to be an indication that the Marine's bowels were emptying at a great speed.

'Oh, Christ,' said the voice from within the closet. 'Oh, Jesus.'

All was indeed not well. What had occurred was later referred to as the Great Loo Throwback, when the tightly packed contents of the outlet were for some reason hurled back into the bowl at some speed. Experts later discerned that this was due to a sudden inrush of seawater from the drain's outlet in San Carlos Water a hundred yards away.

But the evidence of the catastrophe, regardless of its causes, was all too apparent.

'You dirty bastard,' said a Marine as the poor man staggered out of the closet. 'Look at the state of you.'

It was true. The last user of the Settlement Hall privy had received more than he had given. Vainly he had used up the few sheets of tissue paper issued in every rat-pack in a small pouch marked 'sundries'. The unmistakable and foul-smelling evidence of his encounter with the toilet hung around him. Men moved away grimacing. The unfortunate one tried to smile, hoping his mates would not desert him in his moment of need. They did.

He was not the only one, though, to end up quite literally in the mire.

The Paras in and around Port San Carlos had grown tired of constant 'Air Reds' which rarely materialized. Almost every time they got an alert, the warplanes flew over them to hit the anchorage. It was inevitable that one day they would have a change of heart, and they picked on a time when many Toms were too far away from their trenches to take cover in them.

A stick of four Skyhawks came over a low hill in line

119

abreast, blazing away with their cannon. Men took cover wherever they could.

One soldier got out of what he thought was a drainage ditch after the raid and wailed, 'Ah, fuck. It's a sewer. I'm all covered in shit.'

An officer trotting by said, 'Shit is one thing we'll all be in if we keep ignoring "Air Reds".'

During that raid the settlement manager, Alan Miller, had also felt the need to get himself involved with this foul-smelling substance, and was enjoying the blissful tranquillity of his personal toilet.

When he heard the crump of the first 1000lb bomb hitting the edge of the settlement he grabbed his waist band and ran. When the aircraft had gone he came out fastening his belt and said to Captain Bob Darby, 'Do you know, I was having a crap when they started bombing us. I was in the toilet.'

Captain Darby, never lost for the right thing to say, commented, 'Well, if you're anything like me when these things are happening, you were in exactly the right place.'

Again the troops had been amazed that in an air raid the civilians had refused to follow their example and make any attempt to take cover.

Over land the Skyhawks had taken to using a particularly nasty kind of 1000lb bomb. It went off in the air after floating down on a parachute and showered shards of jagged metal over a large area. Informed of this, the civilians still did not bother to protect themselves. Miraculously none of them were ever hurt.

At the end of one raid two men carrying a stretcher bearing the wounded body of a young soldier stumbled sombrely towards a waiting 'cas-evac' Sea King helicopter, which had come in at speed, and was anxious to leave rapidly.

But the raiding aircraft had not gone after all. They had circled for another bombing run on the settlement. As they roared in a stretcher-bearer dropped one corner and the casualty, swathed in a blanket, fell into the mud. Undeterred by whatever pain he was suffering, and spurred on by an indomitable will to survive, he picked up his blanket and ran like a bat out of hell, throwing himself headlong into the gaping door of the chopper.

All around, Paras firing at the aircraft stopped and fell about laughing.

Air raids were beginning to cause more than a little discomfort for 40 Commando at San Carlos Settlement too.

The plan was a simple, and supposedly foolproof one: every time Argentine planes were known to be in the area, the warning would arrive at the Command Post, and a Marine would immediately stick his head outside and yell those dreaded words 'Air Red, Air Red' which were by now as commonplace as a request for a cigarette and treated with as much activity as if someone had instead muttered, 'Looks like rain.'

The plan was that the warning would be shouted down the line of trenches by word of mouth, eventually ending up at the last trench nearly half a mile away from the Command Post.

On one such occasion a distant group of Marines were seen dancing wildly on their trench instead of diving into it. A stick of Skyhawks screeched overhead, and the Marines disappeared underground at speed.

Enquiries were made as to why the warning had been treated with such apparent disdain. The words 'Air Red, Air Red,' had become confused as they were passed down the line, and by the time they reached the end had been changed to 'Galtieri dead, Galtieri dead', which would indeed have been a cause for some celebration.

It was later pointed out that a message had been similarly misjudged in an earlier war. 'Send reinforcements, the regiment is going to advance,' had been received as 'Send three and fourpence, the regiment is going to a dance.'

As the embarrassed miscreants of 40 Commando said

in their defence, 'You can't blame us if methods of communication haven't improved since Kaiser Bill's time.'

'Quite right,' said their sergeant. 'And you can't blame me if you get your bollocks shot off because you've got cloth ears.'

The trenches were supposed to provide an all-round arc of fire at enemy aircraft. Each trench had its sector to cover, and any plane which passed through it was to be blasted with machine-gun fire. It was surprisingly effective.

During one raid tracers from 40 Commando's guns flared upwards, except from one trench where at the vital moment the machine gun had jammed. Small shiny objects were seen coming from the trench instead, accompanied by a lot of bad language. The occupants in their frustration had refused to let the aircraft go by without some dissuasion at least, and were throwing ration tins into the sky, shouting, 'Take that, you bastards.'

By this time 45 Commando, on the flanks of 2 Para, were away from their beach-head at Ajax Bay and dug in on Sussex Mountain. They had survived one of the first air attacks on D-Day from an Argentinian piston-engined Mentor ground attack trainer from Port Stanley which had laced the hillside with bombs and cannon fire.

After the raid a colour-sergeant climbed out of his trench and checked on his men to see if any of them had been hit. As he walked among the trenches he said, 'They are bound to make a film about this. I'm wondering who's going to play my part. I reckon Robert Redford would be just right for it.'

Since the sergeant was a squat fellow with the kind of face unlikely to cause a sensation in a screen test, few of his men agreed.

But in this unit, as in all others, there was a profound sense of camaraderie among the men. On one morning after an air raid a young Marine decided it would be a fine idea to make his battery commander, Major Gerry Akhurst, a nice cup of tea. He was aware that the major had the rare luxury of two water bottles instead of the usual one. What he did not know was that the enterprising Akhurst had filled one with neat Scotch whisky before the landing, to keep up his and his men's spirits on the freezing nights in the trenches.

The thoughtful Marine took the wrong bottle, and poured the contents into a mess tin. He did not think twice about the slightly less than pure colour of the liquid now bubbling over the hexi-stove, as Falklands water is notoriously brackish.

Two tea-bags were dropped in and vigorously stirred, and the mixture poured into a couple of plastic mugs with large amounts of sugar.

Major Akhurst beamed and thanked the Marine. He raised the mug to his lips, sipped, and winced. The awful truth dawned on him in a flash.

'Oi! Come back here,' he yelled. 'Do you realize what you've done?'

The kind-hearted Marine had the error of his ways pointed out in no uncertain terms, and observers remarked later that he had been lucky to escape with his life.

The Blues and Royals had discovered a source of luxury items like whisky, cigarettes and sweets in the small shop at San Carlos. But, lacking the community spirit of Major Akhurst, they tried to keep it to themselves.

The kindly old lady who operated the shop backed them up, as the limited supplies on her shelves were supposed to keep her regular customers going right through the winter. But selling her wares to a 'real English lord', in the shape of Lieutenant Robin Innes-Ker, was too good an opportunity to miss. Lord Robin, who strictly speaking was Scottish, hid the true identity of his antecedents in order to speed up the purchase. But spies from 40 Commando were on hand, and insisted the old lady served them too.

'Where the hell did you get this?' demanded Colonel Hunt when offered a tot that evening.

'Ask no questions, hear no lies,' came the reply.

'Fine,' said the colonel. 'Never let it be said my lads don't have initiative. Cheers. But don't spread it around.'

It was too late. The word had spread, and the San Carlos Store was closed by the old lady after it had been put virtually under siege.

Close to the store, the little stream that ran through 40 Commando's camp had been diverted slightly to allow a constant and plentiful supply of fresh water to be available, purified and stored in a rubber tank above the fuel dump.

The stream, though, was still used by the hardy few who insisted on strip-washing each morning, regardless of the fact that HQ Company and others used the stream as a urinal.

One morning a fearful shrill cry rent the air. 'White bodies. Come and see the white bodies.'

Two young officers had removed their numerous layers of clothing and were scrubbing themselves in the freezing water.

'Daft sods,' said a not terribly impressed and fully-clad observer. 'Come all this way, survive the air raids, and die of frostbite. Personally I'd rather stink and stay warm.'

'True,' said his mate. 'I've never seen two pairs of balls shrivel up quite so small. If they don't get out quick their little cobblers will disappear.'

'Well, you know what they say about officers,' said the first. 'Most of them haven't got any in the first place. These two are obviously trying to prove something.'

'They sure have. Now I have the cast iron proof I've always wanted that officers are completely fucking barmy.'

The young officers hauled their pink and gleaming torsos out of the water, rubbed down and got dressed.

'Shame they've got to ruin it all and cover themselves in cam-cream again, innit?' said the first Marine. 'Mad, completely fucking mad.'

There were more air raids that morning, and again the shipping in San Carlos Water bore the brunt of the attacks.

Aboard the RFA *Stromness* things were not a lot quieter than they were before 45 Commando had got off.

Captain John Dickinson, known to his crew as 'Death or Glory' Dickinson surveyed with some pride the rails of his ship, now bristling with rows of machine guns.

'We can put up thousands upon thousands of rounds a minute,' he beamed. 'Only trouble is, if we fire them all off at once we'll capsize with the recoil.'

As he spoke another pair of Skyhawks screamed past the port side, between *Stromness* and *Fort Austin*. A large white plume of water appeared after a colossal explosion which had shaken both ships.

'Missed me, missed me,' jibed a gunner.

'Bit too fucking close for comfort, though,' said his mate. 'If *Fort Austin* goes up the whole of East Falkland goes with it.'

He was right. *Fort Austin* was the ammunition ship, desperately trying to get her bombs and ammunition ashore to the brigade maintenance area at Ajax Bay. There were wild rumours that she had everything on board from 9mm shells to atom bombs.

More Skyhawks hurtled past, firing cannon and dropping bombs.

'Can't we talk this over?' shouted the gunner at the passing plane. 'There's no need for anyone to lose their temper.'

The gunner had in fact just missed the opportunity of his life, as the belly of the Skyhawk had presented itself temptingly in his sights when his gun had jammed.

Hands, on *Stromness* to phone over a story to London on the ship's satellite communication 'Marisat', incurred the wrath of Captain Dickinson.

'Get out of the way,' yelled the captain at Hands, who was craning over the ship's side to get a better view of incoming planes. 'Nobody's going to mind a bit if you get shot by mistake, but we can't afford to waste the ammunition on you, so give the gunners a clear view.'

The raid passed but the lookouts remained vigilant. Suddenly a shout from the starboard side: 'Here they come again!'

'Fuck,' replied a gunner who was in the middle of reloading his machine gun. 'Tell them to hang on for a minute.'

Captain Dickinson wasn't so sure his ship was under attack. 'Don't shoot,' he called. 'It's only a flock of birds, and we haven't come all this way to shoot the wildlife.'

'But are they friendly birds?' said the gunner, now loaded and ready. 'No Argie seagull is going to shit in my eye.'

No Argie seagull did, but the Skyhawks kept on trying.

Stromness wasn't the only ship in the anchorage to feel that the Argentinian air force was taking a personal interest in sinking it.

In *Fearless*, still the senior Naval ship in the flotilla, the constant bombardment was beginning to take its toll. But no matter what is going on, the correct way of doing things according to the Dartmouth Etiquette Book must never be forgotten.

In the wardroom, officers sat off duty, oblivious to the pandemonium which reigned supreme outside.

'I say,' said one, aghast, as an extremely scruffy and dirty Marine dared set foot across the threshold. 'You can't come in here looking like that!'

The young officer, who had been living in a hole in the ground and was understandably looking forward to a few minutes in the warm, cigar-smoked paradise of the bar in *Fearless* was not prepared to argue over the finer points of procedure.

126

'And I suppose you are going to throw me out,' he said through three days of stubble.

'Well . . . not this time, perhaps,' said the incumbent of a soft chair, realizing that perhaps this was not the right moment to stick to the rule book. 'But next time, you might consider taking your muddy boots off.'

The Marines officer was not impressed. 'Next time,' he said, 'I might consider sticking one of them down your throat. And I won't have taken it off first.'

'Point taken, old man. Have a beer.'

Honour was restored with smiles all round – just in time for another Air Red. The crew of *Fearless* knew exactly what to do. They hauled on their anti-flash hoods and gloves, and scuttled off to their appointed panic stations. Visitors had neither protection nor bolt holes.

'Where the hell do we go?' shouted a newcomer, fresh from the rigours ashore.

'Anywhere you like,' said a well-protected sailor as he rushed past.

Bodies hurtled past in all directions; explosions were heard outside. This was most certainly not enemy sea-gulls.

'Yes! Got the bastard,' yelled a sailor with his eye to a radar screen. A Skyhawk had indeed been downed over San Carlos Water, the pilot having baled out a split second before disaster. On the decks of *Fearless* the remnants of the canopy; in the water the injured pilot, who was soon brought aboard with a badly injured leg.

Suggestions that he be shot on sight, as his infantry colleagues had machine-gunned a British helicopter pilot in full view of 3 Para earlier, were overruled. He was given medical treatment first, then interrogated.

At first the Argentinian pilot refused to believe where he was.

'This cannot be HMS *Fearless*,' he said. 'I know it can't because we have sunk the *Fearless*.'

'Not for the first time,' said his interrogator, 'your intelligence is not totally accurate.'

127

But the pilot had to be shown the ship's name carved into plaques on its side before he at last accepted that his information was not correct.

Those early raids had claimed one more ship, although at first it was not apparent. HMS *Antelope* was reported as being hit, and in bad shape. But men lined the rails of every ship in the anchorage when she was seen limping bravely back, mast twisted, smoke pouring out of her.

A landing craft circled the little frigate, its occupants waving congratulations and encouragement at the Type 21's crew. They waved back, but only later was it realized that the waves were not cheerful replies, but warnings to stay away.

Antelope anchored well away from the other ships.

That night a flash rent the darkness. A fearful explosion followed. A bomb lodged in the ship had exploded, killing a bomb disposal officer. Her crew waited patiently on the flight deck near the stern to be lifted clear before the inevitable sinking.

Ashore, watching sadly, a small group of SAS men watched the drama.

'Please God. Please let them get off,' said one, knowing that friends were aboard.

Another, much bigger explosion; *Antelope*'s main magazine went up showering sparks and fragments of the ship into the night sky. Somehow the crew had managed to get off in time, but the ship was now beyond hope of recovery.

The following morning, shrouded by smoke and steam, she went to the bottom. One crewman and the bomb disposal man had been killed.

Chapter 8

Everyone in uniform was taking cover but them. The men of the Rapier ground-to-air missile batteries around Port San Carlos stayed above ground, poised to do battle with Mirages and Skyhawks as they thundered in low on killing runs across the settlement.

They were coming now, enemy aircraft which had opted to hit the bridgehead hard after running the gauntlet of lead in San Carlos Water.

'Ready when you are, Mr de Mille,' said a sergeant. A young corporal trained the missile launcher to the west.

'Mirages, mate,' said the sergeant. 'Hairy delta-winged bastards you could hit with a bow and arrow. Don't miss.'

On his headset, the sergeant was told, 'Three kilometres and closing fast.'

Then there they were; three Mirage fighter bombers trailed by a fourth contour-flying over the rolling slopes above the settlement, cannon already barking.

With a deafening crump, the Rapier was fired at the lead warplane. 'There goes another fucking bungalow, Sarge,' said the young officer, referring to the £17,000 cost of each missile fired.

'Steady, steady,' said the sergeant as the missile was tracked into the slipstream of the Mirage. 'Bingo! Got the bastard. Right. Any more takers?'

The Mirage bucked in the air and immediately trailed black smoke as it banked hard left and disappeared over a hill-top. A pall of black smoke rose above the distant rumble of an explosion and Paras cheered, knowing for sure that one enemy at least would not be going home.

But three were left and although their flying time from the Argentinian mainland gave them little more than three minutes over the target if they were to retain enough fuel to get back to their bases, they were banking in for a second run on the settlement.

Colour-sergeant Brian Faulkner and his mate Steve had rushed from the regimental aid post in the bunkhouse to their slit trench overlooking the tiny inlet with their light machine gun. They were well in position as the Mirages turned for the next attack.

Brian and Steve, both medical assistants, were comedians as well as professional soldiers. Both put their hands on their heads and simultaneously ducked, chanting the exaggerated word 'OOOh' as they did so. It was a routine they went through during every air raid. Joking apart, they were now ready for the jets as they screamed back, firing cannon once more, causing the water to dance a quickstep towards the settlement.

One Mirage banked, exposing its underside to the two men and Brian screamed, 'Fire, for fuck's sake. Nail the bastard.'

'I'm pissed off,' said Steve. 'I'm not playing. Fucking gun's jammed. It's jammed. Bastard's in my sights and I can't touch him.'

Other guns were not jammed. A private attached to quartermaster Captain Norman Menzies was blazing away like it had gone out of style.

'Yes, yes,' screamed the lad. 'Look, bits are falling off. I've got him.'

Whether he did or not was never confirmed. But the Mirage roared away at a crazy angle using its afterburners to accelerate to safety. So short of fuel at the limit of its range, the chances of a Mirage reaching its mainland base after using its after-burners were remote. If the warplane did not die because of the machine-gun bullets that undoubtedly hit it, then it probably crashed into the South Atlantic on its way home.

The raid was over. A buzz spread through the settlement as the men crawled out of their trenches.

'We've caught an Argie.' And they had. A Para patrol beyond Settlement Rocks had picked up a lone Argentinian soldier wandering towards the settlement. He did not put up a fight.

He had the high cheek bones of a northern Indian, a fit if freezing member of the forces the British troops were there to vanquish. There was nothing remarkable about him. Nothing, that is, except that the prisoner was wearing a sweater with shoulder flashes that read 'Royal Marines Commando'.

A burly Para sergeant said, 'He's one of the cunts who shot down the helicopters. Bastard. Fucking shoot him.'

He was not shot. Instead he was taken into a hut behind the manager's house and he was interrogated by senior officers of 3 Para aided by a villager who spoke fluent Spanish.

'Said he was a private,' said Intelligence officer Captain Giles Orpen-Smellie. 'Anyway, after a little heart to heart, in which I grant you the odd voice was raised, it turns out that he's now a sergeant. Stole the jersey from Mike Norman's lads in Naval Party 8901 after they were overwhelmed during the Argie invasion.

'The chap was a bit reluctant to talk to us at first, but he was encouraged to see the error of his ways and now he's singing like a bird. All very useful stuff.'

To those outside, 'seeing the error of his ways' was a phrase that would benefit from a modicum of elaboration. A sergeant came out of the interrogation shed and obliged. 'Gave the cunt a kicking,' he said. 'Don't have time to fuck about with the niceties.'

Another Argentinian obliged by getting captured over at San Carlos Settlement.

High up on the ridge, 40 Commando's 'A' Company reported to the command post that an unwelcome visitor was in the process of being 'bounced' towards the rest of the unit.

131

Alan Gibson, 40's Intelligence Officer, was almost beside himself. 'Got to do it properly,' he said, smiling, 'have to do our own debrief before we let that lot in *Fearless* get their hands on him.'

Colonel Hunt passed the word that natural enthusiasm was to be curbed. 'I don't want him torn to shreds,' he said. 'This will be a properly conducted questioning.'

The Argentinian appeared, hands tied behind his back, head covered in a makeshift blindfold. Behind him, half a dozen rifles were aimed at his spine in the impossible event that he should make a run for it. Round his neck, pathetically, a blue-white-blue ribbon denoting his nationality.

'Didn't the Jap kamikaze pilots do that?' asked a Marine who had come out of his trench to witness the arrival.

'Yeah,' said another Marine standing next to him. 'Didn't do them a lot of good either.'

The prisoner was brought in and shoved into a shed next to the quartermaster's stores. Alan Gibson strode forth, ready for the debrief he had so much been looking forward to.

Minutes later he emerged, smiling.

'He's a Lieutenant Commander in their Marines,' he said. 'He says his mates buggered off when they realized they'd been spotted, and he was the only one left. Shit scared, he is. Doesn't seem to know what's going on.'

The obvious question, what was he doing there in the first place, was graphically answered a few moments later. Three Skyhawks screamed in across San Carlos Water with pinpoint accuracy towards the well-camouflaged position 40 Commando were holding.

'There's your fucking answer. Take cover!' yelled a voice, as men scattered in all directions.

The prisoner had all too obviously been spotting for the Argentinian air force, and had given the exact grid reference of 40 Commando just before his capture.

Cannon fire ripped up the soil where moments before Marines had been gawping at the prisoner. Now it was all too clear why he had not been too happy to be where he was. He had called the air strike on to the exact position where he was now being held prisoner.

In the confusion of cannon fire and bombs going off all around, the still blindfolded and tied-up Argentinian tried to run away in his panic. He was squealing horribly, but came to earth with a sickening thud as he tripped and sprawled headlong over the prostrate body of a Marine who was covering his head with his hands.

The Marine looked round, and with sarcasm in his voice simply said, 'Clumsy. Watch where you're going.'

The raid passed. It had been the nastiest experience so far for 40 Commando. Two bombs had landed directly on their position, and two men were killed. One, Marine Steve MacAndrews, was still firing his machine gun at a Skyhawk as its 500lb bomb landed directly on his trench. He had died bravely. The other, Sapper Gandhi, also took the full impact of a 500lb bomb. But 40 Commando's main position had been undamaged, although a part of it had to be cordoned off for a day while a third bomb which would have caused far greater damage was defused.

'One day,' said Alan Gibson after his prisoner had been sent to *Fearless* remarkably unscathed by the Marines, 'the Argies are going to learn that their bombs aren't being armed properly. If everything they dropped went off bang, there's a fair chance we'd be wiped out.'

Everyone listening promised on their scout's honour not to tell the Argentinians that they were making a mistake.

The ships, too, had suffered in the air raid. The landing ship *Sir Lancelot* had been hit by a 1000lb bomb which caused considerable damage, but, thankfully, had failed to explode.

Some of the crew, not unnaturally, were not inclined to hang around until it did, and made their way at the trot for the lifeboats. Safely in them, anxious to bid the old ship an albeit reluctant farewell, they waited to be lowered into San Carlos Water for a fast paddle ashore.

It was not to be. 'No-one told you to abandon ship,' shouted amiable Captain Chris Purtcher-Wydenbruck. 'I'll tell you when. Get back on board.'

'But sir,' cried a plaintive occupant of one lifeboat, 'we've been bombed.'

'Back on board,' ordered the captain. 'We've a job to do.'

And they all did it. The next day, the plucky *Sir Lancelot* was to be hit again with another 1000 pounder, which again failed to go off. During her time in Bomb Alley, the men aboard the old ship were to shoot down three Mirages and two Skyhawks with her Bofors gun and Blowpipe missiles, a higher tally than any other ship in the Task Force.

Back ashore, the edginess of fighting soldiers keyed up to get into the fighting, and living hourly with the threat of counter-attack, was underlined by a tragic error in the hills above Port San Carlos.

A Para observation post had spotted what looked like a small force of enemy troops advancing on the settlement. Artillery and mortar fire was called in and platoons of 3 Para were sent into the attack.

This, thought everyone, was it. Contact with the enemy. The first land battle.

Artillery and mortar rounds thudded into the deep peat bog around the interlopers in the area of Fisherman's Valley and Paras blazed away at the advancing troops with their FN rifles.

Then all firing stopped. The mistake had become horribly apparent. Paras were firing at Paras. Several of the so-called interlopers were hit and seriously hurt.

'They were one of our recce platoons,' said Captain Bob Darby. 'It's a bloody cock-up. Mind you, I suppose

134

we learned one thing. Our artillery and mortar fire was bloody good. One guy caught a mortar round between his legs. If it had not buried itself in the peat, he would have had it. As it was, he was blown up into the air and more or less escaped injury.'

The incident did not do the morale of the Paras all that much good, but it did underline once more to each one of them that they were in a killing game. There might have been enemy infiltrators. There still could be. Sooner or later, the fighting would be waged on the ground, as well as in the air.

Even in death, there was humour. A colonel in another unit away from Port San Carlos was pondering how to write the awful letter to the parents of one of his men who had just been killed in an air raid.

'I really don't know how to put this,' he said, looking round appealingly for support.

'It's easy, sir,' said a colour-sergeant. 'All you have to write is "Dear Mrs Bloggs, I regret to inform you that your son is now spread over the following grid squares." '

In Port San Carlos, there was no respite from the marauding Mirages and Skyhawks; no time to dwell on the tragedy up in the hills.

Some men had heard on the BBC World Service that according to unconfirmed reports, the SAS had blown up most of the Mirages on the Argentinian mainland.

'What are they?' shouted a Para as three aircraft screeched towards the settlement on a bombing run.

'Mirages,' came the reply.

'Can't be,' said the Para. 'They're all supposed to have been blown up.'

'Well they're mirages of bleeding Mirages then,' said another voice. 'If you don't think they're real, don't bloody duck.'

The Para ducked. Everyone did. Except the civilians, who still didn't go in for that sort of thing.

The Paras up in the high ground of Settlement Rocks

blazed away at the Mirages as bombs floated down on parachutes and burst in the air across the settlement. Marines on the slopes close to the community followed suit.

'Either those fucking planes can fire sideways, or some bastard up in the hills is shooting at us,' said a Marine from 42 Commando.

Up in Settlement Rocks, the Paras thought the same. Both sides had also let go with Blowpipe missiles at the aircraft, and the air was filled with hot lead and wandering rockets, all in search of Mirages.

The fact was that Paras were inadvertantly shooting at Marines, and vice versa. One Blowpipe rocket that missed its Mirage nearly scored a direct hit on a Marine trench. It hit the turf ten feet away.

From that time on, firing at will from the trenches during air raids was heavily frowned upon.

At San Carlos the trenches were beginning to look a bit more like home. Little comforts like decorations were appearing on the mud walls: a few Page Three pictures, some maps, even family photographs. One trench had 'Mon Repos' on the entrance, and from many came the sounds of tuneless humming and the smells of apalling cooking.

A few enterprising Marines had forsaken the rigours of outdoor life and had squatted in a large sheep-shearing shed on a low hill above the beach-head. A blind eye was turned on this activity by senior officers.

The only trouble with the shed was half the walls were either missing or had been bombed out during earlier air raids, and the roof was a brilliant red.

'All it needs is "target for tonight" painted on in large luminous letters,' said regimental sergeant-major Pearson. It was indeed an obvious aiming point for enemy aircraft, but it was considerably warmer and dryer than a trench.

Before dawn one morning the dreaded sound of

low-flying aircraft was heard by the occupants of the shed. Everyone woke.

'Don't worry,' shouted a reassuring voice in the dark. 'It's got to be Harriers. The Argies can't fly at night.'

A second later two earsplitting explosions shattered the peace.

Half a dozen voices shouted 'Wrong!' in unison as men hurtled outside. Argentinian Canberra bombers, bought in a job-lot from the RAF, were flying very successfully at night. Thankfully, their aiming was not too good in the dark, and their mission only achieved a few large holes in the peat well away from 40 Commando.

Occupants of trenches, however, couldn't resist muttering 'Tee-hee' at the shed-dwellers.

Later that same morning four strangers walked into camp. They looked extremely hard men, each dressed in leather jerkins with bits of weaponry strapped to various parts of their bodies. They were shattered and filthy.

'SBS, sir,' said their leader, making himself known to 40 Commando's quartermaster, Captain Geoff Whitely. The quartet had just returned from a few days up in the hills.

'Doing what, exactly?' enquired a Marine.

'Oh, a bit of this and a bit of that,' replied one of the SBS with a smile. 'Most of it extremely evil.'

'How on earth did you survive at nights?' continued the Marine.

'With some difficulty, but you learn who your friends are, I promise you.'

'What do you mean?'

'It's the only way,' said the SBS man. 'I've got body heat; so's me mate. Combine the two and we both keep warm.'

'You mean you curl up together in one doss bag?' said the Marine, catching on.

'Yes, but it's all right. We're married.'

The conversation was cut short by the old cry 'Air Red, Air Red.' Marines raced for their trenches and their weapons. The SBS contingent didn't. Taking scant cover behind a low wall they aimed their rifles skywards.

'Come on then, you bastards,' said one, who had every intention of attempting to become the first man ever to down an aircraft with a grenade launcher, which was fitted underneath his rifle.

As so often happened, the Air Red failed to develop. The SBS were taken to *Intrepid* by helicopter brought in specially for them.

'I suppose that's it for you lot now then,' said the Marine as the four men walked off to clamber aboard their transport.

'Not quite,' said the leader. 'We were here before you lot got here, and no doubt we'll be here long after you've gone. Piece of piss in the SBS, innit?' he added with a sarcastic smile.

25 May arrived with everyone in high hopes about how the Task Force was going to help Argentina celebrate its national day.

'We've got to get their aircraft-carrier today,' said an officer at 40 Commando's O-Group.

'Not a chance,' said Captain Alan Gibson, grinning. 'They've spoilt it all by renaming it the 25th of June.'

40 Commando had previously decided that the most appropriate way to mark the aircraft-carrier's named day was to fill it full of torpedoes, and for everyone in *Hermes* and *Invincible* to line the rails and sing 'Happy Birthday', as it sank beneath the waves.

But the carrier, bought cheaply from the Royal Navy, was taking no chances, especially on this of all days.

Argentina, though, had other plans, designed largely to increase the sagging popularity of General Galtieri. A concentrated air attack was launched on the Task Force at sea.

The Cunard container ship *Atlantic Conveyor* was still at sea, with, amongst other things on board, a squadron of the massive Chinook helicopters still waiting to be landed.

An Exocet missile launched from a Super Etendard fighter-bomber was intended for one of the British carriers. It was deflected by 'chaff' and veered off towards *Atlantic Conveyor*.

Captain Ian North, the Cunard ship's captain who was affectionately known as Captain Bird's Eye, was among those killed as the missile found its new destination. *Atlantic Conveyor* was abandoned with the Chinooks still inside her. Twelve men had died.

That same day the destroyer *Coventry* was also attacked by Argentinian aircraft and was lost. Nineteen men died.

Back at Port San Carlos the news was greeted with stunned silence. Quartermaster Captain Norman Menzies, nicknamed Norman the Storeman by the men of 3 Para, usually ever cheerful now looked dejected.

He said, 'Fucking hell, I thought we were winning. It doesn't much look like it now. It's time we broke out of the bridgehead and got on with this.'

The loss of the Chinooks was to be one of the most serious setbacks of the whole campaign. They were crucial workhorses, capable of carrying far more supplies at one go than anything else at the Very Senior Officers' disposal. Only one Chinook was now available to them, which put an almost intolerable load on to the shoulders of the already overworked pilots of the Sea Kings and Wessex.

The advance would inevitably be delayed now and plans rejigged as alternative methods of shifting gear overland were pondered.

At Port San Carlos, settlement manager Alan Miller had every available civilian worker driving tractors and trailers loaded with food, ammunition and mortar rounds to outlying platoon and company positions.

There is no doubt that the efforts of these men, and in the days to come similar courageous deeds by men and women all over East Falkland, were to play a major part in enabling front-line troops to press on for the ultimate objective, the capital, Port Stanley.

But now Alan Miller, while doing all he could to help 3 Para, was not in the best of moods. He stalked around the settlement shouting as any British farmer might, 'My fields have gates. Fucking well close them. My bloody horses are roaming around the countryside and breaking into a gallop every time there's an air raid which over this ground is not the best thing that could happen to them. As if I don't have enough to do, I have to go out every day playing cowboys and round them up.'

One Scimitar tank of the Blues and Royals was neatly camouflaged in a thicket of gorse bushes, its position marked only by a white horse belonging to Mr Miller which apparently had convinced itself that here lay a good source of food and water.

How much sugar the horse ate has never been established, but this is one animal which, like the civilians, was seemingly impervious to the bombs and bullets of the Argentinian aircraft.

Another Blues and Royals light tank at San Carlos was hiding in a large garage which was nearly perfect for the purpose, but not quite. Every time an air raid was called, the little tank shot out of the garage to take up its offensive position. Each time it took a little more of the garage with it.

Eventually it stopped looking like a garage; more like a light tank with a few bits of wood over it.

'I hope they can shoot straighter than they drive,' commented one Marine. 'Otherwise we're in for a few own goals.'

Here too the wandering habits of the livestock were causing problems. Cattle on the low pastures were proving more difficult to capture than usual, much to the annoyance of settlement manager Pat Short and his workers.

One day Colonel Hunt received the most unusual helicopter request of the campaign.

' 'Scuse me,' said a large man in a boiler suit and wellingtons, respectfully holding his cap over his waist. 'I wonder if there's any chance I could have the use of one of your helicopters?'

Colonel Hunt, every ready to oblige and sensing some dire emergency smiled back.

'We'll see what we can do,' he said. 'What's the problem?'

'Well, the cows have all buggered off up the valley, and I reckon one of the choppers could be used to shoo them back,' said the farmer.

Officers around the colonel hid their grins. 'It was never like this in the High Chapparal,' muttered one. The colonel, keeping a superbly straight face, pointed out ever-so politely that sadly there weren't any helicopters around at the moment as they were all busy, but as soon as one became available for the purpose he would immediately let the farmer know.

The farmer departed.

'I can just imagine the orders for the Gazelle pilot,' smiled an officer as soon as the farmer was out of earshot.

' "Proceed to grid reference so-and-so, then head 'em on and move 'em out. Most urgent, keep them dogeys movin'."

Surprisingly there were not many of the thousands of sheep everyone had expected near the settlements. The hardly little beasts were out in the rough pastures, either by accident or design, but certainly well out of reach of hungry soldiers.

In 40 Commando another reason for the absence of sheep was put forward.

'Obvious, isn't it?' said a Marine. 'They're off spying

141

for us on the Argies. Could be a bit of a problem debriefing them, though.'

'I think you're wrong,' said his mate. 'The Falklands branch of the RSPCA heard the Blues and Royals were coming and gave them all an honourable death first.'

There then followed a comical sheep impersonation contest over the trenches at the Blues and Royals position.

'Baaa-baaa. Yoo-hoo, over here sweetie!' But the Blues and Royals refused to bite.

Afloat, wandering around like lost sheep, the drivers of the small landing craft and rigid-raiders were having their own problems finding out exactly who was where.

Brigade headquarters was now in a gorse thicket not far from Blue Beach 1 and San Carlos, but what with all the colours and numbers for the different locations, combined with the codewords for various bits of equipment, it was hardly surprising that some of the little-boat skippers became horribly confused.

'Hello Charlie three nine, this is zero. Do you have a mike callsign near Blue 2? Your sponsor has a sunray for three five, over,' was a typically-worded instruction.

'Where is brigade?' asked a young lieutenant to a rigid-raider driver who was supposed to be taking him there. 'Is it Red Beach 1 or Blue Beach 2?'

The driver was passed the stage where he tried to keep abreast of where everything was. 'Fuck knows,' was his reply. 'I just keep driving round until some cunt says we're there.'

It was worse in the dark. The ships kept moving around during the day, and at night with their lights out, many looked the same. The assault ships usually stayed in roughly the same position with *Fearless* up San Carlos Water near the brigade maintenance area, and *Intrepid* at the Fanning Head end of the anchorage.

But frigates like *Penelope* and *Argonaut* had the same profiles. So did the LSLs, and there were more of them.

'Ahoy, *Sir Lancelot*,' called a rigid-raider driver who had arrived in the dark alongside one of the landing ships.

'Next door, pal,' came the reply from an unseen lookout.

The little boat sped off to the LSL 100 yards away.

'Ahoy *Sir Lancelot*,' he tried again.

'Not here,' said another unseen lookout.

'Well, who are you then?' said the exasperated rigid-raider driver.

'Can't say,' came the reply.

'Look, I'm getting pissed off with farting around. Give me a clue,' said the driver.

'Begins with a "B",' said the lookout.

'*Sir Bedivere*?' ventured the driver.

'Spot on,' said the lookout.

'Great. Now where's *Sir Lancelot*?'

'Can't say.'

'Well, fuck you,' said the driver, and left to try elsewhere.

The rigid-raider driver probably did find *Sir Lancelot*, and had he gone on board, would no doubt have been impressed by the cool bravery of bomb disposal man Royal Navy Lieutenant Bernie Bruen, working hard to defuse the two unexploded bombs on board.

The crew of *Sir Lancelot* had by now been put partly ashore and partly on her sister ship, *Sir Galahad*.

Sir Galahad eventually had its own problems. Another 1000lb bomb had hit it, and also had failed to go off. Bernie, who went everywhere with his violin, delicately worked on the *Galahad* bomb for 22 hours. Now and then, he took a breather. Once, impressed crew members said, he put down his tools and went to the deserted wardroom. There, he poured himself a pint of lager, took out his violin, and played the odd tune or two for about five minutes. Then he drank his lager and returned to the bomb.

To his assistant, still close to the 1000-pounder, he said, 'That's much better. Drink and a play every now and then takes away all the tension.'

Ashore, troops were becoming a little excited by a 'buzz' that a breakout from the bridgehead was imminent. If true, it was good news. All of them felt that the sooner they battled their way to Port Stanley, the sooner they could go home.

Major Roger Patton, 3 Para's second in command, said, 'If we're not careful this could drag on for ages. We could have three winters and no summer all in one year. The winter we left at home, the winter here, and the winter at home again by the time we get back there.'

The company commanders came in from their outlying positions for another 'O' Group and Major Martin Osborne of 'C' Company said, 'I'm not saying it's bleak where we are, but if the people who run the Dartmoor National Park find out we've got part of it here, they'll go fucking mad.'

As they spoke, the wheels of the shore-based combat machine were beginning to turn. The first moves in the break-out from the bridgehead had been planned. Men of 2 Para were even now approaching a place called Camilla Creek House, their start line for the strategically vital settlement of Darwin and Goose Green.

Chapter 9

Tense, raring to go, and being human, a little scared, the men of 2 Para were now on their start line, and an historic chapter of British military history was about to be written.

This is 2 Para's story; firstly a story of an heroic battle; secondly, a tale of brave men in action against seemingly impossible odds, men who won through to open the door for the beginning of the end for the Argentinian invaders. Goose Green and Darwin started the domino effect. After that, ground forces swept ahead taking one objective after another, determined to win, and spurred on by the valour of 2 Para.

It was hardly the way Shakespeare would have written it or Napoleon would have wished to be remembered as it got under way.

Lt-colonel Herbert Jones, known affectionately by his family and all his men simply as 'H', had been receiving the latest intelligence reports from the SAS on Goose Green.

He returned beaming from *Fearless* after a final briefing with Very Senior Officers. The officers of 2 Para had been avidly awaiting his return. H kept them waiting a moment longer, then broke the suspense with the simple phrase, 'We're off, then.'

It was the beginning of the British breakout from the bridgehead. H called all his company commanders together, and they got to his command post as rapidly as they could.

'This is it,' he told them without emotion. 'The brigadier wants us to go and take Darwin and Goose Green. And we've got to do it now. The waiting is over. We're on the way.'

Although it was not a moment for jubilation, the company commanders were inwardly delighted.

Colonel H wasted no time in issuing his battle plan.

' "D" Company will move out immediately,' he said, 'and will take Camilla Creek House. You have got two hours on the rest of us. We'll be right behind you.'

And so it was. 'D' Company amid stifled cheers moved due south towards their objective. Their faces were masks of green and black camouflage cream and they 'tabbed' without bergans in fighting belt order only, carrying as much ammunition as they could. They were men in a hurry to get into the first land battle of the Falklands Campaign, knowing that up to 6000 enemy troops lay between them and the liberation of the twin settlements.

The entire Task Force operation, sailing to the South Atlantic, the landing and all, was operating on Greenwich Mean Time, or Zulu Time as the military call it. So everything was happening just one hour behind London time.

At exactly 7.30 pm Zulu, the rest of 2 Para followed in the footsteps of 'D' Company. They tabbed it over night and arrived at Camilla Creek House at 3 am, exactly as they had planned.

The whole of the next day, with the Argentinians at Goose Green still unaware that they had company on their doorstep, 2 Para was being fed information on the objective ahead by their own recce troops and the men of the SAS.

Then Colonel H put forward his six-phase plan for the battle. He wanted to gain control of both settlements in daylight.

'It all went beautifully and according to plan,' said H's second in command, Major Chris Keeble. 'The only things we were unsure about were Argentine mines and the state of the two small bridges we had to cross before coming to grips with the enemy. But just as H had planned, we reached their main defensive line at first light.'

'A' Company turned off from the main attack towards Darwin Hill on the left flank. A major fire base was established to allow a break through the left flank at Boca House on the edge of Darwin. But it was at this point that the whole 2 Para advance could have come unstuck at the most crucial stage.

Enemy machine gunners, well dug in and providing a major problem, had to be disposed of and quickly if the Paras were to continue moving forward before Argentinian artillery was called in on them.

The enemy machine gunners were pouring down withering and accurate fire on the British Toms. The advance was in danger of grinding to a halt.

Six machine-gun positions stood in the way. It should have been left to a platoon commander, a lieutenant, to deal with them. But Colonel H, in his flamboyant manner, decided to lead from the front.

With his adjutant, Captain David Wood, H stormed forward at the head of a platoon, blazing away with a Sterling sub-machine gun. He had decided that desperate measures were needed to win the day. But his heroism exposed him to fire from several Argentinian trenches. As he led the charge up a short slope, he was seen to fall and roll backwards. But although hit, H was not finished yet. With extraordinary resolve and courage, he picked himself up and again charged the enemy trench, still firing his machine gun and seemingly oblivious to the intense fire being directed at him.

He was hit again by sustained fire from another trench he had outflanked and fell for the second time. Sadly, this time he did not get up.

Colonel H Jones was dying, just a few feet from his objective. He had not heard a corporal saying, 'Watch your back, sir.'

In death he had achieved his object. His heroism had

demoralized the enemy in their trenches and inspired his men to charge forward in force.

It was now 1.30 pm Zulu on the afternoon after the advance on the twin settlement began.

2 Para's 'C' Company had meanwhile come through 'A' Company on Darwin Hill and were skirmishing forward. 'D' Company had taken Boca House.

Then the Argentinians hit back hard. Air attacks were launched against the Paras with Skyhawk and Pucara aircraft dropping bombs and strafing. And, shockingly, they used something much more exotic. Major Keeble, who had now taken over command from Colonel H, said, 'They also hit us with napalm.'

It was not the only dubious tactic used by the Argentinians that day. From trenches near the schoolhouse further along the isthmus towards Goose Green from Darwin, one, or possibly two, enemy trenches were seen with white flags of surrender waving over them. A young lieutenant, Jim Barry, moved forward with a section to take the occupants prisoner. What happened next incensed the Paras.

Major Keeble said, 'Our men were fired on as they went forward to take the surrender at these trenches. In hindsight, I do not necessarily think it was deliberate.

'The fire was coming from other trenches. I think in the fog of war there was a misunderstanding. In the bedlam of battle, perhaps it was understandable.'

At the time, though, 2 Para were not prepared to be so forgiving. Little mercy was shown to the occupants of those trenches which had surrendered. In future, the Paras would not trust the white flag, and were inclined to fire first and talk about surrender afterwards.

Relentlessly 2 Para pushed on. They were helped by an innovation suggested by Major Keeble, who was still finding trenches were taking too long to clear if the momentum was to be sustained.

The 'Milan' anti-tank weapon is one of the newest and most devastating pieces of kit at the Paras' disposal. In simple terms it is a small, portable weapon which fires a wire-guided rocket that can be tracked by the firer.

'They didn't have any tanks, but we had Milans,' said Major Keeble. 'So we used them against awkward trenches from 2000 metres, out of the range of their machine guns.'

It was an idea that worked so well that it now has every chance of becoming standard infantry procedure.

Between 6.30 and 7.00 that evening the last card was played to break the Argentinians' will. It was delivered by a Harrier strike, and culminated in 1000lb fragmenting bombs being dropped on the enemy.

By now 2 Para were over-running Argentinian trenches, although getting dangerously low on ammunition.

'It was a bit of luck,' said Major Keeble, 'that they used the same type of rifles and ammunition as we did. As we moved forward we were able to pick up what the enemy had left behind in their hurry to get away, and use it against the ones who were still fighting.'

As the advance progressed Lt Dick Nunn flying his Scout helicopter near Goose Green was spotted and intercepted by two Pucara aircraft. It has since been shown that the Argentinian pilots played a cruel game of cat and mouse before closing in for the inevitable kill. Nunn was trying to reach and pick up Colonel H.

Nunn tried everything he could to shake off the attackers: contour flying, sharp turns, every evasive ploy in the book, and some that weren't. But the Pucaras finally decided to end it, and shot the hopelessly outgunned Scout out of the sky. The coolly professional and immensely likeable Nunn, who had travelled south aboard *Sir Lancelot*, was killed instantly, his crewman severely injured.

149

In the land battle, the final phase was about to be entered.

Major Keeble was considering the option of ending all Argentinian resistance by destroying the settlement of Goose Green and then moving in to mop up anything that was left. At this time it was believed that the civilians of Goose Green had been evacuated, or were at least out of the way. In fact 114 of them were still inside the community hall, right in the middle of the settlement. Such a bombardment, then, could have proved disastrous.

Aware that there just might be civilians still in the settlement, and anxious to prevent further unnecessary bloodshed, Major Keeble decided to give the Argentinians a chance to surrender. He sent two captured NCOs down into Goose Green to inform their commanders that the British were prepared to talk. If the offer was rejected, they would be wiped out.

The pause gave the Paras a chance to regroup and replenish their supplies.

The word came back that the Argentinian commanders were indeed prepared to talk, and Major Keeble and a small party moved into the settlement. Major Keeble, a devout Catholic, told his adversaries that he had no wish to take more lives. He also left them under no misapprehension that 2 Para would not give them a second chance if the talks failed. He even said that a powerful Harrier strike would be called to demonstrate the hopelessness of the Argentinian position.

It was not needed. The soft but forceful sincerity of Major Keeble had the desired effect, and the Argentinians asked only that they could be given the chance to 'surrender with honour'. The request was granted, and the finer points of the surrender worked out.

At first Major Keeble feared something might be going wrong when only the men of the Argentinian air force came out to surrender. He insisted on the soldiers coming forward too, and only then did he and everybody else realize how greatly outnumbered the Paras had been.

As the Paras moved forward into the settlement, Argentinian soldiers, some as young as 15, came out to surrender. Some looked terrified, having been told that the British would shoot them. Then, realizing this was not to be, many young Argentinians fell to their knees, some in tears.

An officer stepped forward, smiling and offering to shake hands with a Para.

'You fought well,' he said. 'But we would have won it we had not been so greatly outnumbered.'

'There are 1600 of you and only 600 of us,' came the reply. 'We were the ones who were outnumbered.'

'This I cannot believe,' said the Argentinian. 'We were told there were over 2000 British, and the way you fought proved us right.'

'Rubbish. See for yourself. This is all of us.'

The Argentinian looked amazed. Instead of the hordes of red berets he had expected, there were indeed just 600 Paras walking tired but triumphant into Goose Green. He wandered away looking dazed.

In the community hall the Paras were greeted as heroes. The population of Goose Green had been penned up inside for over a month with even the basic amenities denied them for some of that time. Now they were free and determined to show their appreciation. Bottles of spirits and cans of beer were brought out as the party got under way. The union flag was pinned above the highest building nearby. Dejected Argentinians trooped off to surrender.

The Argentinian air force paraded smartly, sang their national anthem, then ceremonially laid down their arms before moving off. The soldiers, less enthusiastic for pomp and circumstance, simply dumped their weapons and shuffled away.

The victory, like Trafalgar, had been marred by the death of the man in charge. Colonel H had been enormously popular with his men, and as Major Keeble said directly afterwards, the victory was his and his alone.

'H had planned the battle,' he said. 'I am merely reflecting in his glory.'

H wanted to get his men into battle, and he wanted to lead them. It was remembered that due to a not untypical foul-up in communications, H was the only battalion commander who did not know that Operation Corporate was under way until the assault group was already steaming round into Falkland Sound.

'We've been left out of it,' ranted H. '2 Para have been ignored!'

Of course it wasn't true, but a signal which should have gone to him along with the other unit commanders had been accidentally held up, and H did not know this at the time. He had to be almost physically restrained by other 2 Para officers from hurtling up to the bridge of *Norland* and making a direct phone call to Mrs Thatcher at Number 10 to register his disgust.

Eventually the error was put right, and the signal was at last passed on to H by the frigate *Broadsword* coming alongside and literally firing the signal across the water to *Norland*. 2 Para knew that the war was on seven hours after everyone else because, it is now believed, a cypher clerk in *Fearless* got his wires twisted.

H, a flamboyant character, was not known for his high regard of politicians. He often, as Major Keeble put it, 'blew hot and cold'.

At Camilla Creek House H heard that the BBC's World Service had prematurely announced that the attack on Goose Green was almost under way. He knew the disastrous consequences this might have, and put the blame on the shoulders of Defence Secretary John Nott.

'If one of my lads dies as a result of this,' he raved,

'I'm taking Nott to court and charging him with manslaughter.'

Whether H would ever have carried out his threat will never be known. His close friends doubt it, not because he would have lost his nerve or changed his mind, but simply because it was said in the heat of the moment.

It is recorded that H had a good idea that the battle would be his last. He knew his heroic flair and initiative could end with him being killed, and he said as much on the eve of the battle. In exercises he had led 2 Para in just the same way, often putting his headquarters far too far ahead of where it should have been according to the text book. On exercises H was 'killed' more than once, but he wasn't going to change his policy of leading from the front.

In the words of his own men, 'H was the best there was.'

The battle for Darwin and Goose Green was far from funny. Many men died, many more were maimed for life. But still the irrepressible humour of the British soldier came through.

In the darkness around Darwin, a small group of Paras was pinned down under intensive Argentinian artillery fire. Shells were landing all around them. The men were scared, but knew they had to move on.

'Any ideas, Sarge?' asked a young Para. 'It's getting a bit boring round here.'

The sergeant made an instant decision.

'Right,' he said. 'Up there.' He pointed to a low ridge in the darkness, where shells were no longer falling. The men scrambled up behind him, and took cover in their new position.

Immediately a salvo of shells landed within yards of where the men now were; shrapnel whistled over their heads.

'Oh, fucking nice that is,' said the young Para. 'Who

was the stupid cunt that said it would be safe up here? I know it can't have been you, sarge, because you never get things wrong.'

Another four or five shells exploded around them.

'I hesitate to say this,' said the young Para, 'but any other bright ideas, Sarge? Assuming, that is, that you're not having too good a time here.'

The sergeant ordered another move, this time to a safer location.

In the morning, with the battle still raging and more rather than less artillery fire coming down on the Paras, a section made a run up another low but strategically important ridge between the two settlements.

To their total amazement there was already someone on top, wearing the beret of the Royal Engineers. But instead of digging furiously or directing fire, the RE was trying to keep the wind off his hexi-stove.

Shells again poured down, obscuring the engineer for a moment as the smoke cleared. He hadn't even ducked, and was still looking intently at his stove, over which a mess tin was bubbling away.

'Hi,' he called cheerily to the Paras. 'Come and have a wet.'

The Paras couldn't believe it.

'Where's the safest place round here?' asked one of them.

'Right here,' said the engineer.

'But, and pardon me for pointing out the obvious, there's a shell crater six foot to your right and another one not much further away on your left.'

'Quite so,' said the RE, stirring his tea.

'So how the hell can this be safe?' demanded the Para.

'If I'd been lying six feet either side I'd have been hit, so this is most definitely the safest place,' came the reply. 'Sure you don't want a wet?'

'No, thanks,' said the Para, leading his bemused section away. More shells came down, and the Paras saw the smoke clear to reveal the engineer starting to cook his Arctic-ration Chicken Supreme. He was whistling to himself happily.

By this time scores of Argentinian prisoners had been gathered from the outlying positions around Goose Green. They had been herded together on the beach. Derek Cooper, 2 Para's enormously popular padre, was asked if he shouldn't go and give the captives some spiritual consolation and guidance. Although a chaplain he was also one of the finest shots with a rifle in the battalion, and was known to dislike vicars. He was not too keen.

The sight of this unshaven man of God approaching did not, as had been intended, do a lot for the peace of mind of the vanquished soldiers. On seeing his clerical insignia many of them looked terrified. They were still labouring under one misapprehension as a result of the language barrier. They had been told in simple English, aided by signs, that they were to walk to their place of surrender. This they had understood.

'But if you try to run away,' said the Para sergeant-major to them, illustrating the point by running on the spot, 'we will shoot you.' He emphasized the message by bringing his rifle to his shoulder and shouting 'bang, bang'.

The prisoners had interpreted the instruction as, 'We want you to run away so that we can shoot you.' Consequently they had fallen to their knees and begged for a reprieve.

The arrival of the padre had again been misinterpreted. Instead of expecting what Derek Cooper had come to give, and greeting him with smiles, the prisoners again fell to their knees in stark terror.

'They think you've come to give them the last rites,' said the sergeant-major.

During the night, the Paras had extra problems looking after their captives while the battle was still going on. The British soldiers, not unreasonably,

155

regarded whatever comforts were available as theirs. So the gorse fires which had been started by the artillery were huddled round whenever the Paras had a chance to rest from their labours.

The Argentinian prisoners, meanwhile, were kept away.

'If you bastards want to keep warm, jump up and down,' shouted a para sergeant. 'Go on. Jump, you buggers, jump.'

In charge of the dispirited prisoners was a Pucara pilot who had survived his plane being brought down by the Paras. He was in the habit of shouting political tirades at his fellow prisoners, which involved a lot of arm waving and fist thumping. The word 'patria' featured a lot in his speeches.

The Paras were more than a little upset by the ranting, and one suggested he should be shot on the spot.

A sergeant, smiling, disagreed, 'No, there's a good chance he's inciting them all to escape,' he said. He grinned. 'Let's hope he is. Then we can drill the lot of them.'

The bond between sergeants and their men is strong.

'OK, you lot,' a sergeant had said just before the fighting started. 'If any of you get a chance, don't forget your dear old sarge wants a few souvenirs to remember this little show by.'

The message was not forgotten, even in the heat of battle.

When it was all over the sergeant returned to collect his kit, to find that one of his men had been there already, and had indeed left a little present for his leader. It was not quite what the sergeant had expected. There, at the bottom of his bergan, was an Argentinian foot.

'I knew immediately it was Argentinian,' said the sergeant later. 'It still had an Argentinian boot on it.'

The surrender itself was not without its humourous moments.

When it was all over bar the signing of the surrender document, the Argentinian air force commander asked Major Keeble if he could make a phone call to General Menendez in Port Stanley, 'Just to see if it's all right by him.'

The phone call was made, and the surrender signed.

'Hello, can I speak to the Chief Spic?' said a Para private later, mimicking the call. 'Hello, boss? Goose Green here. We're fucked. OK if I chuck the towel in? Fine. Regards to the missus. Cheerio.'

With the surrender now complete, there was just one last problem. A small patrol of Paras had been out of radio contact and were thought to believe that hosilities were continuing.

They had last been heard of on the radio saying they had encountered an Argentinian patrol and were about to engage them. That was several hours before. Now there was a good chance that they were still 'brassing up the enemy' or even worse had been captured or killed.

Contact was made just in time. They were all right, and were indeed on the verge of 'turning the lights out', as they put it, on the enemy.

'There's no doubt about it,' said one of the patrol later, more than a little disgruntled. 'It's sod's law. Every time you're just about to start enjoying yourself some bastard comes along and tells you to stop.'

An Argentinian commander saved another patrol from disaster as his men were themselves being taken prisoner.

'I strongly advise you make contact with your men up there on that ridge,' he told Major Keeble, 'and tell them to come into the settlement by another route.'

'Why is that?' asked the major.

'Your men are walking right into a minefield,' said the Argentinian.

157

As the celebration party was getting under way in the community hall, a private asked a colleague if the Midland Bank back home would give a fair rate of exchange for Argentinian pesos.

'Doubt it,' said his mate. 'It's a dodgy currency. Why?'

The private produced a thick wad of banknotes he had recently come across.

'Christ! There must be billions there,' said his friend. 'But you'll get sod all for them back home.'

The private looked disappointedly down at his booty. 'Ah, fuck it,' he said, and threw the whole lot up in the air like confetti.

An English-speaking prisoner was taken to one side and asked one of the most important questions of the moment.

'Do you know anything about mines?' asked his inquisitor.

'Yes,' replied the prisoner. 'We have used anti-tank mines and anti-personnel mines.'

'We know that,' came the rueful reply. 'We found quite a lot of them. Now, be a good lad and tell us where you've put the rest.'

'I'd like to help,' said the prisoner with obvious sincerity. 'But the truth is nobody knows where they are. They're all over the place.'

And so they were. Suggestions from angry Paras to make all the prisoners walk up and down until all the mines had been found the hard way, were discounted as being not quite in accordance with the Geneva Convention. Many mines were found, but not all. Explosions in the distance during the next few days marked the untimely end of some of the local cattle which had strayed into unmarked Argentinian mine-fields. One such explosion was greeted by the remark, 'More instant beefburgers' from a Paras' billet.

The prisoners were housed in a large wool shed until they could be moved across to Ajax Bay and eventual shipment to Montevideo or an Argentinian port. Outside the shed was a large pile of ammunition, becoming increasingly unstable as the rain soaked through it.

Under the Geneva Convention prisoners cannot be made to move ammunition, but the Argentinians, realizing they were close to a potential holocaust, begged to be moved elsewhere.

'They've called the shed Armageddon,' said a corporal after the prisoners had made known their plight. 'As in "Ah'm-a-geddin' out of here." '

The prisoners were not allowed to move, as there was no other building available to house them. But they were given permission to carefully move the offending pile of ammunition.

Sadly, one man was hideously injured during the moving operation, when one unstable grenade or mortar round went up as it was being shifted. The man had both his legs blown off instantly, and his insides burst into flames after his stomach had been ripped open. Pitifully, he was still semi-conscious, although without question on the verge of death. A Para medic took the only course of action that was practical and fired four rounds into the man's head. Even the other prisoners thanked him for putting the man out of his misery.

Brigadier Thompson arrived at Goose Green within three hours of the surrender being signed. Major Keeble greeted him outside the community hall. The brigadier offered his congratulations on the victory, and his condolences on the loss of Colonel H and the other men who had died.

A liberated civilian inside the hall saw the brigadier's green beret, and announced to his friends, 'Marines. Late as usual.'

The civilians and the Paras laughed. This was indeed the Paras' day. One of them even became an on-the-spot godfather to one of the local children. The parents had promised themselves during their captivity that the first British soldier to walk into the settlement would be asked to be their child's spiritual guide.

The new godfather accepted his new responsibility happily, after being reminded by his friends that being a godfather did not mean having to be in charge of the Mafia.

The party swung into top gear, with the best food and drink that could be found made instantly available by the civilians.

Major Keeble sought a moment to be alone, and left the party. Outside he stood to look up the hill to where the fiercest fighting had been and where his friend and commander H Jones had died.

Chapter 10

While 2 Para rested and licked their wounds after the battle that was beyond doubt the one to trigger off the headlong advance on Port Stanley, other units were poised to break out of the bridgehead.

At Port San Carlos, amid air raids, Colonel Pike of 3 Para said, 'The breakout is on. We are pushing forward as of now. My men are keen to get into the enemy and win. We cannot tolerate even the remotest notion of defeat. My men have heard how the sanctity of the white flag was flouted at Goose Green and will go into battle armed with that knowledge. We are prepared to play it their way, if that's what they want.'

Lead units of 3 Para, in fighting order only, left Port San Carlos virtually at the trot, heading for Teal Inlet, over halfway to Stanley. As they pulled out, 45 Commando came through Port San Carlos, yomping with full kit towards Douglas Settlement to the north. Both units expected heavy opposition at both locations.

'We'll be knackered when we get to Teal,' said Sergeant John Weekes. 'But we'll banjo the bastards if they stop us getting any sleep.'

So now three of the five units in 3 Commando Brigade were out of the bridgehead and advancing.

By nightfall, the men of 3 Para were tabbing their way across the inhospitable countryside of foot-hugging peat bog, freezing streams, and the ankle-breaking stone slides, literally rivers of rock, that wander down from just about every hillside in the Falklands.

'It was like the blind following the bloody blind,' said Sergeant Chris Phelan. 'It was so sodding dark, you couldn't see that many men ahead of you. When one fell into a hole, you didn't take avoiding paths around him, you followed him into the hole. Very off putting.

'All the time, we had been told that the Argies had units in the area. Their top lads, Unit 601, were supposed to be around somewhere. And their snipers, too.

'We thought we had to get to Teal by daylight, or we'd get a right fucking if we were out in the open at dawn.'

Going overland with the infantry towards Teal was Major Richard Dixon, in charge of a long line of BVs, the Volvo tracked vehicles that had already proved to be adept at crossing the boggy terrain. 45 Commando had some of them. 3 Para did not. Some were going separately, but all were bound for Teal, the jump-off point for the battles for the high ground overlooking Port Stanley.

So good were the BVs at their new role, their crews and others had already conferred on them the not inaccurate nickname of 'The Bog Trotters'.

The Paras, mostly exhausted, swarmed into the Inlet ready for a fight. 'Fuck,' said Chris Phelan. 'The cunts have pissed off.'

The enemy troops had, indeed, left. But it was a coincidence. They actually did not know that 3 Para were tabbing towards them.

Still some way behind were Major Dixon and Lord Robin Innes-Ker with his light tanks. It had not been their fault that the terrain had been so rough or that they had been forced to make their move in the dark.

'It was all right when we had the headlights on,' said one of Lord Robin's extremely fed-up drivers. 'Then we had to turn them off. Quite sensible really, but it had the one disadvantage of making it impossible to see where we were going.

'Sorry we're late but we kept driving into ditches and having to be towed out. I should have stayed in the fucking cavalry. Horses operate quite well without headlights.'

Still at San Carlos settlement, still within sight of their landing beach, 40 Commando were beginning to seethe.

'I had every expectation that we were to be the spearhead battalion,' said Colonel Hunt. 'It's beginning to look ominously as though we might get left behind. And that is not going to make me a happy man.'

After Goose Green, no one wanted to be left behind. Every combat unit wanted to be in on the fighting.

Colonel Hunt listened with interest to the account of the battle of Goose Green. He noted how the Argentinians had fought and where their weaknesses lay. He heard, too, how Colonel H. Jones had died leading a platoon attack – not his job at all.

'It was immensely brave, and typical of H,' he said. 'But I'm damned if I'm going like that.'

At Teal, the men of 3 Para were digging in yet again. Air raids were threatened, but never materialized.

Intelligence officer Giles Orpen-Smellie said, 'The enemy have been here, but they've gone; God knows where. Why they left without a fight is baffling.'

Sergeant Tony Dunn did a recce of the settlement and in pitch darkness came up to his mates and said, 'Never mind. What's the food tonight?'

'Chicken supreme,' came the bored reply.

'Fuck that,' said Tony. 'Done a bit of good here. Put myself about a bit. Who's for steak?'

True to his word, in a community that survives mostly on mutton this tenacious NCO had found three or four large steaks to tuck under his wind-proof.

A member of the Press asked him where he got it. It was not a professional question, merely one born of envy.

'Fuck off and do your own blagging,' said Tony, a man not known to reveal his sources. It was obvious

163

the steaks were not stolen. Somehow, the highly personable Dunn had charmed them from someone.

The green hue of jealousy glowing through their cam-cream, privates and corporals staggered about in the darkness, desperately hoping to see a dim neon sign somewhere in the settlement with the magic word 'Sainsbury's' on it. No luck.

'You don't get to be a sergeant by being a total cunt,' said Dunn, and wandered off into the blackness to his trench.

One Tom, freezing and full of nothing but de-hydrated chicken supreme, muttered, 'That's it then. I wondered how you got to be a sergeant. Now I know.'

Still, the Toms did not fare that badly. From no-one knows where – if they did, there would have been a top-secret classification on it – some gurgled away in their trenches enjoying an elixir wearing the name 'The Famous Grouse'.

'Lowers your body temperature, raises your spirits,' said one sentry. 'Shouldn't really do this on stag, but I'm mean when I drink, so if any unwelcome guests show up here, I shall be fucking unfriendly.'

The people in this small community had been pleased to see the British. The Argentinians had given them an unpleasant time, dropping in by helicopter every now and then to try to take away their radios, which were always carefully hidden each time the sound of a helicopter was heard.

In the dead of one night, Dave Thorsen, a 19-year-old who wanted more than anything else to kill the invaders, heard a bang on the door of his parents' house.

'Fuck them,' said Dave to his parents, a remark for which he was heavily scolded.

'You don't swear in front of us, and you shouldn't swear at all,' chided his mother.

Dave, well rebuked but still angry, said, 'They must

have walked here this time. We didn't hear any helicopters.'

Defiantly, he opened the door at the back of the house, just above a little stream, prepared to be rude to the Argentinian soldier he expected to be standing outside.

Instead, the wind was taken out of the young rebel's sails.

'I say, old chap,' said a frightfully British voice beneath a crown of helmet and camouflage netting, 'is this the road to Stanley?'

Dave was lost for words. In time, he said, 'You're British?'

The officer, a Para captain, replied with a smile, 'Yes, old lad. Pleased to see us, are you?'

Everyone there was.

'Seen a lot of Argies?' asked the captain.

Dave replied, 'One came down here yesterday with a white flag from a hill over there, saying he had some wounded and could we give him some food.'

'How did you handle that, old lad?' asked the captain.

'Told him to fuck off,' said Dave, forgetting his mother was listening to every word he said.

'Did he go away, dear boy?' queried the captain.

'No,' said Dave. 'Well, he wouldn't. He had a pistol and a couple of grenades with him. He wanted food and our Land Rover to go and get his injured. We gave him some red wine and some food. Then he went. Took the Land Rover.'

'Never mind,' said the captain. 'No problem. We've caught them by the sound of things. Up in the hills. Want your Land Rover back?'

The people of Teal had had a pretty good idea that the British were on their way. A young lad from Port Stanley, with considerable courage, had sneaked out of the capital, which was then a closed town, and made his way alone across country to Teal. Patrick Minto, aged 20, had been taken to the capital under guard from Douglas settlement by enemy troops, and kept at the police station.

'They're cunts, the Argies,' said Patrick. 'When they let me out of the police station, I was allowed to wander about Stanley. I saw it all. I know where their guns are, I have seen their Hercules landing every night, despite the BBC saying the runway's been blown up. I know where their food is stored. They are eating fresh food and drinking orange juice. They are doing okay.

'But they are scared stiff. They shoot at each other. I was near the airport and I saw two of their own planes circling. They had been hit and they were in trouble. They just wanted to get down. I suppose they were circling waiting for clearance to land.

'Anyway, the troops on the ground were so jumpy, they didn't bother with all that. They just opened up on one plane with all they had, and shot it down. An own goal. It was great.

'As I walked round the town, it became obvious to me that the Argies were not all that happy. I heard one conversation where one soldier was saying to the other that they had all been told that the British would never land troops. Now they knew the British had landed, they were keen to fuck off home sharpish.'

It was good news for the Paras at Teal. This was the first confirmation that the morale of the average enemy soldier was a trifle lower than the recommended level of what the Toms called 'a lean, mean, fighting machine'.

The manager of Teal Inlet settlement, David Barton, said when the lead units of the Paras came in, 'Good to see you. Glad the British are back. This is not Argie country, really, you know. They don't have the right attitude. It's harsh. They need the home comforts.'

Glad to see the British though he most certainly was, Mr Barton soon began to have reservations.

'Don't go digging bloody great trenches around my house,' he told the Toms.

Darkness fell. The night was peaceful. Then came the dawn.

'Christ,' said Barton. 'No, really. This is not fair.'

His lawn looked as if some strain of giant moles had whizzed in from nowhere and set up home. Trenches had been dug all over the place.

The Paras had to dig trenches, and many had to be close to Mr Barton's house because senior officers of the battalion were based near it. Some of the Paras felt that Mr Barton's lawn was not as important as his liberty and this was their little way of ramming home the point.

Colonel Pike said after his men had slogged 36 hours non-stop from Port San Carlos, 'My men are in fine shape. They are now the British front line in the Falklands. They want a fight. They are ready for one.'

Mr Barton was inclined to give them one.

To dispel his anger, a young Para told him, 'No mate. You don't understand. One's for you and the missus to get in if the shit hits the fan.'

Mr Barton could see the logic of that, but was not convinced that such extensive landscaping of his property had been entirely necessary, or was likely to enhance its scenic beauty.

'That,' said a Para, smiling, 'is what you call tough shit.'

By now the Paras were not alone at Teal. From the hills came strange people, their appearance better suited to the lot of a Mexican bandit movie; men in strange clothing, toting un-British rifles, sneering under monstrous moustaches and wearing their hair long enough to give any typical sergeant-major an orgasm of rage.

'It's the hooligans from Hereford,' said a Para, correctly identifying the newcomers.

167

The SAS, who had been up in the hills worrying the enemy, had come to town.

They looked worn out by days and nights in the mountains checking enemy positions on the next high-ground objectives, Estancia Mountain and Mount Kent. While some warmed themselves by the large Raeburn stove in the kitchen of the bunkhouse at Teal, others automatically began to dig trenches. There had been no air raids on the settlement, but no-one believed there would not be one soon.

Almost every SAS trooper carried an Armalite rifle and most had 66mm rocket launchers slung underneath the barrels.

'Just the job for persuading an Argie to come out if he's hiding in a house or behind a rock,' said one trooper. 'One of these up your arse and, well, your afternoon's fucked.'

While the troopers dried out wet sleeping bags, a recce patrol high up in the hills to the south of the settlement had noticed some newcomers in the area, at Top Malo House.

They reported back to Captain Rob Boswell and his Marines Mountain and Arctic Warfare Cadre, who set out at night, stealthily groping through the darkness for seven kilometres until they were in position near the house by daylight.

Inside were 16 men of Argentina's special forces, Unit 601, armed with Belgian folding-stock FN rifles with tracer and armour-piercing rounds, and grenades. They had been dropped by parachute from an enemy Hercules and although they had finer cold-weather clothing than the British, they had had to kill two sheep for food. Their presence was a threat to Teal and to much of the 3 Commando Brigade advance which was now gaining momentum.

Boswell's men had 66s too, and were not slow to use them.

'We were not sure how many enemy were in the

168

house,' said Boswell, 'and I couldn't see much future in knocking on the door and asking them nicely to give up. So we gave them a few 66s for openers and all hell broke loose.

'The bloody house burst into flames. We'd put a couple right through the window and that woke the bastards up, believe me.

'Then they came out. For a moment I hoped they were going to surrender. Wrong. They started blazing away with everything they had and we started giving them shit back. There was no cover. Both sides were standing up at pretty close range trying very hard to corpse each other. It was like a bloody grouse shoot.

'Still, we killed four of the buggers, injured seven and took the other five prisoner. Four were not there, unfortunately, or we'd have turned their lights out, too. Three of my boys got gunshot wounds but they weren't badly hurt.

'When the fire-fight ended, the Argie captain, wearing a yellowish neckerchief round his throat, came up to me and said, "Perfecto, perfecto." I thought it was pretty good, too.'

But Teal settlement manager Mr Barton most certainly did not. He owned the house. He had supposed it was deserted but it was now little more than a pile of charcoal. Angrily, he stormed around the settlement, finding a more senior officer each time, demanding, 'Why couldn't you take them prisoner? Why did you have to burn it down? Who's going to pay?'

No-one rushed forward with a satisfactory answer and it was clear to all around that Mr Barton did not think he was having a good day. Until two months previously, he and his family had lived in complete tranquillity, like every other islander, but all that was gone now.

'Even when this is all over,' said Mr Barton, 'the British will have to keep a large garrison here. I'm very much afraid that we'll all have to change our way of life now. It'll never be the same for us here again.'

As he spoke, major things were being planned. 42 Commando and one troop of SAS were poised to take Mount Kent, one of the last peaks in the path of the push to the capital, Stanley. 45 Commando, still on a gruelling march through a blizzard closing on Teal, were scheduled to press on for Long Island Mountain, due east.

That night, 45 came into Teal. These crack fighting men, like 3 Para, did all their advancing on foot, and had yomped from Douglas Settlement through the worst weather so far in the campaign. They came in to Teal under cover of darkness, a long column of men with full packs, some carrying more than 100lbs and many fit to drop.

'Fuck,' said 3 Para's Tony Dunn. 'They look absolutely knackered.'

And they did. Yards from their refuge for the night, the large sheep shed beside the jetty at Teal, young men in their teens threw off their bergans and left them to lie in the snow. Some dropped their weapons.

'Looks like the retreat from Moscow,' said Dunn. But he was not laughing at the Bootnecks, as men in the Parachute Regiment are prone to do any time a Royal Marine gives them the opportunity. 'Poor bastards. Let's help them.'

Other Marines helped their weary mates to their feet and carried their packs for them. One by one from out of the darkness came Paras to do the same. The friendly rivalry between the units was momentarily forgotten as one fighting man helped another to shelter.

Well, almost forgotten. One Para said to one deadbeat Marine, 'It's your own fault. If you can't take a joke, you shouldn't have joined.'

Captain John Burgess, 3 Para's doctor, watched the Bootnecks trudge by the bunkhouse. He said, 'It's the same all over. We've had men down with exposure. We're not fighting now. We're surviving.'

It was grim. But even senseless with exhaustion, these men retained the ability to laugh at themselves. In the regimental aid post, hanging above the beds where men were recovering from everything from shrapnel wounds to frostbite, a Playboy gatefold nude beamed lovingly down.

Above the picture of this well-endowed goddess someone had written in large felt-tip pen, 'Good news! If this still turns you on, you are alive.'

Inside the bunkhouse, a civilian farmworker asked a group of SAS men poring over a large map on the kitchen table what they were doing.

A very big man wearing a shoulder holster, smiled beneath an enormous, roguish moustache, and replied, 'Planning something nasty. Now fuck off.'

A few minutes later, the SAS men disappeared into the night. If anyone knew what they were up to, which at Teal was unlikely, no-one said.

Even the SAS did not know everything. Men of the SBS were out that night too. In the coming hours, they were to meet on a mountain side, strangers in the night.

Back at San Carlos Settlement the SAS were in residence inside the sorry remains of the large sheep shed there. These men of 'G' Squadron had also been living rough. Their clothing was filthy, their faces dirty and unshaven and lined with fatigue.

They were enjoying a hot meal and probably the first mug of tea to pass their lips for several days, when in strode an extremely clean fresh-faced young officer. This unsuspecting man was in fact the advance party for the soon-to-arrive Gurkhas of the reinforcing 5 Infantry Brigade, which was in the process of cross-decking from the liner *QE2* to *Canberra* off South Georgia, 800 miles to the south-east. His job was to

171

find accommodation for little Nepalese warriors. The sheep shed seemed to fit the bill perfectly.

He strutted purposefully towards the disinterested SAS men.

'OK, you chaps,' said the young officer. 'You're going to have to clear orf.'

'Oh, really?' replied one of the SAS troopers, without bothering to take his mug from his lips. 'Are you sure about that?'

The man from the Gurkhas pursed his lips and narrowed his eyes at this apparent display of insubordination. 'Quite sure. My Gurkhas are coming and I'm putting them here.'

The SAS still looked very unimpressed.

'Is it true, then,' said one of them, 'that your privates are black?'

The officer looked furious at hearing this old joke. 'Right,' he fumed. 'I want your names.'

The SAS men, too tired to argue or to continue poking fun, decided to put the man in the picture.

'Come on,' said the officer. 'Who are you?'

' "G" Squadron, sir,' said the leading trooper.

The visitor flushed and looked crestfallen.

'Ah, fine,' he said, and shuffled off. 'My mistake, I'll look somewhere else.'

The troopers grinned, but did not feel warmly enough disposed towards the young man to call him back and tell him they were moving out that night anyway.

These troopers had been living at extremely close quarters to the Argentinians. Their job had been to get right in amongst the enemy and report back.

'They are in a right fucking state,' said one of them. 'Don't know whether they're coming or going. The temptation to nip behind one of them and shout "Boo" into his ear is overwhelming.'

At the same location, 40 Commando's spirits suddenly soared. They were moving out at last. 'It may not be very far,' said Colonel Hunt. 'Only to Port San Carlos for the time being.'

Marines rushed around packing their kit and getting ready to yomp out. A 'for sale' sign appeared above more than one trench. One Marine, knowing the Gurkhas were arriving soon, left a note for the new tenant. He had been joined in his underground home by what he described as 'a little furry thing' and he wanted the Gurkhas to take care of it. He still swears it was a vole or mouse, despite his friends' insistence that such creatures cannot survive the East Falklands climate.

'Are you sure you weren't playing with yourself and got hallucinations?' asked his sergeant.

But not for the first time, or indeed the last, 40 Commando's hopes were to be dashed. Another signal was received. The move-out was cancelled.

'Fuck this,' said Lt Mike Hawkes. 'Do they want us to take root?'

Across San Carlos Water at Ajax Bay the medical squadron was re-enacting an episode from M*A*S*H. Casualties were now coming in thick and fast, from Goose Green, the ships, and from other areas across the islands.

Medics were working round the clock in their hospital which was a converted, abandoned refrigeration plant.

Ajax Bay had been badly hit on the same evening that 40 Commando had taken its worst pounding at the beach-head. Medical experts would agree that putting a hospital in the middle of the biggest ammunition dump the British had put together since Korea was not exactly wise, but there was nowhere else. That raid had done a vast amount of damage to the ammunition and other supplies.

The medics had been queueing up outside for their evening meal when the Skyhawks paid them a visit. 'All hell broke loose,' said a leading medical assistant.

'I hadn't even had my first mouthful. It was most inconsiderate of them.'

Ajax Bay had looked from San Carlos like a massive firework display. When it was over everyone got back to work in the hospital.

'There's a hole in the roof,' one of the orderlies told Surgeon Lt-Commander Rick Jolly. 'And there's something sticking through it.'

Jolly went to investigate and sure enough, there was a 1000lb bomb. 'I didn't put my ear to it to see if it was still ticking,' said Jolly later. 'But what could we do? We could not abandon the hospital, and there was no hope with all the other pressures of getting the bastard defused. So we just had to carry on as if it wasn't there.'

It was Jolly's proud boast then, and it was to hold throughout the campaign, that casualties brought into the hospital, no matter how serious, were always to leave it alive.

Behind the hospital, a barbed-wire compound had been erected. Inside, standing pathetically right in the middle, was a solitary Argentinian prisoner. He looked miserable and cold. Around the compound, Royal Marine guards kept an eye on him.

'Poor little sod,' said a passer-by. 'Why don't you invite him over for a chat and a wet?'

'He's staying right where he is,' said a guard. 'He's not getting an inch nearer me.'

The passer-by, a journalist new to Ajax Bay, suspected the prisoner was highly dangerous. 'Haven't you disarmed him yet?' he asked. 'Or is he a specially nasty bastard?'

'The little shit is harmless in that respect,' said the guard. 'But he's got mumps and no Argie is ruining my bollocks.'

From the hospital the ships in the anchorage could be seen clearly, ships that now bore the evidence of battle. Some had gaping holes in their sides where bombs had hit, but not exploded. Others were blackened by those which just missed, but had gone off.

Everywhere, helicopters flew between the ships and Ajax Bay, for it was in this supply area around the hospital that another war was being fought.

Men of the Commando Logistics Regiment were working round the clock to keep unbroken the flow of vital ammunition and food to the front line. The loss of *Atlantic Conveyor* and her heavy-lift Chinooks meant that keeping the supply line open was now a nightmare.

Sergeant Dennis Brown, barking orders to his men, said, 'It's a bastard. People screaming for this, people screaming for that. Everyone wants everything at the same time. Moving it, that's the problem. We've got it, but getting it to the units is a right pain in the arse. And all the time, the bloody Argies come over and bomb the shit out of us.'

But, if not always that quickly, the supplies always did get to the forward units.

Helicopter pilots, flying the kind of hours that would give the Civil Aviation Authority apoplexy, in machines that were crying out for maintenance at much more frequent intervals than they were getting, were literally moving mountains from the stockpiles to keep the momentum of the advance from being lost.

Back at Teal, Colonel Pike was issuing orders to his company commanders and the word spread among 3 Para that they were soon to push forward again.

'We are all set to go now,' said Colonel Pike. 'The sooner the better.'

Sea King and Wessex helicopters droned in over Teal to unload ammunition and mortar rounds, and hundreds of cases of ration packs.

'Oh, shit. How nice,' moaned one Para as the ratpacks were manhandled on to the boggy grass. 'Arctic again. Bleedin' chicken supreme. Has no cunt got any imag-

175

ination? I'll be laying bloody eggs before this little lot is over. It could turn you broody.'

To the east, young Ailsa Heathman had just fed baby daughter Nyree, barely a year old, while her husband Tony chugged around their farm, wondering how he would get his bales of wool to Port Stanley in a war. For the Heathmans, it was the end of their first year on their own farm. Getting the wool to Stanley and selling it was crucial if they were to stay in business. They had seen few Argentinian soldiers since the invasion; a helicopter or two paid them intermittent visits, but that was all.

From her back door, Ailsa had seen enemy activity high up on Mount Kent and the neighbouring Estancia Mountain, the peaks that were the doorway to the capital, from her home at Estancia House, and for that matter from the rest of East Falkland.

She knew the British had landed. She knew they were at Teal. She did not know that a few moments after darkness fell that night, the men of 3 Para would be tabbing in force towards her home, in the first phase of the final push on the heavily defended Port Stanley.

Chapter 11

All was not well at San Carlos. The word was out that 5 Infantry Brigade was about to steam round the point at any moment, and 40 Commando were still there in sight of the beach, Blue Beach 1, where they had landed over a week before.

'It's just not fucking fair,' said Lt Mike Hawkes, still vainly trying to make his trench habitable. 'Everyone else is off having a good time, killing lots of Argies and winning VCs and we're still here.'

Colonel Hunt was in no better frame of mind.

'I thought we were supposed to be the spearhead unit,' he complained. 'Looks like we're going to miss out on the whole damned issue.'

Up on the hill overlooking San Carlos Water, the Rapier anti-aircraft missile battery woke up one morning to see that the *Canberra* had indeed returned, and 5 Brigade were about to join in the fun.

'Cold steel for Johnnie Gaucho,' said the sergeant in charge, borrowing a headline from a recently arrived copy of *The Sun*. The sergeant was smiling. 'Trouble is, the Gurkhas might have an abundance of cold steel, but the poor little fuckers won't like the cold weather.'

The Gurkhas now about to come ashore had trained as best they could for the rigours ahead on the Brecon Beacons of Wales.

'Never mind,' said the sergeant, as he saw the first of the Gurkhas loading into the LCUs that would bring them to dry land, 'give Johnny Gurkha a sniff of action and this whole bleeding show will be over in a matter of minutes. Evil little bastards. Served with them once out East. One thing they don't do is lose.'

Another young Gurkha officer, straight from Eton

and Sandhurst by his accent, was already ashore at San Carlos sorting out the intricacies of the landing.

'How do you reckon your lot will get on here in the freezing deep south,' inquired a friendly Marine officer.

'Shouldn't be too many problems,' said the Gurkha. 'They're all raring for a fight.'

The Marine pointed out that 40 Commando were in the same situation, but were feeling more than a little frustrated.

'Might have a bit of trouble if it comes to a bayonet charge,' said the Gurkha officer. 'They're not awfully good at that.'

'Thought that was your forte, so to speak,' said the Marine.

'Well, in theory it is,' came the reply, 'but they're so psyched up I can foresee it going wrong. Say the word "charge" to the blighters and you might as well go home.' The Marine looked puzzled. 'They set off at a rate of knots after the order, and, to put it bluntly, that's probably the last you'd see of them.'

Traditions and legends about the Gurkhas were rife, but the Marine still looked more than a little perplexed. He asked, 'I'm sorry. I'm not quite with you. What could go wrong? I mean these blokes are supposed to be the bravest there are.'

The young Gurkha officer, beaming with pride, explained.

'You see,' he said, 'once they've set off, bayonets fixed and all that, you can't stop them. There's absolutely no point in yelling "right wheel" or "halt" or anything. They just keep on going, destroying anything in their way. Bloody good, actually, but as you can see, it does have its drawbacks.'

As he was speaking, the first LCU drew up by the jetty at San Carlos. Inside were rows of little Nepalese men, eyes sparkling.

'Jesus,' said the Marine. 'I see what you mean.'

178

The LCU tied up and off streamed the pride of the 1st/7th Gurkha Rifles. The Marines of 40 Commando could only watch, open-mouthed and incredulous, as the newcomers came ashore. It was indeed a sight to behold.

Off they streamed, wide-eyed and excited, small dark-faced men with white teeth. Above them towered bergans that seemed twice as tall as they were. This was what they had come all the way from Nepal for; a chance to get stuck into some heavy action for the British crown.

As they poured along the jetty, rifles to the fore, faces alert and intense, they demanded in high pitched voices, 'Where de Argies? Where de Argies?'

A young Marine, his boring routine shattered, gawped in disbelief. He said, 'Fuck me rigid, are these guys real?'

Just as their officer had promised, once ashore and even without any semblance of an order to charge, the Gurkhas could not be held back. Their enthusiasm was unbounded. They shot off towards Sussex Mountains into the short grass, their bergans high above them, blood-curdling cries of 'Where de Argies? Where de Argies?' marking their route. As one Marine remarked, 'They look like heat-seeking ferrets, the rate they're going.'

One Gurkha had been told earlier to stand at a point on the path running through San Carlos Settlement, as a marker for where the rest of the battalion would turn off into the grass.

The only trouble was that the man had been positioned by his officer quite innocently in the middle of the only track capable of taking 40 Commando's vehicles, which were even now queueing up to get past.

One of 40's young lieutenants approached the marker, and asked him very politely if he wouldn't mind moving just a foot or two one way or the other so that the vehicles could get by.

'No, my officer say I stay here, thank you,' said the Gurkha private.

'Come on, Johnny, shove off a bit, there's a good lad,' said the lieutenant, smiling benignly.

'No, thank you. My officer say I stay here so I stay here, thank you,' came the reply.

'Please, Johnny. I'm an officer too. Do as you're told,' said the now cross Marine.

'No, thank you. My officer say I stay, thank you,' smiled the Gurkha.

'Look, fuck off out of it, you disgusting little dwarf,' said the officer, losing his temper.

'No, thank you. My officer say I stay here. And don't try anything, thank you,' said the Gurkha.

The Marine decided that a tactful retreat was the only way out of the situation, and he left the Gurkha to wave his colleagues by and into the rough country. Within half an hour they were all gone, and 40 Commando was left once again in total charge of the San Carlos Settlement.

If the British were disconcerted by the behaviour and attitude of the Gurkhas, the Argentinians were unquestionably scared stiff. The reputation of the men with razor-sharp kukris had gone before them.

After the campaign was over an Argentinian conscript talked with awed exaggeration of 'doped-up Gurkhas killing each other'. He added that they had been seen advancing in the open and shouting wildly, which certainly would have been an accurate description.

Another prisoner taken later on said, 'I saw some Gurkhas. They are bloodthirsty little things. They are not like men, they are completely inhuman.'

There is no doubt also that the British used the fearsome reputation of the Gurkhas to their advantage. When 2 Para moved out of Goose Green on their push towards Port Stanley, the Gurkhas were left to look after the prisoners who still remained after the epic battle.

The prisoners were by this time getting unsettled and showing the first signs of causing trouble. 2 Para had a simple but effective ploy. Before they left, 2 Para had told the prisoners that the Gurkhas were cannibals and ate people they did not like. The Argentinian conscripts believed what they were told without question, as rumours about the Gurkhas were already rife.

The Gurkhas had no trouble. They had been told to smile at the prisoners every time they looked like getting out of hand. A Gurkha's smile is a terrifying thing. It looks as though he is about to do something dastardly. The prisoners behaved themselves immaculately every time a Gurkha bared his teeth, believing that one false move, and he would leap forward and eat them.

The Gurkhas provided problems for the British troops, though, not least through the password system. They were quite good at coping with phrases like 'Dark Tyrant', or 'Roman Charm' but their arithmetic was not their strong point.

In the early days of their arrival the passwords had been changed to numbers. If the number of the day was 'eleven', a sentry would call out a lower figure, like 'six' and the reply would have to be 'five' to add up correctly.

'Gurkhas can't count, so we're going to have problems,' said a forward-thinking member of 40 Commando. 'I remember having to dive for cover on exercise once after I'd given the correct number in response to a Gurkha sentry's challenge. The little swine thought I'd got it wrong, and was trying to turn my lights out. Be warned.'

The brigade, not unaware of the problem, made sure that all the pass-numbers from then on were low enough so that even the most innumerate of Gurkhas would not be able to miscount.

With the Gurkhas now gone, having passed right through their own position, 40 Commando's morale sagged to new depths.

Colonel Hunt was furious. 'I'm going to see Brigadier Thompson and find out what the hell's going on,' he told his officers. 'They can't leave us here for ever.'

A Gazelle helicopter arrived to take the angry colonel to see his superior. The officers and men of the Commando were heartened, feeling certain that their colonel would return having given the brigadier a piece of his mind, with orders to move out towards Stanley. A conversation earlier involving the brigadier had been overheard when he was quoted as saying that 40 would after all be the first battalion into the capital.

As dusk fell, Colonel Hunt returned. He was no happier than when he had left.

'We stay here,' he said angrily. 'They reckon there could be an airborne attack on the bridgehead, and we're to stay as rear-guard. God knows how the men are going to take this.'

The men didn't take it at all well.

Brigadier Thompson had been a favourite with 40 Commando, particularly as he had been a former commanding officer of the unit, and had openly called them 'the best unit in the brigade' at a flight-deck concert on *Canberra* on the way down. His former fan-club felt betrayed.

The word spread around the Commando, and 40 began to resign themselves to the fact that the war was going to be completed without them.

'Brigadier's Ball. Want to buy a ticket?' asked a sergeant sarcastically.

'It's not a dance, it's a raffle,' he added.

40 Commando's RSM Pearson felt the blow more keenly than most. He had been a fervent admirer of

Brigadier Thompson, and took the decision to keep his unit back almost personally.

'You can tell him from me,' he said bitterly, 'that I resent the £25 I gave for his leaving present. If you see him, tell him I want it back.'

As the campaign continued, and 40 Commando still went nowhere, the wisdom of the brigadier's decision became little more apparent if no more acceptable. Intelligence reports had indeed been intercepted suggesting that the San Carlos area had been earmarked for an all-out attack by an entire Argentinian brigade. Brigadier Thompson, possibly believing that 40 Commando were the best unit at his disposal, had kept them back to deal with it. The attack never materialized, and 40 to this day feel they were cheated out of their rightful share of the action.

They had only a taste when some of them moved forward to reinforce the Welsh Guards after the tragedy at Bluff Cove, and as a feeble consolation, Colonel Hunt was sent to accept the Argentinian surrender on West Falkland when it was all over.

Through the luck of the draw, or the fortunes of war, 40 Commando Royal Marines never had the chance that they craved to prove themselves throughout the campaign.

As one disgruntled Marine said on *Canberra* on the way home afterwards, a voyage which had seen 40 jibed at as 'The Adventure Training Commando' by others; 'God help the IRA when we get back to Northern Ireland. We've got a lot of pent-up aggression to get rid of.'

To rub salt into their wounds, 40 saw the Gurkhas pass by, only to be followed by the Guards.

'Here come the Hooray Henries,' said a 40 Commando corporal, as rows of glistening Welsh Guardsmen prepared to come ashore. 'We'd better sweep the path, we don't want these fairies getting mud on their boots.'

There is little love lost between the Marines and the Guards, and this was not the best of times so far as 40 Commando were concerned for Guards to start leap-frogging through their position.

Afterwards 40 told stories of guardsmen coming ashore with polythene bags over their boots, holding umbrellas aloft. They are unsubstantiated. But beyond doubt is the fact that the Guards had come to war direct from a long period of ceremonial duties in London, and were hardly in the same fighting-fit condition as the Marines.

One guardsman had to stop and rest on his bergan after walking less than a quarter of a mile.

'Why didn't you bring your fucking polo ponies?' yelled a Marine, adding to his mate as he took his arm, 'come on, Cynthia, must wush or the cucumber sand-wiches will go orf.'

The crew of *Canberra* later revealed that the Guards had done little of the physical training on board that the Marines and Paras had done, but had mooned about all day complaining if lunch was late.

The Marines were dissuaded from getting too close to the Guards as they came ashore, lest remarks such as those led to reprisals.

'Go on, fuck off, Woodentops,' called another Marine, using the familiar Army slang for the Brigade of Guards. 'You might find a few pretty sheep left.'

40 Commando were left to their solitude, with Colonel Hunt stoically announcing, 'Well, if this is the job we've got to do, we'll do it to the best of our ability. Nobody will find us lacking. But they won't find us happy either.'

The Gurkhas, meanwhile, had the task of clearing Lafonia. Lafonia is the southern and largely flat half of East Falkland. It is vast, and was thought to be still occupied by at least a company or two of Argentinians. It would hopefully provide ample opportunity for the

Gurkhas to use up some of their seemingly boundless energy and enthusiasm.

In record time, and far faster than anyone could have believed possible, Lafonia was cleared. The Gurkhas, sadly, hadn't found a single enemy soldier to dispose of and had swept through Lafonia like a tidal wave.

'Can't blame the Argies,' said one of their officers later. 'Probably heard we were coming and pissed off like sensible chaps.'

He paused and looked back at his men, still champing at the bit. 'God knows how we'll handle them if we don't find the enemy soon.'

The ships in San Carlos Water were by now enjoying a respite from the attentions of Skyhawks and Mirages. Tension, though, was still high as the Royal Navy kept on its toes. At both ends of the waterway the 'goalkeeper' frigates were keeping their eyes and radars trained on the skies, aware that the most effective air raids usually happened when nobody was expecting them.

In *Fearless* the appalling 'Minders' of the MOD were still living in comparative luxury, with the exception of Alan Percival who was doing his utmost at Ajax Bay to get reporters' copy back to London when military traffic on the satellite permitted.

War-weary and exhausted journalists returning with their stories from the frozen trenches and sheep sheds of the front line found little solace among the Minders. The MOD men, still crisp and clean, were loathe even to allow the journalists to sleep on the carpet of *Fearless*'s wardroom floor while they of course remained firm in their bunks.

Sir Percivale, the LSL with stores still aboard, was ordered round to the new brigade maintenance area and headquarters at Teal Inlet. It was to be a voyage into the unknown.

'We could have a few problems,' said one of *Sir*

Percivale's amiable officers. 'For a start it's a navigator's nightmare through Salvador Water; second we don't know whether or not there are Argies with big guns on both sides of the inlet; third, even if we get it right there will be less than three metres of water under the keel; and fourth, no ship of this size has ever been through before.' He paused, then added smiling, 'Should be a piece of cake.'

In the dead of night, *Sir Percivale* slipped out of San Carlos Water, and began to creep round Fanning Head and Cape Dolphin on the way to Teal.

'Any last requests?' grinned another wardroom joker, turning on the music box. ' "Oh God Our Help in Ages Past" or maybe "Yellow Submarine" seem appropriate.'

It was a long and wakeful night, when the imagination played strange tricks. Was that a torch flashing on the headland? Were we being tracked on enemy radar, about to be attacked at any moment?

Colonel Tom Seccombe, on his way to catch up with the rest of the brigade, had the right idea.

'Another pint?' he asked the guests at his table. The offer was accepted.

Colonel Seccombe, who had been the Military Force Commander in *Canberra* on the way south, had been promoted too soon for his own good if he was to play an active role in the Falklands campaign.

When in charge of a Royal Marines unit, he had done sterling service, and had used his own unorthodox but effective methods in keeping the peace while stationed at Springfield Road in West Belfast.

Now, though, he was a full colonel and could only get into action if Brigadier Thompson was incapacitated. He had not wasted his time, however, and to the delight of his friends had been out shooting.

'Nothing more hostile than the local geese,' he added hastily. 'Bagged six of them, and very tasty they are too.'

When other duties had permitted, Colonel Seccombe had been seen around San Carlos stalking his prey, with a ·22 sporting rifle under his arm.

'Trouble was, I didn't know the habits of geese,' he said sadly. 'Shot one, and instead of the others flying off, the mate of the deceased stood pathetically over it.' It could have been a problem for a non-military man. 'So I shot that one too,' he said. 'Seemed the fairest thing. Didn't know till later that they mated for life.'

The colonel's plunder came as a welcome change for those lucky enough to get a share.

Sir Percivale kept cheerily on her course, with Colonel Seccombe typically taking the potential dangers in his stride.

'No point in worrying about it,' he said. 'I'm going to bed.'

Before dawn, *Sir Percivale* was bustling with activity as she made her way stealthily through Salvador Water towards Teal Inlet. It had been a testing time for the navigator and the officer of the watch, but all was going well.

'Try and raise Teal on the radio,' asked the officer of the watch as they neared their destination, still not totally sure that the settlement was in safe hands.

The radio officer did as he was asked, but could not resist the opportunity to have a joke at his colleague's expense.

Listening with mock intensity to his headset, he said, 'Think we might have a problem.'

'Why? What's wrong?' demanded the excited bridge party.

'There's someone there all right,' said the radio officer, 'but they're talking to us in Spanish.'

'Christ! What are they saying?'

The radio officer could hardly keep the smile from his lips as he replied in a phoney Spanish accent,

'They're saying, "Buenos dias, senors, for you the war is over!" '

It was a tale related with relish over breakfast, as *Sir Percivale* stole silently through the misty gloom of another Falklands morning and dropped anchor a few hundred yards from the jetty at Teal Inlet. The little ship had made nautical history, but there was no celebration to mark the brilliance of the navigator or the daring of Captain Anthony Pitt.

'Right, you lot,' called the man in charge of the shore boats. 'We're here. You can fuck off now.'

A Mexeflote raft, a cargo-transporting pontoon-like creation of linked rigid steel boxes, came aongside, and with more of the tracked BVs and some stores, Colonel Seccombe was taken ashore.

The Mexeflote graunched up against the beach, and with Marines shouting, 'Hiyo, Silver,' the BVs lurched off through the icy water and onto dry land.

The rest of the unloading did not go strictly according to plan, as due to the steeply shelving nature of the beach, the large-wheeled vehicles that had been sent down to assist in the unloading operation could not get aboard.

The drivers tried valiantly to hurl their vehicles at the ramp of the Mexeflote, and even succeeded once or twice in getting their wheels out of the water. But the slippery steepness seemed destined to win in the end, and horrified Marines by the main stores depot could see that the time would soon have to come when they were detailed to spend the rest of the day manhandling the new supplies without mechanical assistance.

'Go on, my son,' urged an observer. 'Get up there!'

'Got about as much chance as a fart in a thunderstorm,' said his mate, already about to do a disappearing act before being detailed to help with the unloading.

But a bit of smart manoeuvring by the Mexeflote skipper saved the Marines' bacon. A new, slightly more accommodating, piece of beach was found, and the big off-loaders could get to work.

Marines collapsed in each other's arms with mock relief.

'It really wouldn't have done my piles any good at all,' said one. 'The good Lord never intended me to be a pack animal.'

'Shame he made such a mess of your face, then,' replied his friend.

Teal was by now bustling with activity as *Sir Percivale* unloaded more supplies that would go into the 'big push' that everyone was expecting. It seemed amazing to all that the Argentinians not only had no idea what was going on, but did not even come to have a look. One well-timed raid could have put the British advance back by days if not weeks.

A forlorn party of pressmen, newly arrived, started looking hopefully for a place to sleep. They found little hospitality at the Thorsen residence.

'Any chance of a table to sleep under, or a floor to curl up on?' asked one optimistic reporter.

'No,' came the curt reply. 'Pilots and medics only in here. Some of your mates are in the shed out the back, but it's full up.'

The bedraggled newcomers found their friends in the shed as promised, and with a lot of good will and rearranging, space was found. Time, thought the hack who had first tried to prevail on the hospitality of the Thorsens, to make a brew.

He knocked on the kitchen door, looking like Oliver Twist with his mess-tin held before him.

'Could I put some water in here so I could make a cup of tea?' he asked in all innocence.

'Use the tap in the garden,' came the reply. 'I've got washing-up in the kitchen sink.'

The journalist shuffled off, hoping against hope that one day a member of the household would knock on his door in England asking a favour.

189

Relationships with the Thorsens improved after a while, but like so many Falklanders they seemed to be treating the whole war that was fought for their liberation as an intrusion on their way of life. Everything was taken in such a matter-of-fact way that nothing, it seemed, could shock, shame or in any way disturb the locals.

While 3 Commando Brigade minus 40 Commando was well on the way to Port Stanley, things were not going so smoothly with the Guards and Gurkhas of 5 Infantry Brigade.

On the one hand the problem seemed to be to stop the Gurkhas hurtling off on their own, taking Stanley single-handed and then swimming the South Atlantic and taking Buenos Aires as well, while on the other, it seemed impossible to get the Guards to move fast enough to keep up with the rest of the land forces.

With 3 Commando Brigade taking the northern route to Stanley, 5 Infantry Brigade were moving round by the south, via the Goose Green area and eventually Fitzroy and Bluff Cove.

At San Carlos, 40 Commando were taking some solace from the 'Flying Postman'.

The mail had a habit of arriving at the least opportune moment, and not all of it was assurances of undying love and loyalty from the folks back home.

'Air Warning Red,' came the old familiar shout, just as Marines were hoping to slope off for a few moments to read the latest batch. The possibility of being bombed was now so commonplace, and letters from home so rare, that hardly surprisingly the mail took priority in most men's minds. The precious envelopes were taken into the trenches to be read in the mud while the 'Air Red' was still effective.

The silence was broken, not by the familiar roar of jets flying overhead, but by a horrified groan from the depths of a trench.

'The bastards!' said the same voice. 'I can't believe it.'

Nothing, it transpired, could stop the flow of the sort of mail nobody likes to receive. The stunned Marine, 8000 miles away from home and sitting in a trench about to be bombed, had received his monthly statement from Access, and was being told by the computer that he owed a lot more money than he had thought. Accompanying the statement was a letter from his bank manager suggesting he ought to give the matter his 'serious and immediate' attention.

'That's it,' he said. 'They can fucking whistle for it. I'll send them a postcard saying if they want it they can bloody well come and get it.'

In the same mail-drop, a young officer received a letter from his aged grandmother in South Devon.

'We're all so proud of you,' it read. 'You have no idea what a great relief it is to us all to know that you are now safely ashore.'

The letter was passed around with glee.

'Dear old Grandma,' said the officer. 'She always gets terribly seasick. Must think that being here getting bombed is better than cruising round the oggin.'

A reply was penned that very afternoon, thanking Grandma for her remarks, and adding, in a sarcasm that would be lost on the old lady, that next time he was bringing his bucket and spade so he could take full advantage of his camping holiday in the Falklands.

Away from the bridgehead the mail was eventually getting through to the other units of 3 Commando Brigade who were considerably nearer to Port Stanley than 40 Commando.

But for these troops, reading the mail had to take second place to vigilance and the delicate art of staying alive.

Chapter 12

The men of 45 Commando were now pretty well rested and raring to pull out of Teal and push forward, knowing that 3 Para had already gone.

The brigade HQ was about to move up to the settlement, and that meant they would be near the rear, not up at the front where all commandos prefer to be.

'Never mind, lads,' Regimental Sergeant-major Pat Chapman told his men. 'Rest now while you can. We'll be off again soon and remember, it'll be a hard slog. There's only one way out of this cunt, and that's through Stanley.'

As he spoke, lead units of 3 Para were overlooking Estancia House. Ailsa and Tony Heathman, baby Nyree, and eleven of their friends who had either fled Stanley after the invasion or had come in from Green Patch Settlement to their north, were asleep.

Some were in the four bedrooms, others were snoring away on the kitchen sofa and floor, toasting near the peat-filled Raeburn.

There was no noise. There never is at night in the Falklands. The wind rarely blows after dark and the sounds of battle had not yet become commonplace here. Typically, it was pitch black outside.

The tranquillity ended when a blaze of light suddenly bathed the farm, and the door of the red-roofed, white-walled house began to shudder under the fist of someone banging on it from outside.

'Christ Almighty,' groaned Tony Heathman, struggling to get his wits together after the rude awakening, and assuming the Argentinians were outside. 'What do the bastards want now?'

One of his friends had gone to the door as he came downstairs. Both of them heard a polished voice calling cheerfully, 'Open up. It's the British Army.'

The door was opened cautiously, and in the dying light of the flare the Paras had put up to illuminate the house and two outlying sheep sheds, Heathman and former Port Stanley policeman Terry Peck saw a bedraggled man in combat clothes with a beaming smile shining from beneath a net-covered helmet across a face painted grotesquely with green and black camouflage cream.

'Mind if we come in?' asked the Para officer. 'It's awfully chilly out here.'

In he went, followed by the kind of men that should have scared the life out of little Nyree, but in fact won her over in seconds.

A burly Para took off his boots and began to dry them beside the Raeburn and Ailsa moved the giant kettle over an inch or two onto the direct heat of the stove in a preamble to making the inevitable cup of tea for the Toms.

In the seconds she took to do that, the big Para had grabbed up baby Nyree and was now bouncing her on his lap, forgetting the screams of war, and chanting in an inane, if disarming way, 'What's your name then? Coochy coochy coo.'

The Paras deployed all across the farm to seek shelter and immediately began digging defensive trenches while a recce platoon went forward several kilometres towards the valley between Mount Kent and Mount Estancia, in case the enemy was close by.

'They have been here from time to time,' said Tony Heathman, 'but they've all pissed off now. Don't have a clue where they've gone. The SAS and the SBS have been around in the hills. I expect they put the fear of God into them. It wouldn't surprise me. From what I've seen of those guys, I wouldn't want to get the wrong side of them. Very nasty-looking lot.'

More Paras were now scaling Mount Estancia, kicking up a hell of a racket as they went.

'You do go in for sound effects, don't you?' said Ailsa. 'I shouldn't think the Argies will stop running till they get to Stanley, after this little lot.'

Three days before, an English-speaking Argentinian officer had knocked on the Heathmans' door and asked to be taken in their Land Rovers to Stanley.

'I told them to piss off,' said Tony. 'Well, that's the impression I gave them, but I grant you I probably didn't use those words. Felt a bit sorry for them. They said they had come from Darwin and Goose Green. Christ, you must have knocked the shit out of them there. They were not in very good shape.'

The Argentinians, he added, were an enlarged company of some 150 men, some of them wounded, who had limped off for the capital before the Paras had arrived.

'Fuck it,' said a corporal who had come to the house to fill his water bottle, and hopefully to scrounge a cup of tea. 'After all that tabbing I was just in the mood to do a bit of zapping.'

The Heathmans turned their radio on and tuned it in to a crackling and whistling BBC World Service. Among the reports was a claim by Argentina that front-line British forces had been lured into a carefully prepared trap.

'Daft cunts,' sneered 3 Para Adjutant Captain Kevin McGimpsey. 'They had more than two months to prepare for us and instead of standing and fighting, they've fucked off. No bollocks. Still, when we get to Stanley, they'll have nowhere to go but into the sea.'

British mortar rounds were now thundering into the peaks of Estancia and Kent ahead of the Paras climbing the former, and 42 Commando preparing to assault the latter.

At Estancia House, Giles Orpen-Smellie read from his own intelligence notes, half not believing them.

'We thought we would have to fight for this ground,' he said. 'But there's no-one here. They've simply run away. All we've found are abandoned positions, weapons and kit. They've even left some of their food, fresh fruit and orange juice.

'After the mortaring, we've found trenches with blood trails leading away from them. There are a lot of field dressings and quite a bit of live ammunition about.'

Then, thoughtfully, he added, 'Frankly, I think they've fucked it. We have much of the high ground now. Nothing can keep us out of Stanley.'

In the next hours, a few Argentinian stragglers were picked up by Para patrols.

'They were lost, tired and hungry,' said Orpen-Smellie. 'They had neither weapons nor radios. How they hoped to keep in touch with their high command, God knows.'

They were not alone. All over the hills, more patrols reported dejected enemy troops by the handful stumbling around in the snow, trying to make their way back to the capital.

'They really are a bunch of dozy wankers, some of them,' said a sniggering private in the recce patrol. 'Just heard on the net that three of the cunts came out from behind a gorse hedge and flagged down one of our Sea Kings. 'Til then, the crew hadn't even seen them. Anyway, they landed, arrested the Argies at pistol-point and bundled them into the chopper. Must be the first time in history that anyone surrendered to a flying helicopter.'

It was now that Terry Peck, a bearded 44-year-old member of the Falklands legislative council, emerged as one of Britain's secret weapons.

Code-named Rubber Duck, Terry was to lead recce patrols to the very perimeter of Stanley, testing the defences and trying to pinpoint the positions of the enemy's 105mm field guns and, more importantly, the

195

longer-ranged 155s, the ones that posed a serious threat to the impending final push to the capital.

Terry liked his new work, and went about it with great vigour. So much so that on one patrol a Para broke all the rules and whispered in the dead of night as the small band edged forward well ahead of the British front line.

'Sarge,' he wheezed, then louder, 'sarge!'

'Shh. Quiet, you noisy bastard,' came the reply. 'What's up?'

'For fuck sake, tell Terry to slow down a bit,' begged the Para. 'Cunt's going like a mountain goat. I can't keep up.'

For Rubber Duck, although he may not have appreciated it then, this was a very high compliment from a man who prided himself on being super-fit and who was very much younger than he.

But Terry hated the invaders. To him, anything that he could do to speed up their demise was to be recommended.

Sometimes, things did not happen as quickly and as satisfactorily as he would have preferred. At the end of one patrol, filthy and worn out, he stood with his back to the Raeburn at Estancia House, drying off his clothes, and looking very dejected.

'Fuck it,' he snarled. 'We were right up on a group of Argies not far off Stanley and I had one slap in my sights.' He propped his FN rifle against a wall, and added, 'One of the Paras told me to hold my fire. Said we didn't want to advertise that we were around. He was quite right. I understand that. But it was like waking up on Christmas morning and not getting any presents. I just want to kill the bastards.'

Rubber Duck and his patrol had not been the only ones creeping through the blackness of that night. The SAS had been observing enemy movements from Navy Point, just a few hundred yards across the water from Stanley itself. Even more of them had been logging

196

Argentinian troop movements in the mountains overlooking the capital. The SBS were doing much the
same kind of work.

So secretively do these crack troops work, that on
one particular night the SAS and SBS did not know
exactly what the other was up to. Regrettably, a patrol
from each group met in the darkness on a mountainside close to Stanley and, convinced that each had
stumbled into the enemy, opened fire. Before the
mistake was realized, one SBS man lay dead. It had
happened before, Briton shooting Briton.

By now, the Paras around Estancia were now anxious
to press on. The weather was closing in and thick fog
shrouding every mountain was keeping enemy aircraft
grounded. With no imminent threat of an enemy air
attack, they were convinced that the time had come to
mount the final phase of the liberation of Port Stanley.

Their appetites had been whetted. Colonel Pike and
some of his senior officers attending O-groups at their
CO's freshly-dug bunker near the summit of Mount
Estancia, and McGowan and Smith who had climbed
up with them, had just had their first glimpse of the
capital.

It was not much of a view, just the edge of the rifle
range on the outskirts of the town. But it was the final
objective and the Paras sensed that if they did not
move on it now, the Marines would do so before them,
and that would never do.

Frustratingly, it was not to be; or not then.

The Paras had already been briefed by Brigade that
their first task before the advance on the capital would
be to secure the imposing peak of Mount Longdon, a
hard climb to their north-west. And, never ones to be
slow off the mark, they promptly set out to take it.

Lead units were already over a low hill and out of
sight of Estancia House when Brigadier Thompson
choppered in with his bodyguard and sternly ordered
Colonel Pike to join him in the command post for a

serious heart to heart while the friends of Ailsa Heathman let their children play outside.

'What's up, then?' asked a confused Tom. 'Go forward, come back, stand still. It's making my bastard head spin.'

'Fucking Marines can't keep up,' one of the officers grunted as he left the CP. 'And when they do, the shits will be given the first chance at Stanley while we piss around in the hills. We're out in front now. We should go and do it now.'

'It's off,' snarled Colonel Pike as he stormed out of the CP with the brigadier. 'As you were.'

Brigadier Thompson flew back to Brigade while a disconsolate Pike returned to his eyrie on Estancia Mountain.

For a few more freezing days and miserable nights, the Paras were to go nowhere.

'Apparently,' said Orpen-Smellie, 'Brigade think that if we take Longdon now, we'd be outflanked and take a hammering. I don't know. Hurry up and wait: that seems to be the game at the moment.'

Back at Teal, the newly-arrived Colonel Seccombe decided he ought to go and take a look at the front-line at Estancia. Why, or what he thought he could do once he got there, remains a mystery.

But colonels being men of some influence, he was able to commandeer a couple of rigid raiders one foggy morning and order the drivers to set course for the little inlet that ends on the doorstep of Estancia House.

Hands, and McQueen of the *Daily Mirror*, were invited to accompany Colonel Seccombe, and that meant Captain Mark Stevens, who insisted on being known as 'PRO HQ 3 Commando Brigade' when a simple 'Mark' would have done just as well, decided he had to go along too.

'Could be a bit dicey, this,' said Colonel Seccombe as the quartet climbed into their raiders. 'We don't know if there are any Argies on the headlands between here and Estancia.'

'There's another problem too, sir,' said one of the rigid-raider drivers. 'It's foggy, these creeks are like Hampton Court Maze, and there's thick kelp just below the surface.'

'All in all, could be quite an experience,' said Colonel Seccombe.

Stevens, known as 'The Clean Marine' due to his ability to look spotless and disgustingly tidy at all times, hefted his Armalite rifle menacingly. He tried to look mean and hard. Colonel Seccombe smiled.

Off into the unknown sped the two little craft, the drivers switching their gaze from the murky waters in front of them to the maps of Salvador Water resting on the controls.

Colonel Seccombe, resplendent in his fur-lined Canadian jacket and carrying his favourite walking stick, looked every inch the country squire.

Stevens looked more than a little edgy.

Inevitably the raiders lost their way several times. Once, with kelp clogging up the propellers, Stevens did the proper thing. He took up the firing position in the port side bow and scoured the misty bank a few yards away. Colonel Seccombe looked suitably impressed, and allowed himself another little smile at this picture of efficiency in the other boat. The smile creased into a grin when he noticed that all Stevens had in his sights was a small group of bemused-looking penguins.

After more wrong turns, more kelp and more terribly impressive gun-toting by Stevens, the raiders ground to a halt.

'That's as far as we'll get,' said the driver of the lead craft. 'We can either go back, or you can get out and walk.'

It was decided to walk, with Colonel Seccombe

striding out in front along the foreshore sharing Rolo chocolates and AB biscuits with the others.

It was two miles to Estancia House, across mud-flats, narrow streams and boggy dunes.

'I assume we do actually control Estancia House?' asked Colonel Seccombe with a twinkle in his eye.

'Yes, sir,' said Stevens. '3 Para have been there for some time.'

'Well, let's hope the place is still standing,' said the irrepressible colonel.

The little party arrived at Estancia to find 3 Para in residence, and not in the slightest bit impressed by suddenly having a colonel in their midst.

'Where's Colonel Pike?' asked Colonel Seccombe, hoping to glean some useful intelligence from 3 Para's leader.

'Up there, sir,' said a Para, pointing into the mist. 'On top of Estancia Mountain.'

The colonel looked a little crestfallen. Having walked a long way already, and with the daylight already beginning to fade, he had no desire to trek up the mountain.

McQueen and Hands, determined to get a look at Stanley from the top of the mountain, hitched a lift on the back of a tractor that was taking up supplies.

Colonel Seccombe radioed for a helicopter and went back to Teal.

On the mountain-top an hour later, the two reporters peered in vain towards Stanley. Visibility was down to less than twenty yards.

At the command post they stopped and called, 'Is Colonel Pike inside?'

From under the drenched green tarpaulin stuck in the rocks a muffled voice replied, 'Oh, Jesus. Not McQueen and Hands,' it said. It was 3 Para's commander. His blond head appeared through a hole in the tarpaulin. He was smiling as he shook hands.

'I'm not telling you two buggers anything unless

you've brought some fags with you,' he beamed. 'Want some tea?'

Cigarettes and tea were exchanged, and Colonel Pike laughed like a drain when he heard the two newsmen had come all that way to see Stanley.

Also in the CP were McGowan and Hudson. The four reporters had not seen each other since two days before the landings. It was a joyful if not ecstatic reunion. Even Hudson managed to force a smile and grunt, 'Hello, then,' to his colleagues.

At the O-group on the mountain top, Colonel Pike said to his officers, 'We need to know if the Murrell Bridge is in enemy hands.' Turning to one of his men, Major Pat Butler of D Company, he added, 'Can we get a small group to take a look at it? If the enemy are on it let us know, but do not engage them.'

The bridge Colonel Pike was referring to controlled the only road west out of Port Stanley. It lay in the valley between Estancia Mountain and Mount Kent.

'Er, small problem, sir,' said Major Butler.

'What problem?' snapped the colonel.

'We're already there,' the major said, and referring to his own second in command, he explained, 'Matt Selfridge was close anyway, and there weren't any enemy on it, so he's sitting on the bridge now.'

Colonel Pike laughed. 'You are allowed to tell me where my men are, you know,' he said, clearly pleased with the initiative taken by his junior officers.

At this point BBC World Service reported that Harriers had been dropping leaflets on Port Stanley, supposedly urging the Argentinians to give up and explaining to them the hopelessness of their situation.

'That puts paid to another fucking rumour,' said one of the officers. 'We're told that no-one can fly in this weather. If the Harriers can, I'll bet they're not the only bastards in the air.'

It was never established if the leaflets had been dropped. Certainly none were found when the troops eventually reached Stanley. But that didn't stop Marines and Paras suggesting what should have been written on the leaflets.

'Dear Johnny Gaucho. You are fucked. Be a good chap and chuck it in, then we can all go home,' was what 40 Commando's resident propaganda expert thought might be on the leaflets.

In fact 'Johnny Gaucho' was a long way from being finished yet.

The reporters on the mountain then had to make their way back down the foggy slopes to Estancia House. It was icy, and wet, difficult country to walk over.

Their path was through unseen company positions, where alert sentries knew that intruders were suddenly in their midst. The newsmen were blissfully unaware of how close to death they were.

Spotted coming over the ridge by one sentry near the farmhouse they were mistaken for an Argentinian reconnaissance patrol. Riflemen were sent out to pick them off.

Five hundred yards from the house a sergeant screamed at them, 'Fucking arseholes, your luck's in. We were just about to blow you away.' The sergeant, sensing the newsmen had learned their lesson and would not go ambling around again, added in a more kindly voice, 'For God's sake, tell us when you go walkies. We really don't want to turn your lights out.'

The reporters apologized and shuffled humbly inside to get warm.

Nightfall found huddles of Paras curled up round the dying embers of carefully concealed fires, and a hive of activity inside Estancia House. All was not well with the forward companies up on the mountain. A radio message was received asking for immediate assistance in the 'cas-evaccing' of a wounded man.

'That's fucked it,' said a Para, warming his toes in

the kitchen. 'The little rascals have come over the top and are attacking.'

No further information was received, and into the main room burst the small but commanding figure of 3 Para's second in command, Major Roger Patton.

'Right,' he announced as though addressing the lowliest of his men instead of the civilians whose guest he was, 'I want two tractors and men to drive them. Got to get a casualty down off the mountain.'

The civilians, who had been working hard all day providing transport for the Paras, did not flinch at the abrupt tone and were keen to oblige.

'Good. Off you go then,' said Patton, leading the way out into the cold darkness. He pointed to A Company's position, and watched the tractors and trailers pull out.

What could it be? Had the Argies really come over the hill? Were A Company even now fighting for their lives against hordes of crack troops making a counter-attack?

Another radio message was received half an hour later, saying the tractors were returning with 'a seriously injured man'.

Still there were no further details, but as the tractors descended, with headlights on, bursts of Argentinian artillery lit up the slopes around them.

A stretcher party was gathered near the house to receive the casualty.

He arrived, and was indeed seriously injured. Barely conscious, he was lifted gently into the farmhouse and through to the back room that the Heathmans had made available as a makeshift hospital.

At last the truth.

'Bit nasty, really,' said one of the medical orderlies, reporting the state of play with a smile on his face. 'Poor sod's in a hell of a state.'

If so, why the grin at the casualty's misfortune?

'Can't see him getting an MC for this one,' said the medic. 'Seems he was having a shit and slipped.'

The unfortunate Para had sneaked away from his trench with shovel in hand, to perform the nightly ablutions before turning in. But in the darkness he had chosen an ill-placed spot.

To save the labour of digging, he had found two rocks with a buttock's width between them, dropped his trousers and started. Sadly for him, the rocks were icy, and he had slid down at least 15 feet, crashing onto the boulders below and seriously damaging his kidneys.

For him the war was over, and his mates were exercising their sense of humour, wondering how he was going to talk his way round being sent home wounded in so novel a way.

'I can see his citation now,' grinned a corporal. ' "For his unfailing devotion to duty, and despite large numbers of enemy forces known to be in the area, Private Bloggs is awarded the VC for attempting to have a shit." '

That same night the tractor drivers from Estancia came under fire again, and were beginning to think that doing what Major Patton asked might result in their life expectancy being somewhat reduced. Two of them burst into the front room at Estancia House, breathless and grinning.

'Jesus, that was close,' said one of them. 'Bloody shells coming down all round us. The Argies are getting a bit too accurate for my liking.'

It later transpired that the two men had been simply in the wrong place at the wrong time, and that the enemy artillery was not quite as accurate at this juncture as they had imagined. They had been aiming not at the frightened drivers, but at what they thought was an observation post two miles away. Their aim had been abysmal, as had their intelligence, as the OP was on Mount Kent, well out of the range of the guns that were firing.

That night the newsmen slept in the attic of the

farmhouse. McGowan, realizing that a nocturnal trip to the toilet would have meant clambering over dozens of sleeping bodies, took a plastic bag in which to relieve himself, should the need arise. The need arose.

Awkward shufflings were heard by his colleagues in the cramped attic as McGowan decanted the evening's liquid intake into the bag. 'Please, God, don't let there be a hole in it,' he whispered.

The following morning Hands woke to find the end of his sleeping bag saturated. He rounded on the man from the *Express*.

'You dirty bastard,' he said, fearing the worst.

McGowan, to prove his innocence, held aloft the still full bag.

'I am not one,' he said, 'to piss on ITN, however much the temptation.'

Hands, suitably informed of the facts, realized that one of the pipes in the loft was leaking slowly, and had caused his moment of panic.

Further south, 5 Infantry Brigade were slowly getting their act together.

Brigade HQ was now established at Darwin, still a long way short of where they ought to be, and causing much uncomplimentary comment from the 3 Commando Brigade at Teal, who felt their advance was being held up while the Guards picked their way slowly forward.

Suddenly, 5 Brigade were presented with an opportunity to redeem their slow progress.

Major John Crossland, commander of 2 Para's 'B' Company, leading the way for 5 Brigade, saw a telephone at Swan Inlet and, using the available facility, called up Fitzroy.

'Are you alone?' he asked farm manager Reg Binney at the other end of the line.

'Certainly,' replied Binney. 'There were Argies here, but they've gone.'

Crossland wasted no time in getting his men forward to Fitzroy, much to the delight of his brigadier, Tony Wilson. This was the famous '50p phone call' which was in fact made free of charge (there are no coin boxes on the islands) and by Crossland, not, as wrongly reported at the time by some correspondents, Wilson himself.

But in one swift move the Paras had pushed the brigade's front line nearly 40 miles nearer Stanley. It hadn't been done without criticism. The only Chinook helicopter available to the British forces on the islands had been 'hijacked', in the words of one senior officer, to assist the 5 Brigade push forward.

But Wilson was making up for lost time. All he had to do now was get the rest of his men up to Fitzroy as fast as possible. That included moving the Welsh Guards round to Bluff Cove in the LSL *Sir Galahad*.

3 Para were ever anxious to keep 3 Commando Brigade's nose in front. As they waited impatiently for their orders to advance on Mount Longdon, they thought long and hard about how they could hurt the enemy, by killing him if possible, but failing that by wrecking his morale

Corporal Jeremy Phillips, one of 3 Para's snipers and a veteran of his trade after duties in Northern Ireland in the South Armagh 'bandit country', had a novel idea.

'The trick,' he mischievously explained, 'when you locate an enemy trench, is not to fire off like it's going out of style but to be patient and wait your moment.

'Sooner or later one of them will come out for a shit, and when he's got his trousers down, you blow him away. Now this tends to discourage the others from coming out. Result: they have to shit in the trench, which after a while is very, very bad for morale.'

Chapter 13

It was at this stage that the Press thought they could take a leaf out of the military's book. McGowan was still with 3 Para at Estancia, and beginning to feel that the war could slip by without him. Hands was back firmly entrenched at Teal Inlet, able to benefit from being in close proximity to Brigadier Thompson.

The man from the *Express* wanted to know what was going on, and realizing that the telephone system had already done 5 Infantry Brigade a lot of good, opted for a similar method of communication.

He first ascertained from the Heathman household that the line was secure, and could not be listened in to by unfriendly ears. He then phoned Teal, and asked to speak to Hands.

'Sorry, dear, he's not in,' said manager David Barton's wife, Coll.

'Never mind,' said McGowan. 'Could you ask him to call back?'

Mrs Barton agreed to do just that, but it wasn't until the following morning that Hands received the message.

Then came a notorious phone call which was made to look at the time as though it had given Argentina victory on a plate. While the troops were having the gravest difficulties in getting messages to each other by radio, Hands and McGowan found that it was ever so easy to bridge the gaps on the islands thanks to the phone system.

'Are you sure this line's safe?' enquired Hands of Mrs Barton before lifting the ancient handset.

'Positive,' said the manager's wife. 'The line is down just the other side of Estancia.'

Hands rang through to Estancia and McGowan was brought to the Heathman's phone.

'Take my advice, old lad,' said Hands. 'Get your arse over this way. Do a runner. Leg it. This is the place to be. If anything happens, it's got to start here.'

'Fine,' replied McGowan. 'What exactly is the state of play at your end?'

'Well,' said Hands, bristling with information culled from the brigadier a few minutes earlier, 'there's a big build-up of gear here at Teal waiting for the big push forward. There's big stuff already going up to the high ground. It's all going on, and the brigadier is confident.'

'Great,' said McGowan, ready to pack his kit and hurtle back to Teal. 'Where are 5 Brigade?'

'On the southern route,' said Hands. 'Not too sure what they're up to, but it looks like a race between the two brigades as to who gets into Stanley first.'

'Who's going to get there first?' asked McGowan.

'Don't know for sure,' replied Hands. 'But both the buggers in charge have got green berets, so I can't see the Guards getting much of a shout.'

'That's it, then,' said McGowan. 'I'm on my way to join you. There's fuck all going on here.'

The call was ended, and Hands walked back into the rain. The awfully red-faced figure of Captain Mark Stevens appeared in front of him.

'You cunt,' he said. 'You've just made the biggest mistake of your life. The brigadier wants to see you right now.'

Hands, stunned, couldn't understand what the fuss was about. Had he forgotten to mention Stevens in one of his reports as being a hero?

'It's not a joke,' fumed Stevens.

In a muddy field, Brigadier Thompson stood pacing angrily as Hands was brought before him.

'I want to know exactly what you said in that phone call,' he demanded through clenched teeth. 'Every

208

word. Every single word. I've got to know what you and McGowan said.'

Hands, completely taken aback, flustered through all that he could remember.

'But why the problem?' he asked. 'The line was secure. We checked. Nobody could have been listening in.'

'Wrong,' shouted the brigadier. 'That line goes straight to the switchboard in Port Stanley. Everything you said was picked up by the enemy.'

Hands, absolutely mortified that the phone call could have cost lives and lost the war, tried again to remember every word.

At last the brigadier seemed satisfied, but no less angry.

'I had every intention of packing you off back home,' he said. 'It's the biggest breach of security so far. You can thank your lucky stars that I'm giving you one last chance.'

Hands left feeling suicidal.

McGowan, meanwhile, had not arrived at Teal. His helicopter transport had flown through to San Carlos Water and landed on *Fearless*. McGowan angrily rounded on Captain David Nicholls, and asked why he was in *Fearless* instead of being at Teal.

Nicholls, like Stevens very much involved in Press relations, replied, 'You're luckier than you think. There's been a blazing row about you and Jeremy Hands making phone calls.'

The two made their way to the ship's wardroom, where McGowan asked Nicholls, 'What's the problem?'

Testily Nicholls snapped, 'Let's be clear about this. You two may very well have cost lives. I think you have cost lives.'

McGowan asked why, and Nicholls explained it all to him.

'I suppose a beer's out of the question, then?' said McGowan, trying to ease the situation.

'Don't be bloody funny,' said Nicholls. 'This is no joke.'

McGowan snapped, 'That line is perfectly safe. I asked 3 Para for permission to use it days ago, just after their lead units had reached Estancia. A senior officer gave me permission, saying the line had been cleared and was perfectly secure to use.'

At this point Nicholls gave a hint of a smile. He said, 'Have a beer. We were just trying to throw a scare into you. Of course the line is safe. You don't think the Press would get to use it before we had checked it out, do you?'

McGowan handed Nicholls a curt memo from photographer Tom Smith outlining his total dissatisfaction with Captain Nicholls' handling of any picture he had sent back for transmission to London. Nicholls read it and said, 'I'm fed up with snotty memos from your photographer.'

McGowan replied, 'And we're all fed up with being treated like cunts by you.' He left the room.

Hands, meanwhile, believing still that his belief in the security of the phone line had caused dire repercussions on the campaign, was getting little comfort from his colleagues.

Max Hastings was telling other newsmen how the indiscretion would certainly be the end of all co-operation between the Press and the military. 'I don't want to stir it up,' he said, 'but we all know who is to blame for this.'

Hands' own cameraman, Bob Hammond, apparently still angry about getting wet as a result of his reporters' insistence that the crew moved out in a rainstorm, rubbed salt into the gaping wound of Hands' shattered life by laughing about the incident in a cynical manner, and referring to Brigadier Thompson as 'Jeremy's best friend'.

McGowan, realizing that his colleague was suffering greatly under his misapprehension, tried vainly to

210

contact Hands and tell him that they had been right all along and the line had been secure.

But due to circumstances beyond their control, the two were kept apart for over 24 hours.

Captain Stevens had assured Hands that nobody else knew about the row outside Very Senior Officers. Yet it seemed to be the talking point everywhere from Teal Inlet to Ajax Bay.

McGowan, at Ajax Bay, was trying to get back to Teal. He too was now being ribbed about the 'indiscretion' on the telephone, and was reduced to suggesting that the next person to make remarks based on inaccurate rumour 'is guaranteed a smack in the mouth'.

Hands, meanwhile, was still in the dark.

Two days later, while on *Fearless*, he tried to find out the consequences of the 'disastrous' call. He asked the commanding officer of the SAS, who he knew as a friend, what had happened.

'Oh, Jesus, haven't they told you?' replied the colonel, smiling broadly. 'Everyone knew the call was perfectly safe minutes after you had made it. The line was down past Estancia.'

Hands left the wardroom, found an empty room and cried his eyes out.

Later he returned in an evil mood, and sought out Captain Stevens.

'You absolute and total shit,' said Hands. 'How could you possibly let me go on believing I was wrong?'

Stevens smiled weakly. 'The brigadier knew minutes after he'd bollocked you that you had been right,' he said. 'But I was under orders not to let you know. He wanted you to sweat a bit.'

The urge to 'do a McGowan' and really be the cause of a Marine officer's death was overwhelming.

But Hands resisted, simply saying, 'I just hope I never ever have to see you again. If that's the way officers have to get promotion, by putting people

211

through the sort of hell you've let me go through, you're welcome to it.'

He left Stevens, who was totally unmoved and probably thought it was all quite amusing.

By now McGowan had got back to Teal, but Hands was not there.

'Who's a naughty boy then?' quipped an SAS man he had met after coming in to Teal a week earlier with 3 Para.

McGowan, conscious of his promise to 'guarantee a smack in the mouth' at the next such remark, very astutely deduced that such an action would quickly despatch him to the 'Great Newsdesk in the Sky' and instead barked, 'Fuck off. Aren't you supposed to be in Stanley being a hooligan?'

The SAS man smiled and said, 'All in good time. All in good time.'

By now most of the Press who had been scattered amongst the units of 3 Commando Brigade were gathered together at Teal, in preparation for 'the big push'. They lived in two sheds.

Hands' desire never to see Captain Stevens again got off to a bad start. Stevens walked into the sheds and called for attention.

'Right,' he said. 'You are all going to return to your units. There are too many of you here.'

In unison, the gathered journalists made their reply: 'Fuck off,' they shouted.

And he did.

To commemorate Hands' return to the human race, it was decided to help him out of his late misery in the traditional Fleet Street way. It is hard to keep journalists and a supply of alcohol apart for long.

Out in the inlet, the LSL *Sir Geraint* lay at anchor. On board was a bar.

'Anyone coming down the pub?' asked Ian Bruce of the *Glasgow Herald*.

'How are we going to get there?' asked Derek Hudson, the pride of the *Yorkshire Post*.

Nobody really knew, but an answer had to be, and indeed was, found. At the jetty, the sergeant in charge of the rigid raiders was pinned up against a wall and asked politely if the Press could borrow one of his boats.

'Certainly,' he said, a grin spreading across his face as an evil plan entered his head. 'But do us a favour, will you?'

'Yes, of course,' said the reporters. 'Anything, so long as you get us to the ship.'

'Well, there's one of my lads who's absolutely shit scared of getting stuck out in the creeks and by-ways in the dark. I'll get him to take you out, but you tell him you're not going to the ship but round to Estancia.'

The Press liked the idea. It was now dark, and Estancia was a good ten miles away through hazardous waters.

The driver turned up looking petrified. 'Do you really want to go to Estancia?' he asked nervously.

'Yes,' chorused the Press.

'Are you sure?' burbled the driver.

'Dead sure,' said the reporters.

'Oh, fuck,' said the driver.

Only when everyone was aboard was he let into the secret. He smiled with relief, and threatened to do terrible things to his sergeant. But such was his gratitude that he even agreed to return in two hours and take the reporters back to shore. The hacks repaid the offer with a promise to get some beer for the driver and his mates, fearful that the joke might rebound and leave them stranded on the ship.

Two hours later, smashed out of their brains after the hospitable crew of the *Sir Geraint* had made their visitors most welcome, the pressmen staggered back into the rigid raider which had returned dead on time.

213

'This is for you,' said one of the reporters, offering a few cans of lager to the driver.

'Cheers, lads,' said the voice in the dark, and the little boat sped off at over 25 knots for the shore, which was somewhere in the blackness.

'How do you know where the shore is?' he was asked.

'I don't,' said the driver. 'I just keep the throttle open until we hit it.'

The press party lurched up the jetty after a bumpy arrival, and staggered up the track towards the settlement, wisely refraining from giving the community the benefit of their favourite songs.

'Halt!' commanded a voice somewhere in the blackness ahead. The journalists froze in their tracks. They knew what was coming next, and knew they had a problem.

'Three!' shouted the voice.

'Waste of time, mate,' said one of the reporters. 'Haven't got a clue.'

'Who are you?' said the sentry.

'Press.'

'Oh, fuck,' said the sentry, wondering how to cope with the dilemma.

'Got a bottle of The Famous Grouse here,' said one of the reporters. 'Is that any good?'

There was a pause.

'Yes, that will do nicely,' said the sentry, mimicking the American Express advert.

The pressmen advanced, and passed the bottle to the sentry, who took one short but loving gulp from it, and passed it back with a smile. He then checked the press cards of his new friends, and asked where they had been.

'*Sir Geraint*, just over there,' said one of the reporters.

'Nice of them to sail a pub round for you, wasn't it?' said the sentry, who then passed on the relevant password. He declined another shot, and waved the party through the gate calling out, 'Careful you don't spill him', as one of their number staggered through.

The pressmen now had the taste, for the first time in weeks, of alcohol, and their shed was destined to see a few more hours of heavy drinking.

Eventually sleep overtook them. So cramped was the tiny shed that some of the newsmen moved to a dilapidated lean-to greenhouse next door. In the tranquil small hours, nothing stirred, except the odd Marine shuffling by as the sentries were changed.

This was the quiet time. The lull before the storm. Men were marking time, getting ready for the inevitable, the major and decisive push to end the war by retaking Port Stanley.

Teal Inlet was now established as the forward headquarters and stores area for 3 Commando Brigade. Back at Ajax Bay, men of the Commando Logistics Regiment were still labouring at their Herculean task of getting all supplies ashore and up to Teal, from where they were taken to the front. Helicopters were lugging 105mm field guns slung beneath them to batteries being set up on Mount Kent and Estancia Mountain, ready for the barrage that would herald the sweep forward to begin the end of the campaign.

'It will be the biggest artillery show the British have laid on since Korea,' said Brigadier Thompson. But he was still worried that without the Chinook helicopters lost on *Atlantic Conveyor*, it was taking too long to get his guns and their shells forward.

From their new mountain-top positions, the guns now had the range to hit the outskirts of Stanley. Soon, everyone knew, the great firepower demonstration would begin, and the final make-or-break battles would be under way.

Records were being broken by helicopters of all sizes. Sea Kings and Wessex were plying backwards and forwards from Teal with the heavy stuff, while the little Gazelles and Scouts flitted around with personnel and smaller stores.

One Scout pilot proudly told of his attempt to get in *The Guinness Book of Records*. 'How many seats in this thing?' he asked some new passengers.

'Four,' came the reply. 'That's one each for you and your crewman and two up the back for us.'

'Quite right,' said the pilot. 'The book says we can get three in the back in an emergency.'

'That would be a bit of tight squeeze,' said one passenger.

'You should have been with us yesterday,' said the pilot, beaming. 'We had nine bodies in this heap. Nearly didn't get off the ground and I was scared stiff people would fall out. Not bad, eh?'

He hastened to add that the 'bodies' were live passengers. 'Just a turn of phrase.'

The Gazelles had been taking risks too. One pressman being flown at low level and at speed towards the ships in San Carlos Water asked the pilot why the perspex screen at the front was held together with masking tape.

'It's all his fault,' said the pilot, pointing accusingly at his crewman. 'We flew into some phone wires yesterday and smashed the front in. Daft sod is as blind as a bat.'

On the ground, there came a welcome respite from the culinary delights of chicken supreme. The men of 42 Commando's echelon had set up a field kitchen near the helicopter landing area.

It meant that for a while, at least, no-one had to do their own cooking. Nobody was more delighted than Ian Bruce. He is not a gourmet.

His own cooking had left even battle-hardened Marines and Paras gaping with disbelief. He knew that to survive he had to consume the entire contents of his 24-hour ration pack. The trouble was, he only got down to eating once a day. And so the dish, known in his honour as the 'Tartan Crapper-Shatterer', was invented. The name not only accurately reflected the colour of the concoction but also what it would do to a toilet bowl, had one been available.

The Bruce Recipe, for gourmets to marvel at, is as follows. Take one sachet of chocolate powder and apple flakes, half a pack of crumbled dry biscuits, a pack of dehydrated chicken supreme and peas, dried rice, and instant tea powder. Place all ingredients into a mess tin and bring slowly to the boil after adding a pint of cold water taken from a murky pond. When simmering, add the rest of the dried biscuits, unbroken this time, and half a dozen Rolo chocolates. Stir with a strong spoon, stolen from SS *Canberra*, and serve garnished with boiled sweets.

'Fucking hell,' said a bemused Marine, watching incredulously as the Scotsman devoured his meal. 'You must have guts like a cement mixer.'

But Bruce was in no mood for jokes about his cooking. He was not well. He had yomped for many freezing miles with 45 Commando and was now suffering from mild exposure. Protesting bitterly, he was cas-evacced out to *Fearless* for a night's treatment in the sick-bay. In truth, it was a quiet period in the war and unlike several journalists who visited the front as frequently as most people win the pools, it was his first, and well-deserved, chance to have a shower and sleep between clean sheets since he had landed more than two weeks earlier.

Some journalists grabbed this kind of opportunity on an almost nightly basis. On one occasion in the wardroom of *Fearless*, the ship's Commander protested to Marine censor David Nicholls that Max Hastings was using the ship as an hotel, while other journalists lived rough at the front.

Later, Hastings was to sneer at such remarks by saying, 'We're not in this to get Eagle Scout badges.'

While recovering in *Fearless*, Ian Bruce was in a

unique position to see for himself the aftermath of a tragic episode in the Falklands war.

All journalists at Teal had been told that the landing ships *Sir Galahad* and *Sir Tristram* had been hit in a Skyhawk attack at Bluff Cove. 'Casualties are minimal,' they were assured by Captain Mark Stevens. 'Under twenty,' he said.

'What absolute bollocks,' protested Bruce on his return to Teal the following morning. 'There must have been about fifty dead. I saw casualties being brought on *Fearless* and I was told many more had gone to Ajax Bay. People on *Fearless* told me it was very bad.'

In fact, 51 men died and another 46 were injured. Of those, 33 were Welsh Guardsmen who died before ever getting the chance to join the battles for liberation.

Later, Guardsman Simon Weston, just 21, said of the disaster, 'You can't imagine it. I was on fire. So were many of the lads around me. I begged my mate to shoot me, I was in so much pain.'

Guardsman Weston lived and was returned to Britain to recover from his injuries.

As ever, the islanders seemed unmoved by the tragedy. At Teal, the real horror of Bluff Cove at last emerged on the BBC World Service. Marines and newsmen, drinking tea in one house, sat horrified when the news was broadcast. There were sharp intakes of breath and pained expressions on their faces, but not noticeably on those of the islanders who were present.

'Did you hear that?' asked one islander, unemotionally. 'Sounds quite nasty.'

The islanders are a phlegmatic lot and a stranger can never be sure if they could not care less, or just don't show their feelings.

The point was underlined when another roving reporter returned to Teal after treatment in *Fearless* for exposure. He had left his precious bergan with all his survival gear in the conservatory of the manager's house. He came back to find the bergan had been tossed out into the pouring rain and was soaked through, an action which annoyed some of the Marines who found it.

Galahad and *Tristram* had been bringing combat troops for the final push on Stanley, and despite this brutal setback, there was to be no delay.

'There are times, and this is one of them,' said Joe Fallaggio, a Marine in 42 Commando, 'when I'm glad I'm Italian and not Spanish. If my parents had got it wrong, I could've been on the wrong end of what's about to happen. For what they are about to receive, let us all be truly thankful.'

Chapter 14

With the blue touch paper well alight, and Argentinians retiring immediately in all directions, Captain Dennis Sparks, commander of 42 Commando's echelon, addressed his men at Teal Inlet.

'It's fucking dreadful up there,' he said pointing in the direction of Mount Kent, where the rest of the Commando was. 'They've been stuck up in the snow for over a week, and are in a hell of a state. But it's been clear today, and you know what a Royal's like when he gets the sun on his back. They'll be perfectly OK by tomorrow.'

Captain Sparks was referring to the Marines, known amongst themselves simply as 'Royals'.

The O-group, in which the worthy captain was explaining the intricacies of the latest plans and events was interrupted.

'Air Warning Red, Air Warning Red,' came the shout from the command post.

'What's it look like?' enquired Captain Sparks, a little annoyed at his briefing being interrupted.

'Fucking enormous,' came the reply. 'Hordes of the bastards heading right this way.'

'Right,' said Captain Sparks, grinning. 'I'd better get on with this before we all get zapped.'

He carried on telling his troops what the state of play was regarding the movement of men and supplies forward.

When it was over, the men ambled slowly back towards their trenches and tents.

'It's still "Air Red",' yelled Captain Sparks.

Still his men showed little inclination towards getting back to their appointed positions with any haste.

'Get your arses below ground. Thin out,' called the captain.

There was reason behind this apparent folly. With the water so close to the surface at Teal, trenches could not be dug to an adequate depth, and had to be built up with sandbags. The more enterprising Marines realized that filling sandbags was a hard and thankless task. It was much easier to 'proff' sandbags from the trenches of more hardworking colleagues. Sandbags had become a type of unofficial currency.

Often the cry of 'take cover' was followed by homeless Marines shouting, 'Where? Some bastard's nicked me trench.'

The deafening roar of jet engines filled the air. Marines and newsmen hurtled into whatever cover they could find, waiting for the expected explosions of Argentinian bombs.

Joe Fallaggio walked nonchalantly past, whistling as though he hadn't a care in the world. He looked down at the cowering newsmen, and smiling, simply remarked, 'Dozy cunts. They're Harriers. They're on our side, if you didn't know.'

Minutes later the evening sky was broken by vapour trails. A Harrier was chasing a Mirage at high level. All below watched anxiously.

The leading vapour trail suddenly stopped. There was no apparent explosion, no ball of flame.

Fallaggio, who certainly knew a lot more of what was going on than many of his superiors, hit the nail on the head.

'That's one less of the bastards,' he coolly and accurately announced. 'One Mirage down, and one more for Galtieri to somehow explain away.'

In the harbour of Teal Inlet one more of the noble knights of the Round Table, *Sir Percivale*, was disgorging more essential equipment. But the crew was depleted, as the entire complement of Chinese on board had insisted on going ashore after hearing what happens to LSLs in the Falklands. The hulks of *Sir Tristram* and *Sir Galahad* were still smouldering at Bluff Cove.

If anybody ever looked out of place, it was these Chinamen in their Sunday-best suits, polished shoes, raincoats and steel helmets wandering aimlessly around the freezing wastes of Teal Inlet.

'It very dangerous,' said one of these men from Hong Kong. 'We not have trenches, and we not allowed to stay on ship. We fucked.'

Every time there was an air raid warning, the little men dived into a drainage ditch which ran through the settlement. It was full of cold and filthy water, in places up to a foot deep.

After one false alarm, the same Chinese complained, 'We still fucked. And we very wet too.'

Since no air raid ever materialized over Teal, none of them were ever hurt there. But staying inscrutable in a drainage ditch is not easy.

The two brigades were now ready to act in unison. 3 Commando Brigade were ready to launch forth on Mount Longdon, Two Sisters, Goat Ridge and Mount Harriet, while 5 Infantry Brigade were fast approaching their objectives: Tumbledown Mountain and Mount William. The artillery was in position below Mount Kent to 'soften up' the objectives. Meanwhile at Teal, the 'REMFs' were left behind with the stores that weren't needed in the first stages.

They passed the time re-enacting the World Cup in a series of football matches against the local children. England always won.

The Argentinians, meanwhile, had beaten a hasty retreat to the very outskirts of Port Stanley, or so it was wrongly assumed.

'They must know they've had it,' said Fallaggio, as the rapidly departing pressmen moved past him on their way to the front line. 'Set me up a pint in the Upland Goose. I'll see you there in a few days.'

If it had been cold at Teal it was positively Arctic on Mount Kent.

The five batteries of the Commando gunners, with their six 105mm guns in each, were now ready to blast off with a total of 1200 shells at their disposal, and the sole intention of giving the Argentinians a headache.

Two days before the main infantry assault, the guns opened up. As one gunnery officer said, 'They're getting a fire power demonstration that they'll be able to tell their grandchildren about – if they live through it, which we rather hope they won't.'

The orders were given to each of the batteries to send over a few shells, which would be spotted by the mountain-top observers. Once the target had been correctly ranged, the whole venom of the battery would fire away, with incredible accuracy, and much to the delight and amazement of the spotters.

Naval bombardments from the ships and air-strikes from the Harriers backed up the 105s.

It was the hope and prayer of the gunners that they would get one order in particular. A 'fire mission battery' was the order to get all six guns firing at one specific target. But never before had these men seen the effects in battle of a 'fire mission regiment', which would have had the outpourings of all 30 guns raining down on one grid reference. To their annoyance the order never came.

'Fucking shame,' said one of the gunners. 'Come all this way and don't even get the chance to do a Guy Fawkes on the bastards.'

After one highly energetic spell of firing by one battery just below 42 Commando's headquarters company, the guns' deafening roar ended and four young Marines stepped out in front of the barrels applauding wildly. The barrage had doubtless had its effect, but

223

the young members of the battery decided that the noise was worthy of praise.

'Well done. Jolly good shooting,' they called with some sarcasm. The gunners replied by stepping forward and taking exaggerated stage bows to their audience.

'All in a day's work,' said one of the gunners. 'We're available for weddings too if you want to book us.'

One of the spotters, watching the rain of death pour down on the unfortunate Argentinians, was Lieutenant Tony Hornby. He returned beaming after one of the batteries had done its job to his obvious satisfaction.

'I was directing their fire on one position which I knew to be teeming with Spics,' he said. 'Then to my amazement, along comes their NAAFI wagon straight out of Stanley with the lunch-run.'

Hornby related how he called a halt for a few minutes while the men who had recently been taking the full impact of the shelling crawled in a bemused state from their places of cover and formed a queue beside the food van.

'I waited until they were all in a nice orderly line, then yelled out for another salvo,' he said. 'It was brilliant. Bodies flying through the air all over the place. Must have greased loads of them. But somehow the van escaped unhurt, and bimbled off to the next location.'

Hornby related how he went through the same operation all over again, waiting for the enemy to leave their cover before calling the fire down on them.

'This time we got the food van too,' he said without too much sorrow.

Another forward observer who got more than he bargained for was Captain Rod Baxter, who effected the most unconventional capture of the campaign.

Baxter had been doing his duty, until the call of nature necessitated his departure from his allotted

224

post. He chose an opportune moment, and disappeared behind some cover, dropped his trousers and began to part company with the remnants of his daily intake of compo rations.

Suddenly the process was interrupted by someone in broken English calling to him, 'We surrender.'

The unfortunate captain did not know whether to lunge for his pistol or his trousers, and realizing the urgency and potential danger of the situation, got into a terrible mess attempting to do both at once. He accepted the surrender and immediately confiscated a pair of trousers.

His pride and dignity were handsomely restored when he returned with his prisoners intact. They had apparently become separated from their patrol some days previously and had been looking for someone to surrender to. An officer with his trousers round his ankles provided the ideal opportunity, and they were in no condition to look around for someone more appropriate to bring their part of the war to a close.

The Argentinians, not being all that slow to cotton on, realized something was happening by this time.

More air raids were launched from the mainland, mainly at places where the enemy wrongly believed the British to be, but sometimes at the ships still in San Carlos Water.

In *Fearless* the dreaded klaxon and 'Air Raid Warning Red' would still be followed immediately by men donning anti-flash masks and gloves and scurrying to their allotted action stations.

An alarming explosion shook the ship and all in her.

But the voice on the Tannoy did not reflect any sense of impending doom. 'The noise you have just heard,' crackled the pipe, 'is an outgoing Sea Dart on its way to meet incoming Dago Airlines flight A4 newly arrived from Argentina.'

Less than twenty minutes later the ever-cheerful

voice crackled back with the news, 'We are pleased to announce that flight A4 has now landed – in four places across East Falkland.'

And thus another attack by the A4 Skyhawks had been beaten off. But not before the frigate *Plymouth* and two landing ships had been hit, though not sunk.

On another occasion, *Fearless*'s ever-popular and immensely professional captain, Jeremy Larken, talked his men thzough another potentially lethal air raid.

This time the enemy aircraft were well inside San Carlos Water, and were taking a great deal of fire from the ships and the guns on shore. All around, it was deafening, the noise made even louder inside the assault ship by the echoes around her steel hull.

In this life-and-death situation the tension aboard *Fearless* was broken by the redoubtable Larken. 'For those interested in cricket,' he announced cheerfully, 'I've just received the latest score in the Test Match from the UK.' He promptly followed up with the details of who had caught and bowled whom and other essential facts that he felt his men 8000 miles from home would like to know.

On board the requisitioned Townsend Thorensen ferry *Nordic Ferry*, the line in 'Tannoy patter' was no less informal.

'Everybody still comfortable?' asked the incredibly smooth voice of one of the Naval officers assigned to the ship. 'Just to let you know we're still in the middle of an air raid. No need to panic. Keep smiling, and stay tuned to this channel for further information.'

Need to panic there may well have been, but with that sort of reassurance, nobody did.

High on Mount Kent the war on land was now being plotted in intricate detail. Brigadier Thompson had moved his headquarters up on the mountain and was in the happy position of being able to pick his moment. His men had won Goose Green and Bluff Cove had not been the setback it might so easily have been. The moment was near. Every unit commander of the front line waited impatiently for the 'go' code which would launch a five-pronged attack to kick open the gateway to Stanley.

Captain Rod Boswell returned to the mountainside with strange tales about Argentinian prisoners he had come across in the makeshift hospital at Teal Inlet.

'It seemed a bit strange,' he said, 'that several of their injured had bullet wounds in the feet and ankles. I asked what had happened and they were reluctant to tell me.

'Eventually they claimed the wounds had been inflicted, not by the British, but by their own officers. They'd been shot in the feet to stop them running away.'

Some of the prisoners lucky enough not to have been maimed by their superiors told woeful tales of how in the middle of the night under intensive artillery fire they had looked for support from their officers.

One told a British intelligence officer, 'We looked round and could not see any of our officers. They had fled. We thought if they could do it, so could we. So we ran away.'

Captain Boswell related too how he had come across an injured Marine. He had been shot in the groin, and was missing a vital part of his manhood.

'You will have to leave the Corps for certain,' Boswell said, quoting someone who was with him at the time.

'No! Why should I?' asked the heartbroken Marine.

'You have to be a complete prick to be in the Marines,' came the reply, which succeeded in making the injured man laugh at a time when he was most downhearted.

Boswell's men of the Mountain and Arctic Warfare Cadre had been securing the hills seeking out Argentinian observation posts, which they knew had to be somewhere around, and which were clearly calling in air strikes on the British front-line units.

Sitting round a little spring of freshwater with his men, Boswell said, 'The longer we wait, the better it is. The longer it takes to find them, the more satisfaction we will get in blowing them off the mountain.'

A young Marine carrying half a dozen water bottles approached this circle of elite Bootnecks, and one of Boswell's men said, 'What can I do for you, John?'

'Want some water, mate,' was the reply.

'No, mate. Our spring, our water. Fuck off,' said the Cadre man, adding, 'There are plenty of pools around full of pond life. Help yourself. This is finders keepers, mate. On your bike.'

Later in the day the sky was alive again with Sea Kings and Wessex helicopters, carrying troops this time and not guns.

The victors of Goose Green, the men of 2 Para, were being airlifted in for the big show, anxious to shake off their unwanted role as support battalion for the Guards and Gurkhas of 5 Brigade.

'Where you going, then?' a Marine asked one of the first Paras to arrive.

'Longdon, mate. Bit of banjoing to do.'

The Marines queried that. 'Surely not? That's 3 Para's job.'

'We're going in support of them,' said the Para. 'After a bit of scrapping we'll tab it past them and nip into Stanley for a result.'

'We have Stanley,' argued the Marine. 'It's Bootneck territory. Brigadier said so.'

'Up your arse, mate,' said the Para. '2 Para or at worst, 3 Para. But no Marines. You'll never keep up. Once we can see it, we'll go like stink while you're still making a wet up here.'

The men of 2 Para were still not best pleased with the aftermath of Goose Green. Before the Gurkhas had arrived to garrison the settlement, 2 Para had received scores of visitors they did not want. It had appeared to the Paras that everyone who could beg, steal or borrow a helicopter had descended on Goose Green with the sole intention of trophy hunting.

There certainly had been plenty of pickings, as the airstrip there was littered with the left-overs of the defeated defenders. It was a looters' delight. There was everything, from helmets to boots, field guns to Pucaras, and everyone in the Task Force, it seemed, wanted something to take home. Believe it or not, a Pucara was actually brought back to Britain by one enterprising unit, carried the 8000 miles aboard a container ship.

'We don't like to call it looting,' said a stranger in the camp with an armful of bayonets and rifles. 'Pillaging somehow seems a little better.'

'We don't mind what you take,' said a displeased Para, reflecting the annoyance of his unit, 'but it would be rather nice if you fucking jackdaws came and said hello to us first. After all, we are supposed to be in charge round here.'

Up on Kent, lead companies of the newly arrived Paras were already beginning to move on in support of their colleagues in 3 Para, who were approaching Mount Longdon. One company remained near Brigade on the slopes of Kent, ready to be airlifted forward when the attack began.

They dug in and began to make the rounds of Marine bivouacs, 'doing a rev-up' as one of them put it.

'Should be all right up here, mate,' promised a Para as he passed one Marine trench. 'Argies ran away when they heard we were coming.'

'Fuck off and play in a minefield,' chided the Marine.

' 'Course, you haven't seen an Argie yet, have you?' goaded the Para. 'Left it all to us. But I tell you, should one come ambling by after we've banjoed his mates, you'll be able to recognize him. They are the ones with the American-style helmets who speak with a Beni-dorm accent.'

'Piss off,' chorused half a dozen Marines.

At another trench, another Para was also at it. 'Tell you what,' he suggested. 'You all wait here, and when the coast is clear in Stanley, we'll ring you up and invite you in. Don't want you getting your boots all muddy, do we?'

'Piss off.'

It went on for many hours, one unit ribbing the other, all men knowing that soon the joking might well give way to the fearful realities. No-one really believed that the enemy was yet beaten.

As everywhere, conditions on Kent were bleak. When it had not been snowing, it rained. Almost every trench had at least a few inches of water in the bottom. The pitiful sight of tough men hobbling like cripples became more commonplace each day as trench foot took a hold. In simple terms, trench foot is the result of human tissue being immersed for long periods in water, causing, in this case, feet to rot and swell.

'It's not my feet I'm worried about,' said one Marine to his mate in the same flooded trench. 'Are you sure there's a cure for trench bum? We've been sitting in water for hours.'

They were in their trenches because yet another Air Red had been sounded. Others were not in trenches, convinced that this raid, like the others that day, would never materialize.

McGowan, chicken-hearted to the end, always believed that air raids would materialize, and was in the habit of scanning the horizon constantly until the alert was over.

Doing just that, but forgetting the proper jargon set down for these occasions, he saw four trails of dark smoke coming from behind what he at first took for British helicopters.

Then it dawned on him that if these were helicopters, they were breaking all speed records.

'What the fuck . . .' he shouted. 'Run like hell.'

Everyone did, just as the terrifying rattle of the Skyhawks' cannon began.

The jets dropped parachute-delayed 1000lb bombs across the brigade area as newsmen and troops alike fell on top of each other in any muddy bolt-hole they could find.

After the warplanes had made their first sweep and were banking for a second, a plaintive Yorkshire voice cut right through the tension and set half a dozen trenches rocking with laughter.

' 'Scuse me,' said Derek Hudson, in all seriousness because he alone had apparently thought it improper to dive for cover without ceremony on top of someone else in a trench. 'Mind if I come in?'

In the raid, Brigadier Thompson and General Jeremy Moore had to dive for cover, too. After the raid the general took off in a helicopter for *Fearless* and the Brigadier jumped in a Volvo BV and sped off for a safer location for his forward headquarters further round the mountain.

'Appears we're moving,' said a Marine, studying the high-ranking activity.

Captain Nicholls said, 'Bastards must have an OP around here somewhere. The only sensible thing to do is assume they knew Brigade was here. That means Brigade has to move. It would be bloody stupid to hang around for them to come back for another go.'

Another far more plausible theory for the attack was suggested by another officer on Kent. 'It's hardly bloody surprising they started bombing the shit out of Brigade,' he said. 'I'm just amazed they didn't try to zap it sooner. All the radio traffic coming in and out must have made this place glow in the dark. It's the classic electronic warfare syndrome. All they have to do is listen in to the chit-chat, get a bearing on the

231

frequency, and send some planes right down the radio beam.'

'I'll never listen to Radio One again,' said a Marine joker as he pulled out, his shovel at the ready, to dig another trench further round the mountain.

As he spoke, another jet screamed in low and Paras on the slopes above him let fly with everything they had. Rifle and machine-gun fire criss-crossed the sky and the aircraft rocketed by.

'For fuck's sake,' shouted an officer. 'Pack it in. It's a bloody Harrier.'

'We know,' shouted a Para, still firing. 'Where was he when we needed him?'

The Harrier virtually stood on its tail and soared away from the gunfire at top speed.

'Did we hit it?' asked a Para of someone.

'Don't think so,' came the reply.

'Fuck,' said the Para, concealing the fact that he was glad he had not.

That night, with Brigade virtually undefended because almost every rifle company was forward at the mountain battle areas, the main fear was one of infiltration by Argentinian units thought to be in the area.

As darkness fell, everyone was ordered, 'Keep quiet. Don't talk, don't cough and don't fart. They won't find us if we don't make any noise.'

It was not to be.

The affable Alastair McQueen of the *Daily Mirror* was sleeping blissfully under a makeshift tent beneath a rock upon which squatted a Marine sentry, shivering and anxious not to make a sound. At first he could not make it out. Dull chortlings and groanings appeared to be coming up through the peat turf. Mr McQueen was snoring. Not many others were. When McQueen snored, few could sleep, it was that noisy.

'For fuck's sake,' whispered the sentry. 'Stop that awful noise.'

McQueen, of course, denies to this day that he snores.

Under cover of darkness, the troops that would be fighting the decisive battles that would lead to the fall of Port Stanley were running forward all along the front.

Artillery fire on both sides had intensified and British Vulcans and Argentinian Canberras were out on high-level bombing missions.

At sea, British warships were in position to start pouring supporting fire into the defences of Stanley with their 4·5 inch guns, and were already pounding the slopes of the key objectives of Longdon, Two Sisters, William, Harriet and Tumbledown, occupied by the enemy.

Helicopters flying at night were taking 105mm rounds to the British guns, and bringing back the first casualties.

On a far ridge near the peak of Mount Kent, the headquarters company of 42 Commando was feeling cheerful. They had witnessed an encouraging gesture: just before nightfall, two Harriers at high altitude etched a Victory-V sign in the blue sky with their vapour trails.

'Nice touch, that,' said a Marine. 'Pity the bastards won't be around tonight to join in the fun.'

The cheerful attitude was short-lived. The company was given a final briefing on what lay ahead. There was no doubt that the Marines would be able to do their job once they got stuck in, but news had just been received that the Argentinians were better prepared than everyone had thought.

'You all thought the airport had been bombed to fuck, didn't you?' said a warrant officer. 'Wrong. As if we didn't have enough problems, the Argies have actually been flying in Hercules right up until tonight. God knows how they got past the warships and the Harriers, but there you are. Tough shit, innit?'

One prophetic comedian suggested that the Hercules had not, after all, been flying in late supplies.

'If they've got any sense,' he said, 'they'll have been coming in empty and packing as many blokes on board as they can for the quick disappearing trick back to Argentina.'

It had been said as a joke, but it was soon learned that the Argentinian transport planes had been evacuating as well as supplying. The senior officers of the 'Malvinas Command' were not among them. General Mario Menendez, the enemy's overall commander in the islands, was sticking it out to the bitter end.

Senior British officers, aided by Dr Alison Bleaney, who was still in Stanley, had been attempting in radio conversations to talk Menendez and his military commanders into surrender. They had failed.

'Can't blame him really,' said a Marines officer on learning that Menendez was going to stay. 'Not much of a choice for him, was there? Give up to us and try and get a passport to Switzerland, or go home and no doubt get topped.'

Sergeant-major Len Cook, of 42 Commando's HQ company was not a happy man. He had spent many long and successful years in the Marines and this should have been his finest hour.

'Instead of which,' he said, 'the rest of the lads are just a few hundred yards up front and in the thick of it, and I'm stuck here picking me nose with the rear party.'

As troops marched into battle, many realized that early guesses about the outcome of the campaign had been wrong. During the quiet period after Goose Green, hundreds of Marines and Paras had taken to walking around saying, 'We'll give Stanley a firepower demonstration soon and then they'll jack it in. Once they see they can't win, they'll give up.'

But, at this point, they had not given up.

The guns of the Commando batteries were now

almost red hot with continued firing. After yet another salvo had gone whistling towards the enemy positions a gunner stepped forward and cupping his hands to his mouth, yelled after the shells, 'Eat lead, suckers!'

Although none of the British could know it then, many Argentinians were doing just that. The accuracy of the bombardment was to win high acclaim during and after the battles. Many enemy troops had wanted to run then, expecting infantry attacks against them at any minute. Some did run, and many of them were officers.

But not every Argentinian soldier was a conscript near the end of his two years in the army, thinking only of staying alive so he could go home and lead a healthy civilian life.

Argentina's own Marines were formidable men, not inclined to run in the face of a fight. And some of the Hercules that had run the gauntlet into the virtually undamaged Stanley Airport had carried men from the crack Mountain Regiment. These units were to be the backbone of the Argentinian defence of the mountain objectives.

Their strength was sorely needed to shore up the lagging morale of the young conscripts, many of whom had initially been told they were going to Argentina's southern border with Chile to deal with a minor insurgence. When they arrived in the Falklands, they were assured that the British would never be able to land troops to put against them.

But Britain had landed its troops, who were even now running forward with bayonets fixed towards the frightened young defenders.

Chapter 15

It was make or break, or as one Para put it, 'Shit or bust.' The high ground had to fall and fall quickly if the British were to succeed. The Very Senior Officers had done their planning, the men were prepared. Now it remained only to see if it would all work when put into practice.

The Argentinian positions had been well softened up by the artillery, and the Naval bombardment. Many of the young defenders were even now cowering in their last protective bunkers, safe from all but a direct hit. They knew, and they were not wrong, that the great British infantry assault was not far behind.

Sergeant Chris Phelan of 3 Para, taking cover with a couple of mates in a trench, was not happy. The Argentinians were, after all, making them fight for every foot of ground, and the enemy artillery was raining in on them with far greater accuracy than they had expected.

'I don't like it,' said Sergeant Phelan, 'I really don't like it at all.'

'What?' demanded his oppo.

'Fucking 155s,' said Phelan. 'Someone should have knocked them out by now. They're giving me the screaming shits.'

While 3 Para were making a frontal attack on a determined and well-entrenched enemy on Mount Longdon, 45 Commando on Two Sisters were playing a stealthy game with their quarry.

45 Commando were 'snurgling', or creeping up on their foe, having crossed the start-line expecting a major battle, which indeed lay ahead of them.

'The last two sisters I knew had 40-inch tits,' said

one of their number, trying to keep up the morale of his colleagues.

'Did you fuck them?' asked a voice in the dark.

'No, but it looks like these Two Sisters could fuck us if we're not careful,' he replied.

42 Commando were also snurgling away on Goat Ridge and Mount Harriet. They had been given the code-names 'Zoya' and 'Katrina'.

'Pretty, that,' said one Marine feeling his way through the dark towards the enemy on Goat Ridge. 'Who gave them names like that?'

'The colonel,' came the reply. 'Those are the names of his daughters.'

Lt-col. Nick Vaux, the CO of 42 Commando, had decided that these two rocky outcrops should be immortalized in his unit's assault by naming them after his two young daughters, now snugly tucked up in bed at home in the West Country.

At this time, before the second and final great infantry battle of the campaign really got started, 2 Para were left cooling their heels on the western slopes of Mount Longdon, waiting to move up in support of their comrades in the Third Battalion.

3 Para had two objectives on Mount Longdon. One, codenamed 'Full-back' was on the eastern side of the summit, and the second, 'Fly-half' was a nearby ridge.

They knew that 'Full-back' was heavily defended by enemy machine-gun posts and snipers. But before they were close to either objective they ran into trouble.

For almost two weeks their reconnaissance patrols had been surveying the six hundred-feet high mountain and were fairly sure they had identified all the open areas where anti-personnel mines would most probably have been laid.

Their plan was for a silent advance at speed with 'A' and 'B' companies moving in a pincer formation to the north and south. 'C' company would be their back-up.

But as 'B' Company advanced to within 700 yards of

the first Argentinian trenches the element of surprise was lost. A young corporal trod on a mine and his leg was shattered. Now the enemy knew they were there and a torrent of mortars, artillery rounds and machine-gun fire swept their position.

'That's fucked it,' shouted one Para, as the company charged forward. 'We're in a bastard minefield. The only way out is through them.'

Fortunately in the initial stages enemy mortar and artillery fire was slightly off target, and before the Argentinians got it right, 'B' Company had raced forward and taken cover beneath a rocky crag within 100 feet of the top of Mount Longdon.

Now the enemy fire was becoming very accurate indeed, and the Paras looked across at Two Sisters and one said, 'Fucking hell, they're taking a pasting.'

The feeling was entirely mutual, as on Two Sisters, 45 Commando were looking across at Mount Longdon and watching the Argentinian shells pour down on the Paras.

'There's going to be a few poor bastards cop it tonight,' said one of the Marines. 'Even the Paras won't be able to walk on water out of this one.'

It was a remark that somehow typified the bitter rivalry yet utmost respect that the Marines and Paras held for each other.

The men of 45 Commando were battling on under supporting fire from the guided-missile destroyer _Glamorgan_ when the men of 42 Commando on Mount Harriet saw a flash of light streak across the beach near Port Stanley and out to sea.

'Oh, Jesus Christ,' said one of 42's Marines. 'It's a fucking Exocet.'

Indeed it was, one of the shore-based missiles the Argentinians had at Stanley, and its target was the destroyer.

Glamorgan's crew saw it coming and fired off Sea Cat missiles in a vain bid to knock it down. Seconds later the missile found its mark. While Paras and Marines fought forward on their respective mountains, *Glamorgan* raced out to sea at 18 knots, badly damaged by the Exocet, and with 13 of her crew killed.

On Longdon the fighting was becoming very fierce with 3 Para slogging forwards doggedly, skirmishing desperately for every foot. It was quite literally an uphill struggle.

Corporal Mick Ferguson was with 'A' Company and the intensity of the battle is best described by him.

'We were going for the rear of the Mount, the slope that runs from the peak towards Stanley,' he said. 'We got pinned down by machine-gun fire for quite some time. We had to withdraw from our position and change direction, back to the way we came. Then we went up to the peak, and assaulted the ridge line we were originally going to take.

' "B" Company managed to get onto the rocky part of the mount and we came in, moved through "B" Company, took the point and cleared out the rest of the objective.

'We had had to go through a minefield to get there. One or two lads in other companies had stepped on mines. That was how we had been pinned down. The idea had been to take them by surprise. There was an explosion as one of the guys trod on a mine, and then all hell was let loose.

'Initially their fire had been going over our heads, and it wasn't until we'd gone about 50 metres that they started to get a bit more accurate. Then we started to take casualties. We were pinned down for about an hour to an hour and a half.

'The hardest bit was the clearing of the positions on the slope that runs off Longdon towards Stanley. We had to clear them bunker by bunker. It was a hell of a position. We didn't appreciate the size of it until we'd actually swept through it. It wasn't until daylight that we realized it was so huge.

239

'In my platoon we had two killed. The Argies hadn't been running away. They'd been standing and fighting. My feeling was they were using determined rifle fire rather than proper snipers.

'We had cleared their bunkers with 66s and grenades. Once we'd gone through the position, that's when they started using artillery on us. In these latter stages I was a little bit concerned,' added Corporal Ferguson in the understatement of the year. 'What frightened me more than anything else was the artillery fire, which was sometimes very accurate, sometimes indiscriminate. We had no way of knowing where it was going to land. That was pretty frightening.

'You do get the old butterflies in the stomach, there's no two ways about it. After we had consolidated we were continually being hit by artillery and big mortars, their 120mm mortars, and they also used their big anti-tank rifles on us. All in all it wasn't the sort of place I'd choose to go for a quiet weekend.'

One enterprising Para had decided that his standard issue of four magazine clips was not going to be enough for the battle of Mount Longdon. At the expense of other less vital pieces of kit, he took with him no less than 18 clips. Even that wasn't enough, as by the time the battle was over he'd used all his own plus seven additional magazines he had found left behind by the Argentinians, a total of 500 rounds fired by one man.

In the height of the shelling described by Corporal Ferguson, another 3 Para stalwart had dived into the first trench he saw. The idea was a good one, but the trench he chose had been the Argentinians' latrine, and he came out smelling dreadfully.

'There goes the old myth about coming up smelling of roses,' said one of his friends, on the verge of deserting him. 'Tatty-bye, Skunk. You're on your own.'

'B' Company found themselves up against a heavy machine gun and a section of Argentinian riflemen

240

pouring lead at them like it was going out of fashion. The position had to be taken out.

Lieutenant Bickerdike moved forward with 'A' Platoon but he did not get far. Lt Bickerdike was shot through the leg and 29 year-old Sergeant Ian McKay took charge of the platoon. He rallied his men and realized the trouble was coming mainly from a bunker 50 yards in front of them. In the attack, Corporal Ian Bailey was shot through the legs and stomach but was still firing as he crashed into the bunker.

Meanwhile Sergeant McKay went round behind the bunker and tossed two grenades into it. It worked, and the Argentinian firing stopped, but McKay had been mortally wounded in his heroic action, and fell dead across the bunker. His heroism was to earn him a posthumous Victoria Cross.

In the closing stages of this, the second major and bloody battle on East Falkland since the British landings, young Paras were at times fighting hand-to-hand with the enemy, often clearing trenches with grenades and bayonets.

The Argentinian snipers were all the time scoring off the advancing 3 Para. One man was shot down, and three others went forward to drag him to safety, each in turn also being hit by the sniper, using US-made night sights far superior to the British ones.

Near the end of the battle for Longdon, a young Para corporal was hit by artillery shrapnel, and went down in agony. 'Christ, I've lost my leg,' he moaned.

His mate crouched beside him and using a humour he knew his injured oppos would understand, he said, 'No you haven't, mate. It's over there.'

The wounded corporal was brought home and was later recovering in a London hospital. He has asked the authors not to name him.

Photographer Tom Smith, unable to take pictures in the dark – flashes being hazardous – volunteered to carry wounded soldiers down the mountainside. He made the trip twice, under fire, no mean achievement for a man with only one lung.

A doctor in the Paras heard an injured man moaning in the darkness and yelled, 'Leave him. He's moaning, so he's alive. He'll be alive in the morning.'

He was, but by then the sniper had been killed.

'Fly-half' had now been taken in six hours. 'Full-back' took another four to secure. 23 Paras were killed in the battle and 47 wounded. The enemy had lost just over 50 dead, most of them 'fragged' by grenades or bayonetted, with 39 taken prisoner, including ten wounded.

'My men looked grim and determined in the light of dawn,' said their colonel, Hew Pike. 'They were moving forward in the mist with bayonets fixed. A lot of Argentinians were killed with those bayonets.'

Over on Two Sisters, 45 Commando had achieved their objective with slightly fewer problems and less casualties.

They had been held for a time by a determined sniper. In the dark, locating him was difficult, and the man constantly moved anyway. But some Marines knew he was close.

In cover, one Bootneck shouted to the sniper, 'You couldn't hit a cow's arse with a shovel.' It was not true, but caused an eerie ripple of laughter across the position.

On Longdon, some Paras were convinced, one of the snipers was an American mercenary. It was discussed many months after the campaign, but never established.

The Argentinians' liking for the heavy machine gun helped bring about their own downfall on Two Sisters. So fast was 45 Commando's advance up the slopes at one stage, the enemy did not have time to retreat with all their equipment.

The Bootnecks stormed one 50-calibre machine-gun nest with such ferocity that the hapless crew had time only to realize their predicament before they died in a hail of 7·62 rifle fire.

To their delight, the new occupants of the trench found the machine gun was not only undamaged, but was mounted in such a way that it could be brought to bear in the opposite direction, against the enemy.

On his radio, the Marine platoon commander reported, 'The big machine guns are causing trouble, but we've captured one and are now using it to good effect.'

The radio message was heard by Brigadier Thompson who was listening to the progress of each of the battles from his headquarters on Mount Kent. Tense and anxious as details of the fighting and the losses came in, he now beamed with relief. 'It made me chuckle,' he said later. 'Even in these desperate situations, the men still have a sense of humour. They are in tremendous spirits.'

There were many desperate situations. During 45's advance, the Marines found an Argentinian who appeared to be badly wounded. He was still conscious, but on closer inspection, the Bootnecks saw that most of his brains were in his helmet. His skull had been split wide open. It was decided that the man still had a slim chance of living. A Marine carefully scooped the brains out of the helmet and put them back inside the man's skull.

'It was incredible,' said one of the men afterwards. 'He was still alive when he was cas-evacced, and we believe he survived and later went home.'

Further across Two Sisters one sergeant was not happy at the speed with which his men were digging trenches. 'As deep as you can get,' he bellowed. 'And don't forget, these things serve two purposes. Deep enough for cover and deep enough to bury you in if it all goes wrong.'

These Commandos from Arbroath had brought with them a few pieces of equipment they had not received in routine issue from their quartermaster. Captain Mike Erwin was obviously a Clint Eastwood fan, as he carried with him in a smart holster on his hip a 3·57 Magnum revolver. On more than one occasion during the advance he was heard to shout, 'Keep up, or I'll give you a 3·57 enema.'

Captain Erwin used his novel firearm against enemy planes, and after one Skyhawk raid was so convinced he had brought his target down, he was on the point of registering his claim with Brigade.

Another of 45's more innovative members sported a cut-down samurai sword, which he had carried all the way across East Falkland strapped across his bergan. It had been the butt of many jokes, but seemed to put the fear of God into the Argentinians when, on Two Sisters, he was seen brandishing it above his head and making blood-curdling war-whoops.

With their headquarters back on Mount Kent, 42 Commando were doing very nicely in their quest for Mount Harriet and one of its strategic features, Goat Ridge. Messages on how the battle was progressing were being fed back to their headquarters where Lieutenant Tony Maclinski was dutifully logging the night's activities.

Suddenly, Maclinski was listening to a disbelieving radio operator.

'You're not going to believe this, sir,' he said. 'Looks like someone has pulled a fast one.'

'Explain,' demanded Maclinski, curtly.

'I'm only telling you what they're telling me up front,' said the radio operator. 'But someone is swearing blind they can see a mushroom cloud over Port Stanley.'

Maclinski grinned, and said, 'The Vulcans are obviously back and trying to make up in a big way for not getting the runway.'

The truth behind the mushroom cloud was never discovered. Far from being an over-enthusiastic Vulcan pilot dropping a nuclear device on the little capital, it was assumed that a British shell had landed in the middle of an Argentinian ammunition dump.

'It looked bloody effective, whatever it was,' said one of the Marines on Mount Harriet later. 'I must admit, it looked as though we were using a hammer to crack a walnut.'

During a lull in the fighting, 42 Commando's padre Albert Hempenstall thought his men might appreciate a little spiritual encouragement. 'I decided to hold an impromptu service,' he said, 'and many men opted to come along. It was a simple affair in the rocks, and because of the activity I had wanted to keep it short and sweet.

'The men gathered in front of me, but before I had a chance to start, one of them said, "Excuse me, sir. Can you hang on a moment?" Naturally, I agreed.'

The fighting men had not forgotten that the day had a special meaning for the padre, even if he had.

'They burst into a loud rendition of "Happy Birthday To You" and I collapsed with laughter,' said Albert. 'I just couldn't believe it. My birthday was already an unforgettable one, but this made it doubly so.'

The song and the little service ended and the men went back to their positions to conclude the battle.

'I'm sure the incident put them in good spirits,' said Albert. 'It certainly did wonders for me.'

Here, too, the Argentinians were not giving in easily. It was by now apparent to all the units that the enemy had put their best men on the mountains.

Colonel Nick Vaux, the CO of 42 Commando, had not forgotten the lessons of Goose Green. He, too, found that Milan anti-tank missiles were very effective against enemy trenches.

'It wasn't the cheapest way of doing it,' said Vaux. 'A Milan, I think, costs about £20,000 a shot. But they were bloody effective.'

Still, snipers were causing a problem, and one of

them had far greater success with one shot than he can ever have imagined. The round went through both legs of one Marine and ended up in the leg of Lieutenant Ian Stafford, a lone Argyll and Sutherland Highlander on attachment to 42 Commando.

The unit was pinned down for a couple of hours under a barrage of artillery shells and mortars before sheer doggedness gave 42 their objective. Despite all the heavy fighting they lost only one man killed and had taken some 200 prisoners.

Colonel Vaux and the brigadier were delighted. The offensive on Stanley was going well.

On Harriet, after the battle, Commandos found a particularly nasty weapon that, fortunately, had not been used against them. Boxes of 9mm rounds used in sub-machine guns and pistols and made in Germany had their heads machine-drilled to give them the 'dum-dum' effect banned by the Geneva Convention.

'If you're hit by one of these,' said a Marine, 'it splits open and makes a fucking great hole in you. It's not at all nice. You tend to die of it.'

As the noise of battle died away on Harriet, young Marines still had a few surprises coming to them. Obviously tense and very pleased to have survived the fighting, they moved around the mountain with their nerves on edge.

'Everywhere they looked, there seemed to be Argentinians popping up like jack-rabbits with their arms in the air,' said Sergeant Dave Munnelly. 'It was most disconcerting. Some of the lads were shitting themselves.'

As dawn came after the battle, helicopters carrying grim cargoes flew low over the mountains towards the field hospital at Ajax Bay, with the British dead and injured carried at times in boxes on the aircrafts' skids.

On Longdon, 2 Para were now moving through their mates in 3 Para, pressing on for their objective, a hill overlooking Stanley called Wireless Ridge. For them too, the going was tough. Argentinian 155 shells were coming in close to their forward company, some bursting in the air, others packed with phosphorus. The British were returning fire with similar hardware, and they were backed by the Scimitar and Scorpion tanks of the Blues and Royals, now moving up to the head of 2 Para's advance.

Eight miles to the South, the Scots Guards were up against one of the finest units in the Argentinian forces. The enemy, crack Marines, were heavily dug in on Tumbledown Mountain in a series of bunkers carved into the rocks.

The Guards charged forward with bayonets fixed, often in the face of heavy machine-gune fire, with fellow guardsmen sweeping in on their flanks to take out the bunkers. One British soldier said, 'We got stuck in with our rifles and bayonets and chucked grenades into their trenches.'

The guardsmen, a young officer, added, 'We used bayonets because they kill people. They are very useful, especially when you fire at a man who's right near you, and you find your weapon is empty. Then you just stick him, and run onwards.'

As the Guards took their objective, they were able to look down on the lights of Port Stanley.

On the mountain called William to their south-east, the gallant Gurkhas were none too happy. The Welsh Guards, swelled by two companies from 40 Commando after the tragedy of Bluff Cove, had moved through the objective that was earmarked for the Gurkhas after the enemy had surrendered almost without a fight, and had pressed on to Sapper Hill, just south of Stanley.

A message to Brigade said, 'The enemy appear to be running at battalion strength back to Stanley.'

All along the new and hard-fought-for front line, the British troops drew breath for the final battle, a battle that everyone was sure would be a desperate struggle against the heavily defended capital of the Falkland Islands: the last battle.

Chapter 16

All along the parapets of the objectives that were now in British hands, the combat troops steeled themselves against the driving snow, waiting for the inevitable command which would send them racing forward to drive the invaders into the sea.

All the fighting units were exhausted but knew that one more massive effort, one more duel with death would end the war in the Falklands.

'That's it,' said a sergeant in 3 Para. 'We've given 'em every chance, and now they've done the worst thing they could. They've upset us now, so we've got to go in and give 'em a fucking. No, we *want* to go in and give 'em a fucking.'

The Marines too were in an indomitable mood.

'It's a pretty convincing scoreline at the moment,' said one of 42's young heroes, relaxing for a few minutes on the slopes of Mount Harriet. 'Do you reckon they'll go down on penalties or try for extra time?'

'If they've got any sense they'll be in the showers and queuing up for the coach home,' said his oppo.

A mountain away on Two Sisters, a corporal in 45 Commando was sharpening his bayonet. Smiling, but resigned to more killing, he said, 'Probably have to use this again. The bastards should have done their fighting out here with us instead of running back to Stanley. Now we're going to have to fight them in amongst civilians, and no matter which way you look at it, some civvies are going to die. Street fighting is like that. Some innocent bastard sticks his head up and gets a round through it.'

Further down the line on Mount Longdon 3 Para had come through the hell of staying put during a merciless

248

artillery barrage, and were anxious to press ahead after their colleagues in 2 Para who were sitting on Wireless Ridge.

'Would you fucking believe it?' said a corporal. 'It's happening again. 2 Para's off, disobeying orders and trying to get into Stanley before anyone else does. We don't mind if they beat the Marines, but it must be our fucking turn.'

A few yards away a sergeant was barking at another young Para, saying, 'What the fuck's wrong with that man?'

The Para was in a trench with an Argentinian conscript who looked far from happy. The Para said, 'Wouldn't get out of the trench when I told him to, Sarge, so I stuck my bayonet up his arse. He'll live. I'm sorry, but I didn't know what state he was in. Some evil cunt on his side had shot him through the legs so he couldn't run away.'

Medics came up and treated the prisoner, who was taken to Ajax Bay, and lived to go home within the next ten days.

In a way, the Marine on Two Sisters had been right. What he did not know, what no-one in the British Forces knew then, was that civilians in Stanley had already been killed during the bombardment on the defences of the outskirts of the capital.

One British shell crashed through the house of the superintendent of education in the town, John Fowler, and burst in the front room. Two women sleeping on the floor, Doreen Burns and Sue Whitney, were killed instantly. A third woman, Mary Goodwin, aged 82 and the oldest inhabitant of Stanley, survived the initial blast with blood pouring from her face.

Fowler's wife, Veronica, was hit in the back with shrapnel as she stood in the kitchen doorway talking to her husband who was making coffee. Fowler himself caught splinter fragments in his lower legs. Mrs Fowler staggered into the front room to comfort Mary Goodwin, who, in tears, died in her arms.

Later General Jeremy Moore went to see the Fowlers and explained that the British were sorry that it had happened. It may sound trite to say that it was a war and these things happen, but General Moore was genuinely saddened by these deaths, the only civilian casualties throughout the campaign. In fact the shell which killed the women had been intended for an Argentinian battery which was firing on the British at the time. Not only had the Argentinians been using the cover of houses for their gun positions, but the British were astounded to discover that the buildings were still being occupied by the local population. Intelligence had led the British commanders to believe that these houses on the outskirts of the town had been evacuated. Not for the first time, British intelligence was proved to be wrong.

To the Paras and Marines on the front line, the order that they knew was imminent was finally given. Adrenalin washed away the cobwebs of fatigue. The assault on Stanley, the final assault, was on.

All troops had been alerted by another 'Air Red'. More Argentinian aircraft were racing in to hit them, and Harriers had been sent aloft from the aircraft carriers on a 'seek and destroy' mission.

Among the units it became a race as to who would get to Port Stanley first. 2 Para took off aggressively and charged off the slopes of Wireless Ridge to do battle on the northern side of the town, which was their task. 3 Para launched themselves after them, determined not to be left out and Marine Commandos from the other mountains ran forward too.

Then the unbelievable happened. Over the radio network forward units were told that the air raid was off, and the Harriers had dropped their bombs into the Atlantic and were returning to *Hermes* and *Invincible*.

One of the Paras, tabbing off Longdon, said, *'Now* what the fuck's going on?'

At that point no-one really knew.

At Brigade, Marines defending the brigadier's head-quarters were having snowball fights. A young man with a radio headset around his neck walked out into the snow and said to a colour sergeant, 'Makes no fucking sense at all. Someone's muttering that they've jacked. It's all a bit garbled.'

The colour sergeant looked at him and laughed. 'Wishful thinking, cunt. Go back and ask them what's going on.'

The young radio operator said, as he walked back to the communications tent, 'Yeah, all right. Doing a brew. Want sugar in it?'

The Marines had now picked teams and were creep-ing around the rocks 'fragging' each other's trenches with snowballs, yelling 'Grenade!' as each one was thrown.

The radio operator emerged from the tent again.

Holding two mugs of tea he said almost apologetically to the colour sergeant; 'Listen, don't have another go at me. It's only what I've heard. They're jumping up and down on the "net".'

'What the hell are you on about?' said the colour sergeant.

The radio man nervously replied, 'It's what I said. Everyone's talking about them jacking. Honest to God, they're saying there's a white flag flying over Stanley.'

The colour sergeant fired across another withering look. 'Bollocks,' he said. 'Check again.'

The radio operator came out of the tent once more. In a faltering voice he said, 'It's official. It's an order. The brigadier has just said that all units will not fire unless first fired upon. That's the order, so I must be fucking right. They really have jacked.'

Five minutes later every unit commander in the two brigades was advised that General Mario Menendez

251

had indeed flown a white flag over his headquarters in Stanley and had contacted the British command and said he was prepared to discuss surrender.

Coming down off Two Sisters, and still preparing for the last battle, 45 Commando found it hard to take in the news. They knew it was possibly still not all over, but the order from Brigade: 'All units to make best speed towards objective', was the best news they'd had since leaving England.

'I just can't fucking believe it,' said one young Marine. 'It can't be true, can it? What about the punch-up on Sapper Hill? What about the fighting through the streets in Stanley? It can't be all over . . . can it?'

At Brigade the snowball fight took on a new vigour. The Marines were cheering as they threw the wet clods of snow, and moved closer towards each other, eventually closing to arm's length and shamelessly hugging each other.

'It's over! It's over!' was the chant. 'We've made it, for Christ's sake. We've won!'

What none of the front-line troops had known was that the British commanders had given General Menendez a message which read, 'There is little point in your continuing the struggle. A decision to give up should be made now. This is no reflection on the bravery and skill of your soldiers.'

Menendez, with his back to the sea and with his army in disarray, had realized he had no option, and in the first instance at least had agreed to talk. He most certainly knew at this moment that he and his cause were beaten and beyond redemption. If he had been able to see for himself the mood and spirit of the British troops he would not have paused even for a moment. Nothing was going to stop them now. The fight was no longer with the Argentinians but in the best traditions of rivalry amongst themselves to see who would be the first into Stanley.

But the time had not yet come when the guard could

be dropped. As each unit headed off at speed towards Stanley, every commander was told, 'Use caution. We are still at war. There has been no official surrender yet.'

This, however, did not have much effect on the Parachute Regiment, who were on a heads-down charge for the capital, with one thought uppermost in their minds: there will be red berets in Stanley before there are green ones.

The Marines, of course, had other ideas, but fortune was not favouring them at this moment in time.

'For Christ's sake stay off the Murrell Bridge,' yelled a warrant officer to the men of 45 Commando, who had thoughts of using the little crossing point to aid them in their bid to be first. 'It's still mined. Let's not fuck it all up now.'

This snowswept morning of 14 June had a deathly air about it. All the big guns were now stilled. There was no noise at all. Back on the shores of San Carlos Water the men in the ships, though still alert, were savouring the first moments in three weeks when they could be fairly sure that they would not be hit from the air. The men in the hospital at Ajax Bay were still at war, however, battling to save the lives of the men from both sides who had been cut down before that white flag was raised.

45 Commando's advance was not going too well. They knew the Paras were almost certainly ahead of them, and now they could see helicopters overtaking them as they yomped with 42 Commando doing an adept leapfrog.

Suddenly the long column of 45 Commando's weary but satisfied Bootnecks saw for the first time at close range the Islands' capital.

'Is that what we've come all this way for?' asked a tired Marine. 'Hardly looks worth it from here. Still, let's hope the pubs are still open when we get there.'

But 45 Commando still had a few miles and several nasty obstacles to overcome before they were home and dry.

'Halt!' shouted a voice at the front of the column. 'Stand still!'

Without knowing it, 45 Commando had walked into a minefield. On both sides of the track, little green anti-personnel mines were scattered. The track itself had more, and underneath had been placed the bigger anti-tank mines.

The eager Marines had to stop, it seemed, every few yards, as disposal experts cleared the path ahead.

A happy chorus struck up from the middle of the column, as deep voices broke into song, 'Tiptoe, Through the Tulips'.

'Shut up!' yelled a sergeant-major. 'Don't put your feet anywhere except in the footsteps of the man in front, and don't for God's sake step off the track. The bastards are everywhere.'

Further ahead a long column of Paras and Marines who had become intermingled after converging on the same track were ordered, 'Don't fuck about. At least ten yards between each man.'

Sergeant Dave Munnelly escorting Colonel Seccombe at the head of the column said softly, 'Pass it back. Spread out. There are enemy still in the hills, and mines underfoot. Look at it this way, if you're close to me and I stand on a mine, you're fucked too. Do I make myself clear?'

Everyone in the column tried in vain to put their feet in the imprints in the snow left by men ahead. It was impossible. All along the column men were heard saying, 'Not now. Not after all this. For fuck's sake, not now.'

A BV from 3 Para's HQ company came down off Sapper Hill and colour sergeant Brian Faulkner said to McGowan, 'Keep your head down. Some of the cunts up on the hill don't seem too keen on giving up.

'We've had a bashing already, and we don't want to lose any more now it's over. Watch your step.'

Along the track towards Moody Brook the column

passed the unmistakable signs of a defeated army in retreat. Burned-out vehicles lay on either side, one jeep pointing towards the mountains but now abandoned, its engine still running.

As the column passed the forward enemy artillery position they saw hundreds of 105mm and 155mm rounds littering the peat bog, both spent and unused. One lorry smouldering beside it was literally laden with the spoils of war: rifles, helmets, pistols and Argentinian quilted cold-weather clothing.

A Para covered in mud and camouflage cream came out smiling and said, 'Naughty, naughty. Don't touch. There's a grenade wired to half a dozen land-mines in the back. It might be the last souvenir you ever take.'

Not far behind, 45 Commando were walking through the valley still taking careful note of what lay beneath their feet and what might be up in the hills looking down on them.

'Harfleag, harfleag, harfleag onnard,' said a Marine trying not to be understood, and begging the question from the man in front: 'What the fuck are you going on about?'

'My great-grandfather was in the charge of the Light Brigade. Shame he's not here to see me now.'

'Your brain's gone,' said the man in front. 'You've lost your marbles.'

'Just quoting. Seems rather fitting at the moment, with us here, and those hills there crawling with Spics.'

'Half a league onwards, into the valley of death rode the six hundred,' said the Marine. 'I know it's a bit more than half a league, but this valley is certainly riddled with death.'

'I still say you've lost your fucking marbles,' said his mate.

Then came the order which ended any doubts.

'Make safe all weapons,' came the shout from the BV with the radio communications set up.

'That means,' said the RSM, Pat Chapman, 'they don't

255

want any naughty little bangs around the place while they're trying to sort out the finer details of the surrender.'

Hands, now feeling an enormous sense of relief, heard whistling from behind him. Looking round he saw a large Union flag attached to a radio aerial protruding from a Marine's bergan.

'What's the tune?' enquired Hands, referring to the whistles.

Suddenly, he didn't need an answer as a break in the wind allowed the notes to reach his ears unimpeded. 'Don't Cry For Me, Argentina,' was taken up by most of the men.

In the streets of Stanley the men of the Parachute Regiment couldn't care less about Argentina, or anyone else but themselves, and were singing to the tune of the hymn 'Guide Me, O Thou Great Redeemer' a little ditty entitled 'God is Airborne'.

The men of 45 Commando were now through the minefield and almost onto the concrete road that stretched from the edge of Moody Brook into Stanley.

'Home and dry, son,' said a sergeant. 'Home and fucking dry.'

Stanley at this time was a divided town. As the victorious were pouring in from the west, the defeated and confused Argentinians were regrouping on the eastern side.

The central sector of the town was declared a no-go area to both sides while General Moore and General Menendez talked behind locked doors, hammering out a document which would end the fighting officially.

'I can see the point in keeping us apart,' said a member of 2 Para. 'But why the fuck have the Argies got all the pubs in their sector? We might have to do something to change that.'

However, the resourceful Paras did have an ace up their sleeves. They knew of a crack team of blockade busters whose indefatigable skill in seeking out and capturing booze was rivalled only by the Toms' own ability to win battles.

Properly briefed in a roadside 'O-group' by the thirsty Paras, a hand-picked team of journalists went to the Upland Goose Hotel in the Argentinian sector, and returned with all the Tennents they could carry.

'Glad you lot all made it,' said one reporter. 'Sorry you lost so many of your mates.'

'Yeah, that's the way it goes, mate,' said a Para, tipping a can of lager into his mouth. 'But you know what they say: paratroopers never die; they go to hell and regroup.'

The Paras had not been overwhelmed by the welcome they had received from the newly liberated population of the capital. Sergeant-major Sammy Dougherty of 3 Para summed it up. 'It's a bloody long way to come and it's been an awful lot of trouble for a mud-heap like this, hasn't it?' he asked of no-one in particular.

All those around him could see what he meant. Only a few locals had come outside into the drizzle to wave one or two Union flags. A few houses were still smoking from hits by British artillery. In the gutters along Ross Road the abandoned bodies of several dead Argentinian soldiers lay roughly covered with single sheets of corrugated iron. Houses painted with red crosses on their roofs to indicate to British warplanes that they were hospitals more often contained huge stocks of enemy ammunition.

One row of houses just outside the city boundary was pock-marked with bullet holes made by outraged Argentinian troops who thought they were firing at their officers' quarters in requisitioned homes, as they marched in ignominy away from the advancing British troops. Sadly for them, the officers had run away too.

A party of newly arrived Marines realized immediately that the Paras had beaten them into town.

Anxious to prevent the men of 2 and 3 Para indulging

themselves in an orgy of self-congratulation, the Marines asked, 'All right, then. Who was here first?'

'2 Para, mate; need you ask? Been here for two hours. Sad, innit? 2 Para always seem to be first everywhere.'

The Marines tried to claw back some of their dignity. 'It's not our fault the brigadier insisted on us doing the job properly and tidying up the road into town after you lot had fucked off. Someone had to make that road safe.'

Both sides smiled. This was not a moment for petty recriminations.

But the Paras could not resist a parting shot. 'Still beat you, though, didn't we?'

The Red Berets moved off singing loudly, 'God is Airborne.'

They walked towards their newly set up headquarters at the far end of Ross Road, past Government House, where General Menendez sat in tears. He had not been allowed to stay with his men and at this time he was being urged by the British High Command to sign the surrender document in front of him. He disagreed with the word 'unconditional' surrender, and that word was struck off the document. He also, at first at least, refused to agree to the surrender of his troops on West Falkland. Haggling over the surrender details was to last until the small hours of the next day, 15 June.

Back at the Upland Goose, officers of the Argentinian elite outfit, Unit 601, were drinking in the bar, knowing they were safely in their own sector of town.

As darkness fell, they were not alone. British combat uniforms were now mingling with Argentinian ones as the journalists from London moved in, covered in the mud of three weeks in the field, intent on doing some serious drinking. After all, while General Moore's men had decided on one overall objective, it was considered only right and proper that the reporters should have a goal too. From the outset, they did; it was the Upland Goose Hotel. And like General Moore, nothing was going to stop them reaching their objective.

The Argentinian troops sat around the bar of the hotel, in which Unit 601 was billeted anyway, cradling sub-machine guns and looking anything but hospitable towards the newcomers. Their mood was not enhanced by the relentless one-line remark addressed to each of them in turn by *Daily Express* photographer Tom Smith, who insisted on pointing at them at close range, saying, 'You lost. We won.'

At last one of the Argentinian officers spoke, in very good English, to the journalists, now half-stunned by free lager given to them by the landlord, Des King. The officer said, 'Gentlemen, you do realize, I hope, that you are in our sector and that the surrender has not been signed. If it is not signed, you will be our prisoners.'

'Better have another lager, then,' said Ian Bruce, phi-losophically.

'And,' the officer added, 'British troops are not going to be allowed to stay in Stanley if that document is not signed.'

David Norris, of the *Daily Mail*, almost choked on his beer. 'Look out of the window. They're paratroopers. How the fuck are you going to get rid of them? They won't be happy about moving out. In fact, if anyone suggests it, it'll bring out the hooligan in them.'

The officer shrugged. He was not amused. He looked outside and saw the Paras walking past towards the British sector.

At Government House the signing ceremony had still not taken place. The appalling Minders from the Minis-try of Defence would not allow the Press anywhere near the place, so a waiting world would have to wait a little longer for the official announcement that the war in the Falklands was finally over.

Angry journalists did what angry journalists always do in times of great hardship: they went back to the pub.

For troops and journalists alike, the dream was one of eating wholesome food and enjoying a hot bath. It never happened. The water supply had been cut off by a British shell and everyone in the town had to go without washing for quite a few more days yet.

Outside one of the official residences at the west end of Ross Road, Paras were looking disconsolate. They were in Stanley, but not all of it, and they still felt slightly frustrated.

'Oh, go on, Sarge,' said one. 'Why can't we go in and finish the bastards off?'

'You, my son,' replied the sergeant, 'will never make it as a diplomat. Now pipe down and do as you're told.'

'All the way through this I've doubted your total commitment,' said the Para, smiling. 'We only want to be allowed to kill a few more.'

They were joking. By now, everyone in the Falklands had had enough of killing. Even the Paras were glad it was over.

In the Upland Goose, an Argentinian military padre was talking to a group of journalists, trying to explain how he, as a priest, reconciled the fact that both sides believed in the same God, and were none-the-less involved in killing each other.

He said, 'You just have to believe that your side is right. Anyway, my job involved more than that. I had to talk to our young men, keep their spirits up. Tell them not to worry.'

How did he do that?

'Well,' said the padre, 'I told them in the beginning that they were going to the border with Chile. It was best at that time not to tell them they were going to the Malvinas. Eventually, of course, they were told. Then I told them that the British would never land here. They wanted to believe it and I think they did. They were also told that many of your ships had been sunk and when your troops landed, they were trapped on the beaches. Now they know differently. I do not think it is telling lies. I think of it as reassuring young men who are frightened. The longer they thought they had nothing to worry about, the longer their spirits would keep up.'

One reporter joked, 'Not like our padres at all. One of them told us we were all doomed.'

The Roman Catholic Church's representative in the Argentinian Army was not best pleased. He left behind him several reams of paper which had been his service sheets, and a meticulous line-drawing of 'The Virgin of the Rosary and the Malvinas' which became the property of one of the newsmen.

His service sheets for the troops certainly were of a propaganda nature. Every few lines included the words, 'Pro Patria!' which left the British padres, soon to arrive in the Upland Goose, with the distinct impression that their Argentinian counterparts were more interested in nationalistic fervour than the spiritual well-being of their charges.

By now, more Royal Marines were getting close to Stanley, and were furious that the orders which kept them out of the town allowed the Paras in.

45 Commando were billeted on Sapper Hill with the Guards, while 42 Commando's new home was to be the former barracks of Naval Party 8901, even further away from the pubs.

'Price you have to pay for being late, mate,' said one Para to a Marine trying to get through a Para roadblock on the edge of the town.

'Don't blame me,' replied the Marine, 'we've been through hell, more than you have. We are faced with the most dangerous thing in the world.'

'What's that?' asked the Para.

'An officer with a map,' said the Marine, glumly.

'Never mind,' said the Para. 'Keep in with us, and we might be able to get you a drink sometime later in the week.'

'Bollocks,' said the disconsolate Marine as he set off back towards Moody Brook.

Major Mike Norman, and many of his men who had fought two and a half months earlier to try vainly to beat off the Argentinian invasion, were now back in their old barracks.

'The place is wrecked,' said Norman, who had billeted his Juliet Company in the shell-shattered building. 'I would have hoped that having come so far my men could have been given a better place to sleep. One of my officers woke up a little after he'd got his head down because he felt something dripping on him. There was a dead Argie in the rafters still leaking blood.'

By now the light tanks of the Blues and Royals had made it into Stanley, with a vast regimental flag draped over the front of one of their vehicles. The Paras looked disbelievingly at the tanks. By rights, they should have been miles behind.

'How fast do those things go?' asked one of the Paras of one of the frightfully aristocratic young officers atop the tank. There was a pause, as the young lieutenant looked skywards as though for inspiration.

'About as fast as the Quorn Hunt on a good scentin' day,' he said in delightfully un-military manner, and in a way that the Para who knew nothing about foxhunting could scarcely comprehend.

'How fast is that?' he enquired, not wishing to annoy the young lieutenant by making fun of his accent. 'About twenty miles an hour?'

'Sines abite right,' said the lieutenant. 'Hi fast do your hinds go?'

The Para looked bemused, and waved the Scorpion through. Paras, as a general rule, do not have hounds, even when known as hinds.

At Ajax Bay, the Medical Squadron were given no let-up by the cessation in hostilities.

Surgeon-commander Rick Jolly strode into the dressing station and said, 'Everyone stand still where you are. I have some news. There are white flags flying over Stanley. It looks as though it's all over.'

Doctors and medical staff at that moment were standing over seriously injured troops, their faces masked, and their surgical instruments in their hands. As one they shouted 'Hooray' and although their faces could not be seen, their eyes creased in smiles. The celebration, said Rick Jolly, lasted no more than three seconds, before the surgical teams went back to their work.

'Even the patients seemed cheered,' he said. 'A whole new and happier mood took over.'

Jolly remembers how the never-ending work of the Medical Squadron had been going on with Argentinian bombs still in the roof of the Ajax Bay hospital.

'General Moore came to see us,' he said, 'and took a look round the place. I must admit it wasn't the way they would have planned a hospital, but it was the best we could do under the circumstances. The general took a look, and with one of his typically incisive remarks, simply said, "This isn't the way I had planned it." He was right, of course, but he laughed like a drain when he saw what we were doing with what was available. It really was just like M*A*S*H.'

The nervousness of the medical staff about the unexploded bombs had been eased by bomb disposal expert Lieutenant 'Bernie' Bruen, who had turned up at Ajax Bay with his violin after defusing the bombs in *Sir Lancelot*.

'He placed sandbags around the device,' said Jolly, 'and saw that we were still not terribly happy. So, and this is typical of the man, he insisted on sleeping on the other side of the sandbags, between the bombs and the protection. The man was amazing.'

Jolly also still tells the story of how Lt Bruen played his violin at a church service at the hospital. 'And then when we were on our own, with the patients having been transferred to the *Uganda*, he put on this superb cabaret for us. It was a great night.'

All the while, Jolly's medical staff were surpassing themselves.

'Doctors had to become surgeons,' he said. 'Nurses

263

became doctors, and orderlies became nurses. Everyone did a fantastic job. I remember at the height of it all, a medic came up to me and said, "OK, boss, that's the practice completed. When do we get on to the theory?" It really was like that.'

Jolly realized that with his men working so hard to save lives, a few old naval traditions could be reintroduced, including the late-lamented 'tot'.

'I remembered from Regulations that "commercial spirit" could be ordered in time of great stress and hardship,' he said. 'So rather than offer Valium, I managed to get some whisky and rum from the *Uganda* for the 120 men in the Ajax Bay Hospital.

'I issued the tot twelve times, and when it was over left a blank cheque on *Uganda* to settle up. It came to £340, which was a bit staggering. But I was able to restore my faith in human nature when the MOD coughed up and reimbursed me later on. If any people in the war deserved a tot it was those lads in the hospital. They worked wonders.'

One of Jolly's lasting memories was of just before the surrender was signed, when some Argentinian Skyhawks flew low over the hospital, in which, as usual, the medical staff were busily engaged in saving lives.

'We had to dive for cover,' he said, 'and one medic said to me, "It's a bloody good job they haven't got their wheels down, or they'd have landed on top of us." They certainly were extremely low, but there was no way we could leave the patients.'

One of the sadder arrivals at the hospital was a Para. 'He had carried his oppo under fire across a minefield,' said Jolly. 'He took him to the RAP, but when he got there found out he was dead. The Para was a bit shocked, and came to us for treatment for that shock. It really does take it out of a man when he thinks he's saving someone's life and finds that no matter how hard he's tried, the man has died on him. But after a while the young lad was OK, and he was redeployed as a prisoner-of-war guard on *Norland*.'

But at the end Jolly finally had one job he was proud and happy to do. Sitting in the shell of his 'hospital' he was writing citations for his men when one of them came up to him.

'Here, sir,' said the young orderly, 'I understand we're all getting the MBE.'

'The MBE?' said Jolly. 'Forget that, mate. There won't be that many to go around.'

'No, sir,' said the orderly. 'The MBE – Mind Boggling Experience!'

'You're not getting that,' said Jolly. 'You've just had it.'

As Jolly spoke, he and his men were as far away from the British troops in Stanley as the men who had landed on 21 May had been from their ultimate objective 23 days before.

In Stanley, an historic document dated 14 June 1982 and timed at 23.59 hrs GMT had just been signed by Major-general Jeremy Moore and Major-general Mario Menendez. Both men saluted each other and shook hands, and the surrender of the invading Argentinian forces on the Falklands was sealed.

In fact the document was signed at 02.00 hrs GMT on 15 June and was followed by a message General Moore sent to the warlords in London which read, 'In Port Stanley at 9 pm Falklands time, tonight the 14 June, Major-general Menendez surrendered to me all Argentine armed forces in East and West Falklands together with their impedimenta. Arrangements are in hand to assemble the men for return to Argentina, to gather their arms and equipment, and to mark and make safe all their ammunitions. The Falkland Islands are once more under the Government desired by their inhabitants. God Save the Queen.'

Chapter 17

15 June dawned to reveal a typical Port Stanley day in one respect. It was the usual Falklands mixture of rain, snow and driving wind, calculated to make everyone feel miserable. Today, though, was different.

The Argentinians moved out of the Upland Goose Hotel, now once again under the control of the British – so long as they could afford Des King's rates. The population of the little town still found it impossible to show any enthusiasm for their liberation, but the British troops wanted to unwind a bit before going home.

The defeated army were to muster near the airfield, where 42 Commando were in charge of relieving them of their weapons.

Major Mike Norman's Juliet Company were given this task, but first Norman had to fulfil his promise. The flag that had been stolen from Government House by the Marines before the Argentinian invasion was dutifully put back.

'We said we'd put it back, and now we have,' said Norman with a smile. 'Now our job's done.' And he went off towards the airport to gather up the Argentinian weapons.

There, ahead of him, the incredibly scruffy-looking Lieutenant Tony Hornby had already struck up a friendship with an Argentinian officer who was helping make the laying down of arms go smoothly.

'Smashing bloke, this,' said Hornby. 'Give him a kiss and he'll do anything.'

Lines of disconsolate Argentinians dumped their arms and moved out towards the airfield. Hornby politely but firmly hurried them on their way.

'I'm doing this because I can speak Spic,' he said with a smile. 'Not very well, got most of it from Fawlty Towers. But it beats digging holes.'

The piles of FN rifles, pistols, bayonets, grenades and long knives grew by the minute. Major Norman arrived to find British troops looking for souvenirs. They were picking through the hoard looking for their favourite trophies.

'When you've finished fucking looting,' screamed Norman, above the howl of the wind, 'can we get on with disarming these men? I want to get this over with as fast as possible.'

Wretched columns of now unarmed soldiers, draped in blankets, filed towards their holding positions, waiting for the ships that would take them home, a welcome but ignominious return to Argentina.

Argentinian officers, under the terms of the surrender, were allowed to keep their pistols until they were put on the ships, as it was accepted by all sides that they were likely to be attacked by their own men.

'Can't blame the Spics, really,' said a Marine at the arms dump. 'If our officers had let us down as badly as theirs, we'd be queuing up to shoot them.'

'Wouldn't waste the bullets myself,' said his mate with a smile, making sure Major Norman was just out of earshot.

At the airport, lines of freezing Argentinians huddled together against the biting wind.

'Serves the fuckers right,' said a Marine without any compassion. 'If the cunts hadn't sunk the *Atlantic Conveyor* they'd have lots of nice little tents to live in.'

It was true. Apart from the Chinooks and other vital equipment, *Atlantic Conveyor* had been carrying the prisoner-of-war tents, embarked in a moment of optimistic foresight by the British. Now the beaten Argentinians had to fare as best they could.

A Mercedes four-wheel drive 'jeep', driven by an Argentinian officer, with another sitting next to him, was flagged down at the check-point by Major Norman. He looked angry that the enemy were enjoying motorized luxury while he and his men were still on foot.

'Stop and pull over,' he commanded. Then he smiled and looked exasperated. In the back of the vehicle were Hands and the ITN crew, returning with the first pictures of the airfield.

'I don't believe it,' said Norman, grinning. 'Go on, piss off.'

Norman and his band of Marines had every right to be a little testy. Theirs was a thankless job in driving snow, a job which kept them out in the open after three weeks of living at the mercy of the Falklands winter.

But if it was bad for them, the 6,200 Argentinian prisoners shepherded into a makeshift POW camp at the airport were faring even worse. General Moore was concerned for the welfare of his prisoners, not just those at Stanley, but another 1,800 on West Falkland.

He was keen to send them home and the *Canberra* and *Norland* were even then being made ready for this task. But General Galtieri, who had just faced an angry crowd in Buenos Aires which had indicated to him that it was not over the moon about the feat of their troops, refused to allow the ships into any Argentinian port.

'Great, isn't it?' said a Marine. 'Our lot seem far more interested in getting the Spics home than us.'

The Paras, too, were itching to go home. Sergeant-major Sammy Dougherty, of 3 Para, clung to a vague impression that the Geneva Convention dictated that victorious troops must be withdrawn from the battle area within 48 hours of victory.

'If that's true,' said one of his officers, 'then we are doing what everyone seems to have been doing over here: we're bending the rules, because it doesn't look as though we're going anywhere for a while yet.'

The sullen attitude of the Paras was quickly noticed by the Marines, who were delighted that the waiting was taking the edge off the barbed sense of humour of their fêted colleagues in red berets.

'Nice to see them looking pissed off too,' said one. 'Cocky buggers have had it all their own way so far. I s'pose you might say that each and every one of them is looking as sick as a Para.'

They were not the only ones. The locals were not that happy with life either. Their elation at being liberated had not only been scarcely noticeable; it was also short-lived.

The first thing they did to show their appreciation to the gallant British troops was ban all of them from the local drinking holes.

Each bar sported a hand-written sign which proclaimed, 'Magistrates' order. From today, all bars are closed.' In fact, those people, largely the Press, who were staying in the Upland Goose were allowed into the bar there as residents, and the traffic in illicit alcohol to the Toms and Marines they had befriended continued apace.

One landlord, full of that truth serum called Scotch, broke down in an emotional fit of honesty a little later and confessed, 'It's not really an official ban. We all got together and decided to keep them out. We were worried they would wreck our pubs.'

Had the Toms known that, there would have been no cause to worry. They *would* have wrecked their pubs.

But the military commanders had no alternative but to honour the ban. Military policemen were posted close to each of the town's bars, and a dusk-to-dawn curfew was placed on the troops.

'Fucking savage, that,' said 3 Para Sergeant John Ross, handing his mate a can of Tennents. 'Just makes it all the more of a challenge to get the stuff. Cheers.'

Stanley was like a powder keg now. The locals, not overflowing with the milk of human kindness towards the British troops, were even more anxious for a spot of revenge against the Argentinian prisoners.

Because of the accommodation headache with the POWs, it had been decided to embark hundreds of them aboard *Canberra* and *Norland*, in readiness for the hoped-for go-ahead from Galtieri to accept his defeated army back home.

So at night long columns of prisoners were marched down from the airport to the public jetty to be ferried out to the two ships.

While they waited in the cold, their numbers tailed back along Philomel Street, past a line of their own Panhard armoured cars, and the Globe Hotel. No-one could have known it in advance, but this was a trifle undiplomatic, to say the least.

What those in authority had apparently forgotten was that the men of the Falkland Islands have two major pastimes – if you overlook work, as they often do – fornication and drinking heavily. There being no television station, no discos, no bowling alleys and no drive-in movies, the former is understandable, if you accept that to enter any one of the women into the Miss World contest is about as worthwhile as sitting around waiting for a penguin to fly.

'I wouldn't say they're ugly,' said 42 Commando's Tony Hornby, 'but this has to be the world centre of double-baggers.'

A 'double-bagger', in Marines' parlance, refers to the amount of visual protection needed before coming into physical contact with a member of the opposite sex. 'A single-bagger,' explained Hornby, 'is so ugly that you have to insist she wears a paper bag over her head before going anywhere near her. A double-bagger is so unspeakably disgraceful that you have to wear a paper bag as well in case hers falls off.'

So, it is not altogether surprising that men of the Falklands drink. On one particular night after the liberation, they had been doing just that. Almost all night.

And so it came to pass that when they were eventually persuaded to go home, the first thing they saw outside the Globe Hotel, was a column of people for whom they did not have any great affection.

The locals, their brains on auto-pilot, began to jeer at and be generally insulting to the POWs. Something had to give, and it did.

While MPs looked on helplessly, fist fights broke out and the odd skull was cracked. Then it spread like wildfire.

Up and down Philomel Street, the noise of battle had returned. The handbrakes were released on the Panhards, and they went careering downhill towards the jetty, hitting walls and houses as they went.

'Fucking arseholes,' screamed an MP. 'Get us some support here before they wreck the town.'

In minutes, the Globe Stores was ablaze. Once it had been the town's largest provisions stores. Now it was crammed with Argentinian supplies.

Help for the MPs arrived in the form of a delighted group of beaming Paras for whom the chance of a good punch-up is never to be missed. Their job was to restore order, to stop the fire-raising, the fighting and the looting in the immediate area. They succeeded in double-quick time and, amazingly, without inflicting fatalities. At the height of the riot, an RMP sergeant with a Sterling sub-machine gun bellowed into the ear of an Argentinian officer, 'Tell your men to pack it in, or I'll blow your fucking head off.'

The officer complied instantly.

The fires, however, had spread to neighbouring streets. Dawn broke to the crackling of gunfire, and many drowsy residents feared that the war had started again. In fact, piles of discarded ammunition were ablaze.

As the morning wore on, and the snow turned to

271

rain, downtown Stanley looked worse than it had at any time during the campaign, and prisoners waiting to go to the ships were ordered to clean the streets of debris.

Through the night, a handful of homes were looted. Some residents said the Argentinians had done it. Others were convinced it was the British. Mrs Lillian Stacey, a frail 86-year-old, was trembling inside her little house, trying to get her little stove alight to make a cup of tea. Outside, in Fitzroy Road, fires still smouldered. Fences were broken. Sometimes sobbing, she said, 'Some men were in here in the night. They broke the window to get in and I heard them wandering about. They ransacked my house. Two clocks that I treasured have been taken and some binoculars and some food. I've been broken into three times now in three months. I didn't have anything that was worth much, not to them. It was just worth so much to me, and it's gone.'

If the British were involved, it has never been established. But in one later incident, they were. Some Marines clearing up the Governor's house had decided to help themselves to a few valuables, when an officer caught them. 'Just put them back and we'll forget it,' suggested the officer, and they did.

But beyond a shadow of any doubt, the Argentinians were responsible for wholesale looting and vandalism while they occupied Stanley. In the Junior School, troops who had been sent children's comics, in Spanish, to read while away from home, had defecated throughout the classrooms and cloakrooms, beneath little paintings of cars and animals, and compositions entitled 'My holiday' and 'My Dad's job'.

Part-time fireman Joe King helped Paras clean the school, pointing out that almost every desk was crammed with fragmentation and white phosphorus grenades, rifle rounds and mortar shells. Outside in the playground near the teachers' common-room window was an anti-aircraft gun, its ammo live, and on the roof was a large red cross.

'This was an arsenal,' said King. 'You couldn't bring your kids here. Apart from that, the Argies made it compulsory for them to learn Spanish, so all the kids stayed away. They've had a long holiday. Now it'll take months to clean up.'

A Para popped up from beneath the floorboards in one classroom. 'Leg it,' he suggested. 'They've got everything down here: bombs, anti-tank rounds, grenades, the lot. Got to get the engineers down here. Could all go up if some cunt tosses a fag in without thinking.'

Almost everyone nosing around the school at the time was smoking.

In Government House, General Moore was giving the casualty figures for his men during the final battle between 12 and 25 June. 33 men had been killed and 140 injured. Then he said, 'My young men fought like lions. I am enormously proud of them. Let anyone complain about the youth at home and I would say, by golly, you should have seen them here.'

If he was impressed by his valiant men, whose average age was a mere 19 years, there were some that were not.

In the Upland Goose, now a hotbed of hard drinking, stealthy journalists still running black-market booze to rank-and-file troops not allowed in, the tension was mounting.

Some officers had been invited in by the £20-a-bed, three-beds-to-a-room, journalistic guests, and it was clear that this was not a popular move. Des King, the landlord, had been drinking for some hours, and had been scowling from his bunker behind the bar. Now it was time to open fire. His face red with rage, he launched a salvo at point-blank range against the chiefs of 2 Para, Lieutenant-colonel David Chaundler and his number two, Major Chris Keeble.

'First the fucking Argies,' he stormed, 'now you lot. When are you going to clear off and leave us in peace?'

When one of the officers, not unnaturally, was on the point of demonstrating just how paratroopers clear enemy trenches, he was dissuaded by a group of sympathetic bystanders, one of whom defused the situation with the cry, 'Forget it, he's not worth it.'

The moment passed, but word got around. Some Paras wanted to level the hotel. Some Marines wanted to help them. Others decided that guile was the finest weapon in this new campaign.

'Was here a week before the Argies jacked,' said a Marine guest to one of the locals in the bar. 'Sniffing around, picking up info, having a drink, getting the lie of the land for our boys to come in and finish it.'

'You mean,' said a very impressed Islander, 'that you sneaked in under the noses of the Argies? In here? Into Stanley?'

'Get us a drink,' said the Marine. 'You'd be surprised at what's going on when no-one's aware of it.'

The Islanders returned with two cans of beer, eager to learn more.

The Marine took a hefty swig, and continued, 'Been in several times. Was drinking in the Globe one night. Full of Argies it was. Very dicey.'

'You were in there?' said the islander, wide-eyed. 'In the pub with the Argies?'

'Any chance of another beer, mate?' said the Marine. 'Left me money in me bergan.'

Back came the Islander with two more beers.

' 'Course,' added the Marine, and he was probably biting his tongue when he said it, 'had to banjo a couple one night. Got into a row outside about whose round it was and my not speaking Spanish and all, well I thought they were being rude, so I topped them.'

'Christ,' said the Islander, begging for more. 'Then what happened?'

The Marine slung down the rest of his beer. 'Well,

274

couldn't leave them lying around, could I? So I tipped them into the harbour, just under the jetty down there, and buggered off a bit sharpish.'

'How did you manage to get into the town?' asked the Islander, almost on his knees now.

'Er, couldn't touch you for another beer?' said the Marine. 'Or better, make it a couple. Keeps breaking up my train of thought, you wandering off to the bar and all.'

Back came the Islander, this time with four cans of beer.

'How did I get in, you ask?' said the Marine. 'Well, not allowed to go into all that. Classified. But I'm glad it's all done now. Gave me a chance to get my hair cut.'

Realization dawned on the islander. 'Christ. I know. Yeah, long hair.' Then, conspiratorially, he whispered to the Marine, 'SAS?'

The Marine sucked breath. 'Shit, leave it out, mate. Say no more. Let's have another drink and change the subject.'

The Islander bought the Marine quite a few more that night. After an hour or so the Marine, well refreshed, ambled out into the night and wandered back to the warehouse where he and the rest of the Commando Logistics Regiment were billeted.

Still inside the Upland Goose, civil war was on the verge of breaking out amongst the journalists. The hacks should have been in the best of spirits. After living through the war, they could surely relax now, safe in the knowledge that their stories on the fall of Stanley were safely in London. It was not the case.

Messages were now being received from inconsolable Fleet Street offices that only one story on the surrender and liberation had arrived.

'Whose?' chorused the irate newsmen, already fearing they knew the answer.

Martin Helm, the chief Minder, at last went to a

front-line position, his immaculate camouflage clothing showing no sign of the mud and filth of combat conditions. He hesitantly confirmed the awful truth.

'Well,' he simpered, 'Max Hastings was the first one with the story.'

'Bollocks,' replied the hacks. 'We all sent our stories with him! He swore blind that he would take our stories as well as his own to the Marisat [satellite telephone] ships. There's no bloody exclusive here. We were all here at about the same time.'

Helm, stumbling, said, 'Well, Max did take the trouble to come back with it, and he was saying that he had an exclusive.'

'Crap!' the chorus replied. 'What exclusive? The *Daily Mail* was here first with 2 Para, and their copy hasn't been sent either.

'What the fuck happened to Dave Norris's story? What the fuck happened to ours? Hastings promised in front of the brigadier that he would take it all back to you people and make sure it was sent.'

Faltering under fire, Helm repeated himself by saying, 'Max did take the trouble to come back to the ships to file his story.'

In turn the pressmen challenged, 'Only because there was only one helicopter seat available, and only one man could go. We could have turned it into a riot, but we trusted him and you to get our stories home.'

Then Helm introduced an argument. He said, 'There was a 24-hour news blackout ordered by CinC Fleet and there was nothing we could do.'

In fact it transpired that Mr Helm and his cohorts had misread a signal from London. There had been no blackout on straightforward reports from the Press that Port Stanley had fallen and the war in the Falklands was effectively over. It was another Ministry of Defence Minders' bungle, the kind which had haunted every journalist with the Task Force during the campaign.

What angered the newsmen most was not that their

copy had not been sent. That was serious enough, but was overshadowed by the revelation from officers in *Fearless* who had come ashore at Stanley and who said how much they had enjoyed reading their stories in the wardroom. They said the reporters' copy had been passed around at breakfast, obviously not having been sent to London first.

The mechanics of sending stories to London were that they had to be censored in *Fearless* and then passed to any available ship with the Marisat satellite terminal on board. *Fearless* did not possess one, but many of the requisitioned merchant ships in San Carlos Water did.

Journalists now suspected that Hastings had ratted on his promise to ensure that all correspondents' stories were sent to London.

Hastings, in his own defence, said that his was the only story to get away before the blackout was imposed. He said he had taken it to the Marisat ship himself, having left the others' copy on *Fearless* with the censors. 'At that point it was out of my hands,' he maintained. 'I'm not as treacherous as you seem to think.'

More than one of those on the spot found this hard to believe however, and one was determined to take revenge.

Ian Bruce of the *Glasgow Herald* took up one of the many 'trophy' bayonets lying around the bar of the Upland Goose and set off in search of Hastings. It was a short hunt. The man from the London *Standard* was sitting in a back parlour of the hotel when Bruce found him. Other journalists alerted by loud screaming and threatening remarks in a Scottish accent headed for the action.

They found Bruce, shoulders arched, apparently ready to plunge the blade into the chest of the ashen-faced Hastings.

Bruce's colleagues dragged him off with shouts of 'He's not worth it,' and Bruce returned to the bar while other newsmen lambasted Hastings, saying that they agreed with Bruce's sentiments if not his tactics.

It was not just sour grapes. The journalists were not the only losers, simply because their stories were not sent, and just one was. A waiting audience of more than 50 million in Britain were aching for on-the-spot accounts of a major British victory. They only got one on the day that mattered. It was hard, in the circumstances, to believe that this was all coincidence.

But there were weightier matters at hand. The troops were still banned from the bars, and as a Victory 'V' formation of helicopters flew over Stanley trailing Union Flags, a tightly-knit group of tenacious Marines had planned a new offensive.

Their objective was the Globe Hotel, already the scene of some post-surrender hostilities. A full frontal assault on the stocks of alcohol was out of the question. There were too many military policemen in the area. Losses would be too high in the attack, so if there were to be casualties in this particular mission of liberation, they would have to be acceptably low.

A political solution was sought. A sergeant of the Commando Logistics Regiment, employing inimitable logic, suggested that the ravages of war had taken their toll and that the hotel 'couldn't 'arf do with a lick of paint'.

Sergeant Sandy MacLeod put it to the landlord that, 'My lads could do you a favour here.'

The landlord readily agreed.

In a matter of a day and a half the hotel inside and out was transformed from a rundown dockside bar to the 'in' place in town. And, of course, the objective was achieved. The landlord paid in kind during and after the act of unmistakable community service. The booze barrier had been broken.

'Mind you,' said MacLeod mischievously, 'we've left our mark. It's not called just the Globe anymore.'

And he was right. The Globe now sported a laurel wreath surrounding a globe, the badge of the Royal Marines. It is now called The Globe and Laurel in grateful recognition.

Major Ewen Southby-Tailyour, his work done, now had another mission. It had long been his ambition to seek out the truth behind a rumour of an Elizabethan galleon that had been wrecked off a remote island to the north west of West Falkland.

Falkland folklore is not the most reliable of sources, but this particular story had fascinated the amiable major during his sojourn in the islands before the invasion. He was determined to get to the bottom of it.

With a helicopter pilot agreeing to aid the search, he set off, and did indeed return with evidence of a shipwreck. It was in fact dated as being eighteenth century, but nonetheless substantiated the rumour. Parts of the 'find' are now in the National Maritime Museum in Greenwich.

But the gods of the military do not smile on helicopters being requisitioned for such purposes, and from their lofty perch they decreed that Major Southby-Tailyour must suffer for such frivolous misuse of military equipment.

The ingenious treasure hunter came into land at Stanley Racecourse in a Wessex, where some inconsiderate litterbug had left a large polythene bag unfettered. As the helicopter came into land, the sheet of plastic was drawn up by the draught, and sucked into the tail rotor-blades.

The Wessex immediately went out of control, and bounced about like a kangaroo that had been stung by a wasp in a sensitive place.

It bounced, it lurched, and inevitably it crashed. The helicopter was severely damaged, but Major Southby-Tailyour and everyone else on board clambered out, white faced and shattered.

A group of Paras, waiting sombrely to fly out to Goose Green for a memorial service, watched in awe.

'Serves them right,' said one of the Paras. 'It's about time the Bootnecks learned that only Paras can fly.'

Rumours were now rife that Mrs Thatcher and the Governor, Rex Hunt, who was soon to be downgraded to Civil Commissioner, were due to fly in any time. No-one really believed that Mrs Thatcher would come, but it was obvious that Mr Hunt would return at the first possible opportunity.

Wary townsfolk, already well accustomed to the social graces lacking in some of the Marines and Paras, enquired in a resigned manner of a Marine guarding the secretariat, 'When's the Governor coming back, or should I go and fuck myself?'

The Marine smiled, and having had his obvious answer denied to him, gave the true one.

'Two days from now,' he said. '*Now* you can go and fuck yourself.'

Visitors were now arriving in the town on a regular basis from the ships in the Task Force. Smart naval officers and ship-borne personnel were landing at the jetty by the Falkland Island Company's store, anxious to see what all the fighting had been for. They were not impressed.

'I say,' said a Dartmouth accent. 'Where are we, old chap? I mean this is obviously the caravan park, so where's the town?'

His misgivings were confirmed by one of the first sights to greet him: that of a mangy brown horse which had grazed in Ross Road uninterrupted and untethered throughout the conflict.

By now homesickness was becoming epidemic among the combat troops. The Paras and Marines had learned that the SAS and SBS were to be given priority, because, as one Marine put it, 'Old Maggie wants her bodyguards back.'

They had little to do but wait for the order that would mean they would head north for leave and the remnants of the British summer.

'Can't be soon enough for me,' said 3 Para Sergeant Tony Dunn. 'This is a fucking one-horse town anyway.'

'No it fucking isn't,' said fellow Sergeant Chris Phelan. 'Some cunt hit Dobbin with a jeep last night and he's lying with his legs up beside the secretariat. It is an ex-horse.'

And sadly, Sergeant Phelan was right. The late-lamented horse was seen that day being carried in state in the bucket-scoop of an army bulldozer with its legs protruding out in front.

A party of Marines outside the cathedral watched it go by.

'Poor old nag,' said one. 'He was the only one to give us a real welcome.'

'Don't always assume that things are as they appear,' said his mate. 'I'll bet you it's made of wood, and that's the SAS inside it on their way out on *Canberra* with the prisoners to do something evil in Buenos Aires.'

'What the hell will the Argies want with a dead horse?' asked the first Marine.

'The Trojans fell for it, and they were a bunch of dagoes, weren't they?' said his friend with a smile.

Stanley was now graced by a Royal presence, in the shape of Sub-lieutenant His Royal Highness the Prince Andrew. The Royal Family are renowned for their love of guns, and Andrew is no exception. In his camouflage wind-proof he was seen walking through the town with a captured Argentinian Para's folding-stock FN rifle under his arm, as though on his way to a grouse shoot.

He was in fact on his way to the RFA *Sir Bedivere*, which, with its Marisat telephone on board, was a popular spot for all servicemen with enough cash in their pockets to make a call home.

In the radio room of *Sir Bedivere*, Andrew waited while a pressman finished a call to his office in London.

'Would it be OK if I used a credit card?' he asked pleasantly.

'I can't see that you'll need it,' came the reply. 'In your case there's a fair chance they'll accept a reverse charge call.'

Andrew and the others present laughed, and the Prince was able to call London, in a conversation later described by a radio officer as being 'just like any son would talk to his mum after three months in a dodgy place.'

Andrew was later interviewed about his part in the campaign, which had been as a co-pilot in a Sea-King operating from HMS *Invincible*. Referring to Stanley, the Prince said, 'Not a bad place to come for a honeymoon.'

A passing Para heard the remark, and when safely out of earshot simply remarked to his mate, 'He must be fucking mad.'

At last the word came that the fighting troops would soon be on their way back home, but not as they had arrived.

The Marines would have *Canberra* all to themselves, as it was felt that with the Paras still blaming the Bootnecks for being slow in crossing East Falkland, there might be a few extra battles fought on the way home. So 2 and 3 Para would fly home, while 40 Commando, 42 and 45 were to go home on the Great White Whale.

After being the first to land back on the Falklands, the disgruntled 40 Commando had had only one other highlight during the campaign: the acceptance of the surrender of the Argentinian forces on West Falkland.

The news of impending travel home brought out the best spirits of all the men. In their billets, Marines felt moved to burst into song, in their usual irreverent way. They sang, what at first seemed a surprising choice, a well-loved Easter hymn:

> There is a Green Hill far away
> Without a city wall.
> Where the dear Lord was Crucified,
> He died to save us all . . .

Two, Three,

> For he's a jolly good fellow
> For he's a jolly good fellow,
> For he's a jolly good fellow
> And so say all of us.

And in Britain the long-awaited birth of a child to the Prince and Princess of Wales had been announced to swell the joy of the British public.

The *Daily Express* in London, anxious for a reaction to the news of the birth from the newly liberated islanders, fired off a telex message to their men on the spot.

The message was handed to photographer Tom Smith who looked at the faces of his colleagues in the bar of the Upland Goose and composed a reply.

It read, 'Everyone here pleased it's white.'

Perhaps fortunately, the reply, inspired by many weeks of contact with the Parachute Regiment's sense of humour, was never sent.

The news among the troops was met with the usual wisecracks. The best and most typical came from the Marines: 'Good on 'em. Let's hope they've got a sense of occasion and call the little lad Stanley.'

Chapter 18

Beyond the shores of the Falkland Islands, one man was not in a singing mood: General Galtieri, president of Argentina, had been ousted by other strong men in his military regime. Just before he was kicked out of office, Galtieri promised the British safe passage for the *Canberra* and *Norland* to carry the bulk of his vanquished army back home.

It was to be no hero's return for the beaten soldiers. Indeed, they were destined for the lonely port of Puerto Madryn in Patagonia. When they arrived the ships had the disconcerting experience of being chaperoned into port by two ships of the Argentinian navy that until then had not dared to leave port.

'It was weird,' said *Canberra*'s deputy captain, Mike Bradford. 'We all knew that the warships were just putting on a bit of a show and would not attack us. But at the time we kept a wary eye on them. Technically, we were still at war.'

On the quayside there was no rapturous welcome from tearful relatives or senior officers glad to have their army back. The crew of *Canberra* watched pityingly as the 4104 POWs ambled down the brow and were loaded into trucks on their way to obscurity in the eyes of the Argentinian public.

Canberra's adjutant, Major Bob Ward, became the only British soldier openly to set foot on Argentinian soil during the whole campaign. He stood on the dockside by the brow ushering off the prisoners.

'I couldn't resist it,' said Ward. 'I just had to be able to say that I'd been to Argentina. But the reception committee didn't like it at all and I was politely invited to get my arse back on board. It was one of those occasions when you don't argue.'

The crew of *Canberra* had made many friends among the prisoners, particularly the wounded ones. But the soldiers were so anxious about what was going to happen to them when they returned, that they all walked straight off the ship, grim-faced. Only one, a man on a stretcher, leaned back and waved goodbye. The whole crew cheered him and waved him good luck.

Another prisoner, as he reached the top of the brow to go ashore, said, 'You British will probably not understand the way it is for us now. If you had lost, you would still have gone home to a welcome for heroes. That is your way. But for us, to lose is unforgivable. We will not be popular in our communities, or in our units.'

Captain Bradford realized only too well that *Canberra* was not altogether welcome. He and the other senior officers still half suspected that the Argentinian navy might have a trick up its sleeve. 'We couldn't wait to get out of it, and back to our friends in Stanley harbour,' he said.

Not all the prisoners were allowed to go home immediately, including many of the officers. At this time, General Menendez was still held in the padre's cabin in *Fearless*, amid rumours that he didn't want to go home at all.

In Stanley, more smiling Argentinian troops were filing onto the jetty on the first leg of their repatriation, aboard their hospital ship, *Bahia Paraiso*.

One of them, an officer named Raphael Enrique Lugo, spoke through a military policeman who spoke Spanish. Still arrogant, he said, 'No matter what the British may feel, we were right to take the Malvinas. They are our islands, not yours. This time, we lost. But had we been better led by our senior officers, we could have beaten you. I would not like you to think that this is an end to it.'

'Got that?' said the MP. 'Man's a cunt, of course.'

The Paras were still enjoying leading little work parties of prisoners around the town. The main task was clearing up the debris and mud which lay everywhere. Sadly, a working knowledge of Spanish is not a prerequisite for service in the Parachute Regiment. So the British soldiers reverted to the old habit of shouting unintelligible instructions in a Spanish accent.

'Oi, hombre,' yelled one sergeant. 'Movo your fucking arso, or you will get my booto up it.'

The message was got across one way or another.

Sergeant-major Cameron March of 42 Commando tried a more subtle approach with his work party.

'Work 'em hard for an hour,' he said. 'Then give 'em a fag and a cup of water and they're as good as gold.'

A certain camaraderie had now built up between victor and vanquished. British troops were swapping some of their combat gear with Argentinian troops, a move that was to cost them when they finally reached home. On hearing of it, Brigadier Thompson said, 'It's always the same. You take them on an exercise with the Americans somewhere in Europe and they come back looking like men in the 82 Airborne Brigade. Wrong windproofs, wrong weapons. Happens all the time.'

'What size booto, amigo?' asked one Para of a smiling prisoner, half his size. 'Footo, how big?'

The Argentinian smiled. He didn't have the faintest idea what the Para was talking about. 'Que?' he shrugged.

'Like Fawlty Towers, innit?' said the Para, to no-one in particular. Then, pointing at his own feet, he added, 'Booto. Swappo.'

The smile drained from the Argentinian's face, and he cowered.

'Ah, fuck, no,' said the Para. 'Prick thinks I'm going to give him a kicking. Only one way out of this.'

The Para unlaced one of his boots and, pointing at the prisoner's feet, said, 'Swappo, OK?'

In a moment, the Para had one of the boots he desired in one hand, and one of his own in the other. Sole to sole, he realized that this was to be a bad deal. 'Fuck, my cat's got bigger feet than him.'

The Argentinian was smiling again, but the Para handed back his boot.

'No goodo,' he said, and walked away looking for bigger game.

The young prisoner, now totally confused, scratched his head and shuffled off in line with other Argentinians towards the jetty.

One Marine had discovered an abandoned pile of something nasty on the road to the airport. Closer inspection revealed that he had stumbled upon four or five Exocet missiles. As the souvenir-hunting game was now in full swing, the Marine thought it would be an ideal opportunity to go home with something different. He asked an engineer standing nearby what the chances were of 'having it away' with one of the missiles.

'No chance, mate,' said the engineer. 'These bastards have all got to be accounted for.'

But the Marine was not to be outdone. He said, 'You show me where it says I can't go home with an Exocet. I know the Customs regulations, and although I might have a bit of trouble sneaking through with a pistol or a grenade, I can assure you there's nothing mentioned about guided missiles.'

'Don't care about that,' said the engineer. 'These things stay where they are, and that's that.'

Daily now, RAF Hercules transports were flying low over Stanley to drop supplies and mail.

One Para was reading a letter by the football field next to Government House, which had been addressed

287

to 'any Para'. When he opened it, he assumed it was just another letter from a girl back home, seeking a pen-pal. But it wasn't. The Para chuckled and read it out. 'Says here it's from a bloke in the Royal Regiment of Wales. They're in Aldershot now. He says, "It's all right for you lot out there, but while you're away, we have had to fight the locals alone." Never mind, mate, help's on the way.'

Other Paras, and Marines, gazed longingly at the Hercules during each sweep they made, looking like anglers staring at a float in a quiet stream, waiting for a fish to bite.

'Why don't the bastards land?' asked a Marine. 'We could go home on those.'

'Fucking crabs, mate,' said a Para. 'Argies landed every night under fire but the crabs don't think it's a safe bet. Daft buggers. They must still believe their own intelligence. I bet they think all those fucking Vulcans hit the runway. Cunts only hit it once in 63 goes.'

Eventually, the RAF did land their Hercules transports, but it made no difference to the Marines and Paras. They were destined to go home by sea, and that was that.

Tragically, while all the combat troops strained at the leash to get back to Britain, the suffering had not ended. The Argentinians had scattered mines indiscriminately across East Falkland, and the job of clearing them soon claimed young engineers, several of whom lost feet at the start of an operation that senior officers predicted would last for many years.

Sergeant Eirwyn Jones of the Welsh Guards lost both his legs when, as he said later, 'A Sidewinder missile got fired by mistake by one of our Harriers at Stanley Airport, after the war was over. You don't like it much when you look down and see you've got no legs.'

But 'going home fever' was sweeping 3 Commando Brigade now, and had infected the journalists attached to it. The game was afoot. First chance of a ride home, and it was every man for himself.

Just such a moment came on a frosty afternoon six days after the fall of Stanley.

'You've got about five minutes to get to the jetty for the boat going out to *Resource*,' said an imperious Ministry of Defence Minder, Roger Goodwin, to a group of newsmen having lunch at the Upland Goose. 'And you must hand in all your kit before you go.'

Very few bothered to do that, treating the man and his order much as one would a five-year-old with a toy gun saying, 'Stick 'em up'. But the scramble was on, and lunch was left uneaten. But the run for home was cut off at the pass, momentarily, by landlord Des King, who barked, 'No-one leaves without paying their bill.' And no-one did.

Resource, a large supply ship lying at anchor just outside the harbour, had been one of the main ammunition carriers during the campaign. Now, to the journalists, she was a beautiful, hulking, grey-painted paradise of good food, hot showers, a Chinese laundry and a pleasant cruise north for sunnier climes.

Or that, at least, was the idea. But as with everything else during the Falklands campaign, nothing went according to plan and the 'get rid of the hacks' manoeuvre by the MOD Minders was doomed to failure.

'For a start, there are no fucking beds for you lot,' said a ship's officer as the pressmen clambered up a rope ladder on to the deck of *Resource*. 'They only told us you were coming five minutes ago, so you'll have to rough it.'

'Roughed it up until now,' said Alastair McQueen, 'so a little longer won't hurt.'

'Don't know why you want to come aboard anyway,' said the officer.

' 'Cos this lovely ship is taking us to Ascension,' said

289

McGowan, 'and from there we can fly home and forget this rat-hole of a place.'

The officer laughed. His moment had come. The unwanted passengers were about to get their come-uppance and he was the lucky man who would give it to them.

'Wrong!' he boomed, delight etching smile lines across his weather-beaten face. 'Fucking got you. We're going to South Georgia. Other fucking way. 'Ware icebergs. Ever been had?'

'Shit,' said one hack.

'It never ends,' said another.

'I'm off,' said Pat Bishop of the *Observer*, and within an hour or so he had fled the *Resource* and was back in Stanley. The remaining journalists decided to stay aboard and consider the situation carefully, using the objectivity they are trained to employ. They went to the bar and got outrageously drunk.

The next morning, the destroyer *Glamorgan* and the frigate *Plymouth* came close by and fired their guns in salute.

'They're going home,' said the same ship's officer, revelling in the unhappiness of his media charges. 'Be home before you lot. Still, look at it this way. Will they be able to say they've seen Antarctica? No. But you will.'

Later, the carrier *Hermes* came close and McQueen, in a vain gesture of defiance, threw his Marine helmet at it.

'Missed,' said the officer of *Resource*.

'Should have thrown it at you,' sneered McQueen, not in a happy mood.

'I've called you up here,' said the captain, in his sea cabin, 'because I feel you gentlemen of the Press have been inconvenienced as much as we have, and I ought to put you in the picture. We are not going to be going to Ascension for quite a while. We still have supplies aboard and other ships want them, so we will be stooging around doing just that.'

'Where exactly are we going now?' said Charles Laurence of the *Sunday Telegraph*.

'Well, we've turned around,' replied the captain. 'We are returning to San Carlos Water.'

'Where we came in,' moaned one journalist. 'And where we're getting off.'

That night, Captain Rod Boswell of the Royal Marines Mountain and Arctic Warfare Cadre said, 'Know how you feel, lads, but my men are staying put. One way or the other, we're off the Falklands and going home. Doesn't matter how long it takes.'

'Ready for a scrap?' Ian Bruce asked McGowan.

'Yeah, why?' said McGowan.

'Cunt over there is giving us shit. I'm going to hit him.' Then, turning to Boswell, he added, 'Rod, could you and your boys see your way to staying out of it?'

'Of course,' said Boswell. 'We'll just sit over here so we can watch.'

'Bottle's gone,' said McGowan to Bruce, as the ship's officer who had angered the redoubtable Scot appeared none too keen on getting a back-hander from him.

'Think I'll thump one anyway,' said Bruce. But the moment had gone, and most of the hacks drifted off in search of the crew's bar.

Having found it, they were amazed that word of the impending battle had already reached the lower deck.

'You get one?' asked a burly crewman. 'Hurt the cunt, did you?'

'Never came to it,' said Bruce.

Easily a dozen of the crew put down their beer mugs and as one chanted, 'Fucking pity.'

There, at least, the hacks found a welcome. It was a long night of risqué jokes and gallons of beer.

The following morning, accurately deducing that the journalists would not be much in the mood for it, a voice over the ship's Tannoy commanded, 'All journalists to the flight deck at the rush. Helicopter standing by for Stanley. Do not, repeat, do not, rush past the purser's office. Pay your mess bills.'

Few bothered.

Minutes later, the hacks, and Rod Boswell, were airborne, heading for Stanley.

Then, a new drama. The big Sea King put down fast in a valley and Boswell whipped out his Browning 9mm pistol.

'Argies,' he shouted, eyes lighting up for the kill.

And in a moment, he was gone.

In another moment, he was back.

'Fuck,' he smiled. 'That was a near thing. Not Argies at all. Bloody SAS.'

With that, a group of cold troopers climbed into the Sea King and within minutes Port Stanley hove into view.

The newsmen were not best pleased to be back where they had started. Worse, they were back at the place that most of them had hoped never to see again.

At the Upland Goose, Hands, who under instruction from his London office had been unable to join in the mass exodus, watched the sorry party arrive. He almost fell about the hall of the hotel laughing.

'I thought we'd got rid of you lot,' he said. 'What's wrong? Homesick already?'

His laughter stopped when he saw the scowls and glowers from his colleagues.

'One more word out of you and I'll split that pretty little face of yours,' said McGowan.

Even sorrier to see the journalists back was Des King, who had hoped Fleet Street's finest had gone for ever.

'I suppose you'll want your rooms back,' he scowled. 'Well, I'm not sure that you can have them. I've got other people in here now.'

'Rooms?' queried Hands. 'You don't really call those things rooms, do you? Any problems, gentlemen, and you can crawl into our grot.'

The journalists all found a place to either lie down on, or to unfurl their sleeping-bags in. Whatever, the price of £20 a night was not open to negotiation.

Express photographer Tom Smith was not happy to see his reporter McGowan back on the premises either.

'Sorry, Ace,' he bumbled. 'I've nicked your boots. Didn't think you'd be needing them any more.'

'I don't,' said McGowan. 'They're yours. There are four things that I won't be sorry if life doesn't push my way again, and army boots are one of them. The other three, if you're interested, are ocean cruises, camping holidays and chicken supreme.'

A Reunion Party that evening in the hotel bar ended, predictably, with several journalists staggering upstairs in a state of some inebriation.

The following night was not a red-letter occasion in the annals of Alcoholics Anonymous. In the bar, some men in camouflage clothing had been imbibing as guests of the press, and were quietly reminiscing through a beer and smoke screen about the preceding events of the campaign. One of the guests, a senior officer in the SAS, had had enough of it all, and had curled up on the floor for a quiet doze. Dave Norris, well tanked up by this stage, and making a spectacular attempt to stagger towards the door, paused for a moment and gazed down on the prostrate body.

'If there's one thing I can't abide,' he hiccupped, 'it's drunks.' And with that he delivered a swift kick into the backside of the sleeping tiger.

Breath was intaken sharply all around the room, and all conversation stopped.

Alastair McQueen suggested, 'Fucking hell, Norris. You'd better leg it.'

But to the stunned witnesses it appeared the advice had come too late. The SAS man, as a testament to his training, sprang to his feet like a coiled spring and was ready for action.

'He didn't mean it,' pleaded McQueen. 'He's drunk.'

'It's OK, boss,' said another SAS man. 'Bloke over-stepped the mark, but he's away now, fully aware that in this life there are things that you don't do even when you're drunk, always supposing that you want this life to continue.'

The now awake and alert SAS officer said, 'Serves me right for kipping in a nest of vipers. Time to go, I think.'

Des King, meanwhile, had been watching horrified from his perch behind the bar, realizing that he had been right all along to discourage the army from entering his premises. But he was wise enough by now to accept that there are times when a landlord should not make too much fuss.

By now most of the Task Force knew that departure was imminent. Even the journalists realized that however hard the MOD Minders tried on their behalf, they would still get out somehow.

But first the troops had the solemnity of remembrance services to attend in Stanley Cathedral, Goose Green and Bluff Cove.

The Welsh Guards at Bluff Cove stood fighting back the tears in the freezing wind as *Sir Galahad* was consecrated as a war grave. The bombed-out hulk of the LSL was later towed out to a point 80 miles off the Falklands and scuttled with the bodies of those who had died in her still aboard.

At a hillside overlooking Goose Green and Darwin, 2 Para gathered to remember their fallen comrades as a last act before sailing for Ascension in *Norland*. A simple cairn had been erected by the locals, with a black iron cross surmounting it.

The men of 2 Para arrived by Chinook helicopters from Stanley, and stood in silence during the short service. Of the population of Goose Green, perhaps two dozen joined them. A lone Gurkha piper played a lament after a bugler had sounded the Last Post. The piper paused during his slow walk across the barren hillside at the spot where Colonel H Jones had fallen.

Some of the Paras openly wept, tears of sorrow in victory.

In Stanley beneath the red spire of Christ Church Cathedral overlooking the harbour, the men of 3 Para attended their own memorial service. On each side of the altar were British flags; the Union Flag to the left, the White Ensign to the right.

In this short but moving ceremony yet more Paras wept for the loss of their mates who had fallen.

There had been another sad occasion in the cathedral, when the three civilian women who had died hours before Stanley had fallen, were remembered by the entire population of the capital and the servicemen who had battled to liberate it.

At the end of the service, three pine coffins were borne from the little cathedral by two civilians, two Marines and two paratroopers in each case. In the congregation sat members of the SAS and the SBS, and when one woman broke down and cried an SAS man put his arm around her shoulder to comfort her.

'This is also the moment,' said Senior Administrator of the Islands' Government, Harold Rowlands, addressing the congregation, 'when we should say that the events leading up to the deaths of these three women were regrettable. But I am sure that none of us would hold the British responsible for them.

'It is also a time for us to remember,' said Mr Rowlands, 'the British dead and wounded, and for us all to express our gratitude to them for liberating us.'

The men of 2 Para returned to *Norland*, the little ship that had brought them to the Falklands. They knew that the ship would discharge them at Ascension Island, and that they would fly home from there.

'Typical,' said one of their number. 'Remember all the fuss they made of the *QE2* when she got back after not having even reached the Falklands? Well, just think of what it will be like when *Canberra* gets back with all the fucking Marines. We'll get fuck all when we get back to Lyneham.'

In fact the Paras were anxious, like everyone else, to get back as soon as possible.

Canberra sailed off with her cargo of Marines soon after *Norland*, and for those who remained there was a feeling of anti-climax.

Rex Hunt, the man who left as Governor, came back as Civil Commissioner. The top brass were waiting for him at the football field when his helicopter touched down. It was a dreadful afternoon, with driving rain, but Mr Hunt might understandably have hoped that his welcome might have included a few more of his former charges to turn out to greet his historic return than the hundred or so who actually did.

He beamed from ear to ear, almost gurgling with delight as he hugged and kissed the residents, who waited impassively for him to walk over and say hello.

'All I want now,' he told Hands, 'is to get back into my home and warm my feet in front of my peat fire.'

Meanwhile the first party of journalists were already back in London. The plane that was to take, amongst others, McGowan, was the one that brought the former Governor back to the Falklands. In their last moments on the islands, a group of them posed by a burnt-out Pucara plane on the edge of the runway. A small party of SAS men booked on the same flight stood back and watched. They were invited to join in the group photograph, but declined.

Alastair McQueen went up to them after the shot had been taken and asked them why they hadn't stood with the journalists for the last picture. McQueen had expected the usual SAS reply about being shy of publicity, but he received another answer.

'Unlike you,' said one of the SAS troopers, 'we're not complete cunts. That Pucara is still booby-trapped.

296

That's why some sensible chap went to the trouble of putting white tape all round it.'

McQueen blanched at the revelation, then joined the rest of his colleagues, and the trooper's friends in 'G' Squadron boarded the Hercules and prepared for take-off. One journalist had to be restrained from making a last gesture towards Port Stanley. He had intended to hurtle down the runway exposing his backside at the Falklands in the time-honoured manner known as 'doing a moon job'.

On take-off the plane's loadmaster shouted above the noise of the four engines, 'Sorry, gentlemen, there is no booze on this flight, which will last about 13 hours. But we do have sandwiches for you.'

'Wrong,' screamed McQueen, pointing at McGowan crouched on the aircraft's floor, cuddling his bergan. 'Unveil it, Ace.'

Inside the bergan was an Aladdin's cave of lager and Scotch whisky. If the SAS had not been friends with the press before, they certainly were now. Conversation in the bedlam of the spartan hold of the Hercules was impossible. But the sign language of happiness and gratitude on receipt of a can of lager or a swig of The Famous Grouse is universally understood.

Hands flew back four days later with another batch of SAS men, and endured a similar hell, again made bearable by copious amounts of illicit alcohol stowed away.

'I wouldn't worry about it, mate,' shouted one of the troopers, noticing Hands' disquiet about breaking RAF regulations. 'There's fuck all they can do about it apart from diverting to Brazil. And let's be honest, that's not terribly likely. Cheers.'

The bulk of the victorious 3 Commando Brigade was now on its way home. The mood throughout was not one of elation, more one of quiet satisfaction and a longing to get back to families and loved ones at home. They'd come to do a job which they knew they could accomplish. They had done all that had been asked of them, and weren't sorry to be on the way out.

The thoughts of what had happened and what was about to happen filled the minds of all inside the cramped and noisy Hercules planes. Everyone, it seemed, forgot that Ascension Island was in the tropics; hardly the place to go walking around in four layers of arctic clothing.

The regular inhabitants of Wideawake Airfield on Ascension could not suppress a smile as the heroes of the Falklands staggered out of the back of the transport planes dressed for the North Pole.

The newly-arrived troops realized their mistake, and shed much of their clothing. The feel of the sun on their skin was something they had almost forgotten; a sensation that was to be savoured.

All around were the 'top secret' planes and equipment that the Minders from the MOD had forbidden any journalist even to look at on the way down.

'What's the big secret here, anyway?' asked McGowan. 'All I can see is the same load of planes that were here when we were going down.'

'Nothing's changed,' said an airman. 'There was never anything untoward here in the first place.'

McGowan and the other newsmen realized that once again there had been a major panic amongst the Minders for no purpose whatsoever.

Absolutely nothing happens on Ascension Island, and all human life revolves around an oasis called The Exiles' Club.

'At sunset,' said one of the barmen, 'if you look very carefully, you see a green flash as the sun dips below the horizon.'

One homegoing soldier replied sourly, 'The only green flash I want to see is the one that comes moments before I fall into unconsciousness after I've had a skinful.' And with that, he and his mates liberated the bar.

Ascension Island began to take on the aura of a magical South Seas paradise, as for all troops it represented the last stepping-stone on the way home.

The bulk of the brigade sailed straight past in *Canberra* and across the equator, while the Paras and other units disembarked from *Norland* and other ships and flew to RAF stations at Lyneham and Brize Norton.

Chapter 19

There was a certain edginess among the men of the Falklands Task Force on their journey home, an uncertainty at what lay ahead of them. True, they could be confident that they had done the job they were sent to do, but none had been able to gauge the reaction of the people at home during the three months they had been away. All they had learned was from heavily censored reports on the BBC World Service and from very out-of-date British newspapers. Would they arrive to a hero's welcome? Or would the public by now believe that the whole enterprise had never been worth the cost in lives and hard cash for a group of islands which few doubted would eventually be handed over to Argentina anyway?

There had been rumours that *Canberra* would call in somewhere on the way home to 'let the boys have a run ashore'. It was decided, though, that it would be unfair to inflict the three Commandos on any port in the world except their home one.

'Let's be fair about it,' said 42 Commando's Joe Fallaggio. 'We'd tear the place apart. I bet they're bolting their doors in Gibraltar just in case. No, all we want to do is get back home and give the wife a seeing to.'

It was no pleasure cruise as the Marines volunteered themselves for continuing keep-fit circuits of the quarter-mile promenade deck of the liner. There might not have been the break-neck enthusiasm of the journey down, but some habits are hard to break.

Nobody was sorry that the Paras had gone home by other means. They, too, were keeping fit aboard the ferry *Norland* on their way to Ascension, as were the

Marines under Rod Boswell's command aboard *Resource*. True to his word, Captain Boswell had clung to *Resource* as though it was a life-raft. 'Slow boat home it might be,' he said. 'But at last it's going in the right direction. When we get home doesn't matter. Finally getting there does.'

There was no problem keeping up the men's spirits in *Canberra*. Each mess echoed loudly far into the night as the three Commandos celebrated their deeds in the Falklands and looked forward to the reunions ahead.

'I'll bet the bastards steam straight on past Plymouth just because the bloody *Canberra* lives in Southampton,' said one of Fallaggio's Mafia. 'Tell you what, though. There might be a few holes in this ship after all if we see the Eddystone Light go whizzing by.'

But P&O had the last word, and the authorities accepted that it would be Southampton. There were groans aboard *Canberra* as the Tannoy announced, 'Those on the port side can see the lights of Plymouth. No jumping ship, you'll be there soon enough, anyway.'

A light aircraft was heard buzzing around the stern of the ship in the warm evening air. The Tannoy crackled into life again. 'The light aircraft above us now has aboard civic dignatories and local MPs.'

The Plymouth-based Marines on the upper deck rose to the occasion in the time-honoured way. Hundreds of two-fingered gestures were waved at the plane and the still night air was rent by the sound of a chorus of raspberries.

'Shame we haven't got the machine guns still mounted on the rail,' said one Marine.

As the great ship glided homeward off the Devon coast, car headlights could be seen flashing a welcome from every headland. 'I reckon someone 'as let the cat out of the bag and knows we're coming,' said a smiling sergeant.

The Tannoy announced in true cruise-liner style,

'Ladies and gentlemen, we will be passing Dartmouth, Torbay, Teignmouth, Dawlish . . .' He was interrupted by three sergeants shouting in unison, 'And all stations to Bognor Regis.'

The man on the Tannoy was obviously no Devonian. The little town of Teignmouth was pronounced 'Tyne-mouth', which led one Geordie Marine to jump up and down in mock delight, shouting, 'Tell me Ma, they're dropping me off special. They'll have to come back to Southampton to dump you buggers later.'

On the flight deck, the Royal Marines' band gave an impromptu concert as the lights of Devon and Dorset's seaside resorts faded into the night. It was a raucous occasion with spontaneous dancing as the band went through a medley of favourites ranging from the compositions of Rod Stewart to James Last.

'May I have the honour of the next dance,' said a smiling Marine, bowing low to his mate.

'No you fucking can't,' said his mate. 'I've been trying to tell you for three months. I really don't fancy you.'

The one remaining fear for the Very Senior Officers was that the Marines would get rolling drunk and disgrace themselves when they landed. Accordingly, the bars on board were closed at 10 pm.

'Seems pointless to me,' said a corporal in 42 Commando. 'We're gonna disgrace ourselves anyway, or die in the attempt.'

That night on television Colonel Malcolm Hunt appeared on the news, picked up on the liner as she was so close in, but nobody heard what he said amid the jeers and catcalls.

The big question now for all aboard was just how big would the welcome be in Southampton. 40 and 42 Commandos knew that soon after they had landed, they would be piled into coaches and sped off back to Plymouth. It was different for 45 Commando, as they would have to take planes from Eastleigh north to their base at Arbroath.

'I just hope it's not the crabs flying us,' said one of their sergeant-majors, 'or they'll never hit the runway. Could be a hell of a way to go home.'

42 Commando returned to the flight deck for another burst of song and dance. They were in ebullient and wicked mood.

Hands was standing innocently by when he was grabbed by the RSM and thrown bodily into the pack. The tune changed to 'Hold him down, you Zulu warrior', and Hands and his clothing parted company. The Marines proceeded to throw the naked hack into the air, catch him and throw him aloft again.

'Either he's very cold,' said Sergeant Norman Clark, 'or his wife married a wrong-un. Like two little walnuts they are.'

Hands was eventually allowed to recapture his clothing, and with all dignity gone, he addressed the Marines. 'I'd like to say it's been a real pleasure knowing you bastards,' he said, smiling. 'I'd like to, but I can't.'

Colonel Nick Vaux had been watching the fun, but suddenly glowered apprehensively as his men prepared to burst into 'The Malvinas Song'. Phrases like 'We're gonna kill a Spic or two' and others prominent in the song were not considered politically proper before a television crew on the eve of the homecoming.

'Don't you think "When the Saints Go Marching In" would be a little more in keeping?' suggested Colonel Vaux. And so the unsaintly men of 42 Commando did as they were bidden.

'Right, you lot,' called Sergeant Clark at the end of the song. 'It's a big day ahead. Time to turn in.'

The Marines did not entirely agree and broke into the chorus which had haunted Clark throughout the campaign, 'Norman is a wanker,' they chanted, over and over again.

In fact Clark was one of the most popular NCOs in the unit, having done more than his fair share to entertain his men during the long days at sea, both heading south and coming home.

It was now late into the last night at sea, and nothing was going to stop the celebrations. The bars might have been closed, but not before ample quantities of alcohol had been secreted in cabins all round the ship.

For once the military policemen were turning the nearest thing they knew to a blind eye. The sounds of merriment and the chink of glasses and cans would have given them a field day on any other occasion. This time, though, some of them even joined in.

Canberra spent most of that last night stooging around the Channel off the Isle of Wight, waiting for the right moment to begin her grand entrance into Southampton Water. It nearly all went wrong as dawn broke to reveal a curtain of thick sea mist enveloping the ship. The first vessels in the welcoming armada could not be seen.

A Sea King laden with journalists touched down on the big ship's flight deck shortly after dawn, and Marines immediately cross-examined them.

'What's it like in Southampton?' asked one.

'Quiet,' said McGowan. 'No one about. Shouldn't be any trouble getting in and off home quickly.'

'What, no one?' asked a chorus of clearly disappointed voices.

'No one,' repeated McGowan. 'I expect that with all the fuss the *QE2* got, it would be a bit of an anti-climax to do it all again now.'

'Fuck,' chanted the chorus.

It was a mischievous lie. Possibly the greatest welcome ever given a home-coming ship awaited *Canberra* beyond the mist.

Soon it became clear to all that McGowan was not the most trustworthy of reporters. First an ITN launch came close alongside; then, as if it was a curtain being raised at a theatre, the mist slowly lifted.

Everywhere little boats darted among each other to get in close to the Great White Whale. Sirens blared, flags were waved, people cheered.

'You wanker, McGowan,' came another chant from astounded Marines. 'Knew all the time, didn't you?'

Openly elated, it took them a very long time to take in what was happening around them. Southampton Water was almost choked with little boats. The sun burned off the remaining mist on this morning of 11 July, and to the joy of the Marines it appeared to burn off a little more than that.

'Fuck,' sighed an incredulous Marine. 'I'd forgotten what they looked like.'

'What?' came a handful of queries.

'Tits, mate. Bloody tits,' said the Marine. 'Look down there. Tits. Fucking great follolloping titties. Beautiful boobies. Come closer. Gimme a handful. I love you.'

It was to happen several times again, but on this occasion, four lovely girls had stripped off their T-shirts to reveal their charms.

'Don't stop there,' screamed the Marines. 'More, more; much, much more.'

The first audible band ashore was playing 'Westering Home' and the first of hundreds of signs could be seen on tower blocks and warehouses, signs like *'Canberra's* Got a Lotta Bottle'; a huge pointing finger suggesting 'Wash and brush-up this way', a friendly reference to the big ship's unkempt appearance; and 'Every One a Winner'.

How a series of major collisions was avoided must still be anyone's guess. Little sail boats at times lost wind almost directly under the liner's massive bow as she slipped resolutely on towards her berth. Fire tugs sent plumes of water high into the air and parachute flares burst into life on either side of the liner.

'Can't fucking believe it,' said Joe Fallaggio. 'Who

would have believed all this would happen? I can't take it in. It's bloody marvellous.'

The Marines managed to maintain some semblance of order as they stood, awe-struck, at the rails. The P&O crew were less restrained. Ship's telephonist, Mrs Anne Taylor, was craning out of a port hole, with several of her colleagues trying to see out past her wildly waving balloons and streamers.

Against the endless tide of craft of all shapes and sizes going up Southampton Water with *Canberra*, a brave little flotilla of about ten canoes passed by, butting through the wakes of the armada, heading towards the Isle of Wight. It looked suicidal but brought a rousing cheer and great applause from the Marines.

Amid the hullaballoo, a Wessex helicopter of the Queen's Flight settled on the *Canberra*'s flight deck, and Prince Charles stepped out, in the uniform of a Royal Navy commander.

'Trust Jug Ears to get in on the act,' said one Marine. 'Shouldn't someone tell him his brother's on *Invincible*?'

The Prince must not have heard that. Smiling, he said repeatedly, 'All these men have done the most fantastic job.'

More banners on the shore could now be seen. One, stretching the point slightly, proclaimed: '*Canberra* walks on water'. Another vowed, 'We love the Great White Whale'.

The Marines had made their own, and they were now draped over the side of the liner. 'Call off the rail strike, or we'll call an air strike', read one. Another boasted '*Canberra* cruises where *QE2* refuses', a pointed observation that this liner had frequently been in the heat of battle, whereas the big Cunarder had ventured no closer to danger than South Georgia, after that island had been recaptured.

Other banners from the Marines were less inventive,

but nonetheless, sincere. 'We went, we fought, we conquered'. Others were simple greetings: 'Hello, Mum', or the presentiment 'Lock up your daughters, the Bootnecks are back'.

Above them a Victory-V formation of naval Lynx helicopters crossed Southampton Water.

By now the relatives of the Marines waiting at Shed 106 could see the great looming hulk carrying their loved ones. The police had at first tried to get all the welcoming visitors to the town penned in an orderly fashion, well back from the quayside. They realized from the start of the day that they stood little chance.

As the sea of bodies surged past one thin blue line trying valiantly to hold them back, a sergeant was heard to mutter, 'Fuck it, lads, we've got no chance. Let 'em through.'

Now the relatives, almost all of them clutching red roses for their particular Marine, were almost at the water's edge. A man with a heavily-laden cart waited to hand thousands more to the men when they stepped ashore.

Canberra was now being nudged towards her berth by three tugs. On the quayside, and now clearly audible, the band from the Royal Yacht *Britannia* burst into 'Rule Britannia' and 'Land of Hope and Glory'.

Several Marines, knowing they were only minutes from their loved ones, wept unashamedly. Young Bootnecks slapped each other on the back, saying, as though they couldn't really believe it themselves, 'We've made it. We've made it.'

The honour of being the first ashore was to be given to the youngest Marine in the Task Force, fresh-faced and smiling Martin Tait, just 17 years old.

The heaving lines were thrown, bridging the last gap between three months and what had been left behind. The P&O gangplanks or brows were pushed against the rusting sides of the *Canberra* and to all intents and purposes she was back.

Sergeant Major Bob 'Buster' Brown looked at the quayside, and summing up the mood of every man on board, said simply, 'Bloody marvellous. We really are back.'

The band struck up with renewed fervour, the cheering from the quayside intensified. But there were still one or two formalities to go through before the Marines could set foot once more on English soil.

With Marine Tait went the brigadier and the commanding officers of the three Commandos, all having to endure the formal handshakes from the dignitaries on shore, when each of them wanted only to get away and back home.

At last the procession started, with Marines trooping gallantly down the brow and onto the less than inspiring dockside. Every man was given a rose from the patriotic gentleman who ran a florist's shop somewhere in the south of England. But each man had his hands full of kit, and so the Marines' return looked more like a succession of victorious toreadors clenching blooms between their teeth than an Army coming back from a victorious campaign.

The relatives and loved ones burst through, to embrace, kiss and cuddle the men who had been away for so long. Tears flowed, brave men wept, and the police gave up.

Marines who had expected 'a thorough going over' by the Customs officers, and had thus thrown captured Argentinian ballistics overboard in the Channel, now regretted their cautious behaviour. The Customs men, just like the police, had conceded the occasion to emotion. No kit was checked for improper equipment, no illegal weaponry was found or confiscated.

'Sod it,' said a member of 42 Commando, watching other Marines pass unobstructed by officialdom into the bosom of their families. 'I got rid of a couple of Argie 45s off the Canaries. Could have got them through with no bother after all.'

On the quayside, Marines were finding that kissing a long lost wife with a rose in your mouth is not easy.

A young daughter rushed up to her father, encumbered by bergan and suitcase, and gave a typical welcome.

'Daddy!' she exclaimed. 'Where have you been?' Daddy, one of the hard-drinking, hard-swearing stalwarts of 40 Commando could not reply. He was in tears.

Southampton Docks became a cacophony of wailing welcomes. The Bootnecks realized that after all, they had been wrong in wanting to sail into Plymouth. All Plymouth, it seemed, was in Southampton.

'I still can't believe it,' said one of 42 Commando's Marines still waiting for his chance to get ashore. 'This is fucking unbelievable. And we've got to go through it all again when we get to Plymouth.'

Coaches were indeed waiting to take the Marines back to their bases. Other Marines, and members of other units, were luckier, and could disappear from the ship and slink off with their wives or girlfriends.

At the Post House Hotel, where it had all begun for the hacks on board *Canberra*, a young man in camouflage uniform strolled through the front doors with his lady on his arm. He looked shattered; she looked expectant.

'Darling,' she crooned. 'What would you like most to do now, if you could choose anything?'

The Marine, for such was his calling, did not hesitate.

'A bloody great pint of beer straight from the tap,' he said with feeling. Bootnecks tend to get their priorities right, and a decent pint takes precedence over all else. But his lady was not of the same mind.

'No you don't,' she said, steering him past the bar and towards the lift. 'Up to the room first.'

The Marine, three months away from home, and too tired to disagree, did not argue. Two hours later, and looking even more tired, he was seen in the hotel bar pouring bitter down his throat while his lady sat next to him looking loving and far from disappointed.

The Post House Hotel was the scene of many such re-consumations. Trust House Forte, not unaware of the benefits that could be wrung from such an occasion, reduced their prices for all rooms booked for guests who were coming to meet the *Canberra*.

That afternoon, *Canberra* looked like a ghost ship. The streamers still hung pathetically over the side, but the celebrations were over. The Great White Whale had enjoyed her moment of glory, and now waited sadly by Shed 106 to be taken round to the graving dock where her refit would be undertaken. The cabins and corridors which hours before had been alive with the sounds of joyous Marines were empty. The welcoming crowds had dispersed.

Only Captain Mike Bradford and a skeleton crew remained on board, the noise of the reception still ringing in their ears.

'Seems strange,' said Bradford on the bridge. 'It's all over. In a funny way it hardly seems that we've been away at all. Everything seems so normal now.'

Doctor Sue West, 31 year-old bachelor girl, was one of the last to go ashore. The P&O assistant surgeon said while leaning over a rail, 'When I joined P&O I thought I had nothing more serious to do than treat people for sunburn. How little I knew then.

'I'm glad I did it, and I'm glad it's over. I've got used to the kind of humour that you get from a man giving blood who says, "Now take good care of it, because I'll probably be popping back for it in a few days' time." I thought being one of only 14 women on a ship with more than 2000 soldiers would cause great problems. It never did. They were all perfect gentlemen who just enjoyed our company. Never before has each woman been given so much attention by so many for so little.

'I'm glad to see England again,' said Dr Sue. 'Down

in San Carlos Water I spent a lot of time looking at the floor-coverings of the *Canberra* while I was taking cover in the air raids in Bomb Alley.

'But there were happy memories too, and a few that are difficult to forget. On the way down I went out on deck in a bikini to do my exercises, but what I didn't know was that a group of troops were doing theirs in the same place. Obviously I brought the entire class to a roaring halt, much to my extreme embarrassment. I melted away feeling like a mixture between an idiot and Miss World.'

The *Canberra*, one of the undoubted heroines of the war, was ready to reclaim her place in the list of top-line cruise ships. But first there was a lot of work to be done. The spartan trappings of a troop ship had to be taken out, and the plush palm-court atmosphere of a cruise liner put back.

The ship, which would forever hold a place next to the heart of Marines and Paras, would never be quite the same again.

As she sat quietly at her berth in Southampton waiting for the refit to begin, a solitary Marine looked up at the liner which had been his home immediately before and immediately after the campaign on East Falkland.

'You're not a bad old bitch,' he said, in a remark that was taken completely the wrong way by the wife on his arm. 'Lick of paint, bit of tarting up, and you'll be as good as new. Good luck, old girl.'

' 'Ere, what are you on about?' said his wife.

The Marine said nothing, but smiled, and walked off to start the rest of his life.

The homecoming of *Canberra* was the last spectacular show of joy from the British public, but greetings awaiting the return of other units was to be just as warm and every bit as genuine.

Sergeant John Ross of 3 Para arrived by RAF transport back in England with the rest of his battalion on a sunny afternoon a little later.

In the restricted confines of an RAF base the public, even if they wanted to, could never have got close enough to give the Paras a proper welcome. It didn't matter.

Ross, with his child in his arms, said, 'None of that stuff matters. We're home, and the only people who really count are our families, and they're all here. Look at me,' he added, nodding at his young child hugging him. 'Anyway you look at it, there's no better welcome than this.'

Following the Paras, other Commando units flew back from Ascension to the English air bases. They too were met only by relatives.

But, said Sergeant Sandy MacLeod, 'You cannot believe the welcome we got from everyone in Plymouth. I swear if you wore a green beret and robbed a bank here, they wouldn't even report it to the police.

'We knew our families would be pleased to see us, but the welcome we have had is unbelievable. I'll never forget it, and neither will any of the lads.'

Around the home ports of the Task Force ships, welcomes just as warm were being prepared. *Canberra* might have had the lion's share of the mass emotion on behalf of the Great British Public, but no ship and no man came home without an ovation.

The ships, once either anonymous or at best virtually unheard of, were now known by their nicknames.

Invincible, with Prince Andrew on board, was greeted by the Queen and hundreds of other mums. But she had become known as 'HMS Invisible', entirely without prompting from the Minders. The *Hermes* was now known as 'Herpes' (a form of venereal disease) or as Private Eye named her 'Hermesetas – dissolves in hot water, Geddit???.' The nuclear submarine *Conqueror* was called 'Clobberer' after her sinking of the *General*

Belgrano, and the twin assault ships *Fearless* and *Intrepid* were dubbed respectively, 'Fearful' and 'Insipid'.

The frigate *Argonaut* was affectionately known by the Paras as 'Argie-nought', and the other P&O liner *Uganda*, used as a hospital ship, was referred to lovingly as 'The Mother Hen'.

She and the ambulance ships *Hecla* and *Hydra* still have a special place in the hearts of the Task Force troops, both those who came home in one piece and those who did not. The work they did in keeping men alive until they could be flown home from Montevideo was nothing less then heroic.

Welsh Guardsman Simon Weston, one of the casualties in *Sir Galahad*, said, 'I owe my life to so many people: the people at Ajax Bay, the guys on the *Hydra*, and the crew on *Uganda*. If it wasn't for them, I wouldn't be here now.'

Recovering from third-degree burns over 45 per cent of his body in a London military hospital, Simon said, 'Thanks to these people, I have got a life to lead, when on *Galahad* I spent some time in agony pleading with my mate to shoot me.'

And every one of the fighting men who returned sound in mind and body would be annoyed if their mates killed and injured were forgotten in the nationalistic euphoria of the welcome they received when they came home.

Sergeant-major Sammy Dougherty of 3 Para said in London, 'None of us have lost sight of the fact that we got back in one piece when some of our mates lost arms and legs, and some didn't make it at all. If we got a hero's welcome, really it's for them. They've given a lot more than we did.'

Denzil Connick, a corporal in 3 Para who lost a leg to artillery shrapnel on Mount Longdon, said, 'It would be easy to be bitter about it now. A lot of the lads who are like me could be very pissed off. But we're not. We didn't join the Army for nothing. It could have happened in Northern Ireland, and for a lot of lads it has. We had a job to do, and we did it bloody well.

'You do get depressed from time to time,' he added. 'That's not really surprising, is it? But I'll be getting a new leg and the other lads will be fixed up too and most of us are being kept on by the Army. So it's not worth dwelling on. We just told ourselves we were going to get better, and we have found that works.'

The administrator of that particular hospital, Lieutenant-colonel Ron Welsh, said, 'These are remarkable men. When we got them here, we expected them to be depressed, and we expected them to get more depressed as time went by. If they did, and they probably did, they never showed it. They are very, very tough men with very tough minds. You have to admire them.'

The indomitable spirit of the men was never better typified than by the injured men who used up their energies in wheelchair races around the wards, much to the sympathetic annoyance of the nursing staff.

They also found that it was not impossible to slip out of the building at night and spend a few well-earned pennies in the local hostelries. The hospital staff, who never ceased to be amazed at the ingenuity of their charges, turned a blind eye when they found hospital beds still empty at closing time down the road.

On one occasion the Toms nearly overstepped the mark, and tried unsuccessfully to get back into the hospital without being noticed after a night out as guests of the City of London Police. Many drinks had flowed that evening, and even the inventive and wily Paras found that sneaking up on the Argentinians was one thing, but getting past the staff nurse when drunk was quite another.

No action was taken by the long-suffering, worldly-wise professionals who run the Queen Elizabeth's Military Hospital in Woolwich.

*

Weeks after all the front-line troops were home, Major David Collett, company commander of 3 Para's 'A' Company, said after a memorial service in Aldershot, 'There is no doubt about it. The British Tom is the finest fighting soldier there is. Anyone would have been proud to have been alongside them in the Falklands.' Although a Para would never say it, it wasn't just the British Toms who were being honoured by that sentiment. Paras have an undying but unspoken respect for the men of the Royal Marines.

The Marines too had learned the lesson that the elite of the British Forces have to include the Parachute Regiment by definition. The Marines now had a new understanding of the men they once called 'The Parasite Regiment'. They had learnt that their new colleagues had referred to them as 'The Royal Latrines'.

But for one unit of the Task Force, there was to be a bitter twist at the end of the Falklands Campaign. Lieutenant Mike Hawkes, 40 Commando's 'schoolie', summed it up. 'Someone, somewhere, doesn't like us,' he said. 'As soon as we get back, we're in training again.'

He was absolutely right. 40 Commando were brought down to earth with a bump. They were to undertake a tour of duty for five months starting in January 1983 at Bessbrook in South Armagh, Northern Ireland.

Epilogue

The people of Britain had, rightly, shown the returning men and women of the Task Force their gratitude and admiration. Much like the spirit of Londoners in the blitz of World War 2, people at home were by and large united by a desire for a successful outcome to the campaign, and for a safe return for all who had gone to the South Atlantic. That desire outweighed concern for the Falkland Islanders themselves, for the sake of whose liberty the Task Force was despatched.

For the people at home, this was the Falklands Factor, a factor that could not in any way identify with the realities of a group of peat-covered rocks 8000 miles away.

It would be argued by many in the Task Force that the wishes of the islanders that they maintain the right to decide their own future was reason enough to do the job. Many would also argue that the islanders themselves were not. The Falklanders proved by the way of life they had chosen that they like to be left alone. Their legacy now is a way of life that can never again be what it was before Argentina invaded. Many of them did not appreciate the presence of the handful of Royal Marines who comprised Naval Party 8901 in the first place, even as their protectors. At least one bar was closed to them, well before the invasion. Now they will have to live alongside a large permanent garrison which has transformed their lonely paradise into a fortress.

Freedom was the watchword for the islanders, freedom to live in peace, freedom to roam the hills and valleys at will. The Falklands War gave them back freedom with one hand, and robbed them of it with the other. True, the islanders have been liberated. But, because of the thousands of land-mines which litter the peat bogs and mountains, it will be many years before they can roam their islands without fear of tragedy.

As the last long glorious days of summer in Britain faded into autumn, so did the Falklands Factor. It was over now, best left to history. Rail strikes, wage demands and Days of Action reclaimed the headlines. The Middle East and Northern Ireland resumed their places, temporarily occupied by the Falklands War, as the frontrunners in the daily diet of violence and death.

The cabins aboard *Canberra* and *QE2*, once occupied by Marines, Paras, Guardsmen and Gurkhas, were given back to fare-paying passengers. The ships of the Royal Navy returned to normal duties, or were laid up for their war damage to be repaired.

The troops went on leave, then returned to a peacetime routine.

Some of the dead were returned home at the wishes of their relatives. Others were buried at a new cemetery overlooking San Carlos Water. The living and the dead were remembered by the largest presentation of honours since the last World War.

Even as the last sounds of gunfire blew away on the wind, the thunder of argument among those who were never there reverberated through the corridors of power in Westminster and Whitehall.

In financial terms over a billion pounds had been spent. Two hundred and fifty-six men died. Seven hundred and seventy-seven were injured.

Cheap at half the price? Perhaps. The British High Command had been prepared to accept a fatality rate of up to one thousand. As this book shows it was hardly their fault that that figure was not reached – indeed, surpassed. Some thanks is due to the Argentinians.

But all that aside, one thing stands out: if Napoleon's army marched on its stomach, Maggie Thatcher's Task Force yomped – or tabbed – on its sense of humour.

FIGHTER PILOT

Colin Strong and Duff Hart-Davis

Based on the BBC Television series, *Fighter Pilot* is a portrait of million-pound pilots in the making.

Many may feel called, but few are chosen. Of the 34 candidates for fast-jet training who attended the RAF Selection Centre at Biggin Hill, only 6 were to pass through the aptitude and medical tests and be chosen for pilot training. Their average age was 22, and the story of these young men as they underwent the exacting 3-year training schedule has become not only a fascinating television series, but an absorbing, compulsive and bestselling book.

Futura Publications
Non-fiction
0 7088 2193 6

THE BOER WAR

Thomas Pakenham

The war declared by the Boers on 11 October 1899 gave the British, as Kipling said, 'no end of a lesson'. It proved to be the longest, the costliest, the bloodiest and the most humiliating war that Britain fought between 1815 and 1914.

Thomas Pakenham has written the first full-scale history of the war since 1910. His narrative is based on first-hand and largely unpublished sources ranging from the private papers of the leading protagonists to the recollections of survivors from both sides. Out of this historical gold-mine, the author has constructed a narrative as vivid and fast-moving as a novel, and a history that in scholarship, breadth and impact will endure for many years.

'This is a wonderful book: brilliantly written . . . the reader turns each page with increasing fascination and admiration.' – A. J. P. Taylor

Futura Publications
Non-fiction
0 7088 1892 7

All Futura Books are available at your bookshop or newsagent, or can be ordered from the following address:
Futura Books, Cash Sales Department,
P.O. Box 11, Falmouth, Cornwall.

Please send cheque or postal order (no currency), and allow 45p for postage and packing for the first book plus 20p for the second book and 14p for each additional book ordered up to a maximum charge of £1.63 in U.K.

Customers in Eire and B.F.P.O. please allow 45p for the first book, 20p for the second book plus 14p per copy for the next 7 books, thereafter 8p per book.

Overseas customers please allow 75p for postage and packing for the first book and 21p per copy for each additional book.